WINNING WAYS

A PSYCHOLOGICAL REVOLUTION FOR EXCELLENCE IN LIFE, ART & SPORT PERFORMANCE

PHIL JOHNSON
PSYCHOLOGIST

VisionWeaver Press

Published by VisionWeaver Press

Typesetting by Riverside Publishing Solutions

DISCLAIMER

This book is for educational and informational purposes only and is not intended to replace professional medical, psychological, or therapeutic advice. The sports psychology techniques, mental health discussions, and performance strategies presented are based on general principles and should not be considered a substitute for professional consultation.

Readers should consult qualified healthcare professionals, licensed psychologists, or therapists before implementing any strategies contained herein, particularly when dealing with mental health concerns, trauma, or working with minors.

The author and publisher disclaim any liability for adverse reactions or consequences resulting from the use of this information. Individual results may vary significantly.

If experiencing a mental health crisis, contact emergency services immediately.

The views and opinions expressed in this book are those of the author and are based on his professional experience and research.

Praise for Winning Ways

Dear Phil, thank you so much for helping us again. We are also grateful for your kindness and compassion. We have been lucky to have found you, as these last two years have been incredibly dark, but you have given us a light to see by. You've given us something very precious—we have hope. ~ **C&H**

*

Thank you for all your help the last few months. You truly changed my life, and I feel more happy, connected, and balanced than I have ever been. I can breathe. ~ **LH**

*

I just wanted to take the time to write a deep and sincere thank you to you. Meeting you and receiving your sessions has really changed my life. I did feel dizzy and energy changing around my brain for around three days, and now it's beginning to settle. But I feel totally different! I feel like I can feel my brain! I feel grounded in both sides and have noticed a difference in the intensity of my ADHD symptoms—less intense. I want to thank you with my whole heart. Thank you. ~ **AD**

*

I have so much gratitude for you and what you have enabled me to do. I am, to quote my wife, "a totally different man, and back to how I was before the accident," and she is so happy to see the silly side of me come back out, making people laugh again and randomly singing to myself without thinking about it. It's amazing—I haven't used or felt the need to use my walking stick since our sessions, and although my weight loss hasn't continued, I am much more active and regularly do things without struggling at all. ~ **MB**

*

D is doing amazing, and I love how he is progressing. We are very grateful for your help and guidance—it has made the biggest difference in our lives. Thank you! Thank you! Thank you! ~ **AS**

*

For me, Brainspotting was the key to letting go of events from my past that I was dragging along with me. It was releasing weight I didn't even realise I was carrying until we took deep dives into my memories. The result has meant developing fresh perspectives of things that happened to me, or understanding why people might have acted that way towards me. Every time we did Brainspotting, it was like I unlocked an invisible door that I had created in front of myself, and I could finally move forward again.

  ~ **LS**
  Olympic Gold Medallist & World Champion

*

We knew I was capable, but I'm so, so excited I finally did it. We think my run time was a new world record! Thank you so much for everything you've helped me with. I've had a really great year, and I'm absolutely loving training and competing. I've been practicing all the processes and breathing I learnt from you, and it's made all the difference.

  ~ **JV**
  World Champion

SUPPORTING
PARENTS – ATHLETES – COACHES

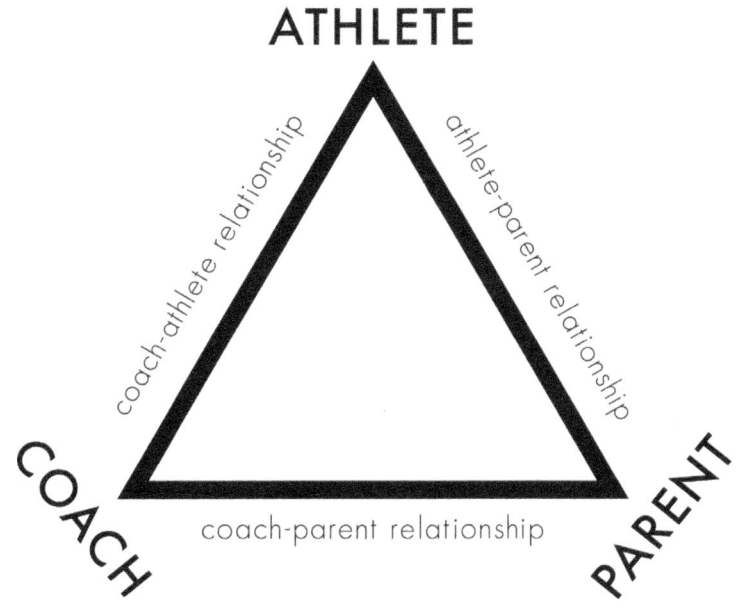

ACKNOWLEDGEMENTS

I dedicate the book with love to my son Peter, an architect and Brainspotting™ practitioner and budding author, to my one-year-old granddaughter Maggie and her architect mum Emma. They also represent two of the generations and I hope this legacy of knowledge benefits them in some way in years to come. I am indebted to my brothers Malcolm, Pete, and my sisters-in-law Christine and Sue, for their love and our shared life experience. Our parents, Eddie and Rose, passed on many years ago but left the three of us a unique legacy themselves.

To Glenis Jones, Football Secretary for Easton-in-Gordano FC, who in 2000, introduced me to Sport Psychology training, and for my opportunity to become a UEFA Football coach, and Bristol City FC Academy for hosting my studies and development. A life changing paradigm shift. To Valerio Zuodar for hosting me in Geneva to write 9000 words in 3 days.

My profound thanks are to my own mentors who believed in me and supported my efforts. Dr Alan Goldberg, Amherst USA sport psychologist, for introducing me to Brainspotting, and directing me to Dr David Grand, (NYC) the developer of Brainspotting (BSP), who trained me, and created BSP; his gift to humanity — a genius. Dr Dina Glouberman, another genius, clinical psychologist, another New Yorker, who introduced me to Image work, psychotherapy, personal development, psychology, and unconditional love. Dr Barry Cripps, my initial sport psychology mentor and the first Fellow of Sport and Exercise Psychology Division of British

Psychological Society in the UK. Simon Elliot, who, together with me as the Founder, has sustained and expanded The Ski Exchange in Cambridge — a business enterprise creation I am truly proud of — and for his determination and passion to give it new and extended life since 1995.

My co-trainers and life teachers in Brainspotting, Agnita Bok, (Amsterdam), P (V and Louise Love (Bristol, England); and my close and lifelong friends Mick and Fran Fuller, Jon Hutt, Martin Hayes, Geoff Holland who understands me and shares my love of sport and music, Barrie Corteen, photographer, and Filips Dhondt, CEO AS Monaco FC.

Appreciative of the culture of the North-West of England — between Liverpool and Manchester – for sport and music influences. My first guitar at the age of seven was more than an instrument; Good Vibrations by The Beach Boys, remains my top song, alongside John Martyn and Haevn music. The discovery and participation in football and skiing have illuminated and dominated my life, along with psychology.

In my portfolio career of being a helper and in service to over 3,000 patients and clients, I wish to thank them for my learning and their willingness to be vulnerable in my presence — and to the ten clients whose anonymised life stories are expressed in the book. To Professor Jo Maher, who, along with Karen Carney OBE, MBE, expanded Brainspotting and Sport Psychology into their domains of Education and professional football, with its uniqueness to impact on a wider world.

To Anna Vanickova and Petra Van De Linden-Brussen, at Mary Magdalene Mystery School, Vezelay, France for their teachings in spirituality, and their unconditional love personified.

To Sally-Shakti Willow of VisionWeaver Press for bringing this to fruition with true vision, Tina Dubois for her masterly editing,

Estella Hayward, Project Manager, in bringing this to press and Wayne Bridgehouse, Mya Castillo & Rachel Goddard for marketing 'The Knowledge'.

— Phil Johnson, Bristol, England, March 2025.

To Barry

My sincere thanks for all the support you gave me in my early development. I hope to book rescuators with you.

God Bless You

CONTENTS

PREFACE

Why Seek Clinical Sports or Performance Psychology for Your Child or Yourself?

Performance anxiety is the major reason why athletes and performers refer themselves to, or are required to seek assistance from, sports and performance psychologists. The major source of referrals are 'performance' managers, parents, athletes, and performers themselves. It's not simply being anxious about a competition or musical performance in itself; it's the loss of performance, the extreme worry, sleepless nights, fear of failure, humiliation, the frustrated coach or teacher, the worried parent, and, in some cases, spectators and sponsors. As parents, there are very few manuals to guide us at each step of the way on what to do with and for our children, especially those with developing talents, whether in sport, the performing arts, or academia/school. **Parents may be out of their depth**, simply unsure what to do next or how to manage the situation, and they can feel alone and unsupported. Indeed, they may also be traumatised by their children's trauma — caught in an unwanted and often unrealised state of powerlessness, accompanied by immobilisation, even shame.

This scenario of worrying about our children doesn't stop at the age of 18 or 26. Those early experiences, which may well have been devastating, can continue to interfere with life and performance beyond the integrated family. Indeed, it may also have been that family life which contributed significantly to the worry and the performance deficits, given that almost a third of marriages end in divorce and that the high expectations of parents themselves are contributory factors to their child's performance (1).

To help and support parents, coaches, teachers, educators, performance managers, athletes, and performers within such situations requires a range of knowledge, skills, and actions that can measurably sustain positive change for all concerned. What if simply talking about the issue doesn't work? Who is likely to have knowledge of working with families, children, and adolescents; professional musicians, footballers, and swimmers; or issues such as trauma, injury, chronic fatigue syndrome (CFS), burnout, loss, death, grief, personal boundaries, early dysfunctional child attachment, rejection, abandonment, depression, eating disorders, addiction to drugs, alcohol, sex, gambling, post-traumatic stress disorder (PTSD), and physical, emotional, or sexual abuse? And is it true that personal disappointment, embarrassment, and humiliation form a major part of trauma?

To meet such criteria, someone would need to be a psychologist, social worker, systemic family therapist, teacher, or university lecturer; a professional sport coach with knowledge of nutrition and exercise physiology; and an expert in mental health psychology, the treatment of trauma, injury, and broken relationships. That person would also need to offer a safe, secure, and indeed 'loving framework' in which to support people in their journeys and transitions towards successful sports and performance. They would guide young people and adults to a more successful, **winning way** of living their lives, which then impacts significantly on the performance zones of their sport, music, dance, artform, and relationships.

Calder Kaufman, clinical psychologist and Brainspotting Trainer in the USA, states in *The Power of Brainspotting* that "contemporary sports psychology does not typically utilise clinical (mental health) knowledge readily at the disposal of trained clinicians, and most certainly does not incorporate 'conversion disorder' (physiology) or similar ideas into its assessment of sport performance problems" (2).

And so...here I am, and this is your guide to support your children and young adults in enhancing their success through the **Winning Ways** I share here. I'm Phil Johnson, and I'm qualified in four disciplines of psychology: Clinical Mental Health Psychology; Sport and Exercise Psychology; Coaching Psychology (Equestrian); and Performance Psychology — recognised by the British Psychological Society (BPS) and the Health Care Professions Council (HCPC). I am also a qualified Clinical Social Worker.

I am a certified Union of European Football Associations (UEFA) Professional Football Coach, with a Diploma in Psychology for Football. I am a Ski Instructor, Systemic Family Therapist, Eye Movement Desensitisation and Reprocessing (EMDR) Practitioner, and Brainspotting Master Practitioner and Trainer. I am a couples and relationship therapist. I have a Teaching Diploma in 'Image-work', and a European Certificate to Practice Psychology. I am a former lecturer in Nutrition and Exercise Physiology, Applied Sport Psychology, Mental Health Law and Practice, and Equestrian Psychology. Additionally, I am a Fellow of the Higher Education Academy.

I have been contracted to work with the staff of a UK University College to oversee their mental health strategy since 2020. I have been a practitioner member of the British Association for Performing Arts Medicine (BAPAM) since 2016, working specifically with the Music in Mind charity. From 2012 to 2014, I worked for Association Sportive de Monaco Football Club (AS Monaco FC) for two seasons with Claudio Ranieri. I created a communications and business strategy consultancy during my remaining time in

Monaco until 2019. It was in Monaco that I first started writing this book, originally for the Football Academy, when a then less well-known Kylian Mbappé was a young player in the Academy, and later transferred to Paris Saint-Germain for €200 million.

In essence, I am a trauma therapist, helping remove barriers to performance. I was a World Class Performance Psychologist to the British Ski and Snowboard Team, British Modern Pentathlon Team, British Swimming, and England Women's Football (including for the Olympic Games from 2010 to 2024), as well as the British Equestrian Carriage Driving Teams. I am a French speaker, based in Bristol, England, and I see clients online across the European Union, Switzerland, Scandinavia, the USA, and South America. I have worked in 25 different sports and participated in 15. I am also a recreational guitarist, with a passion for music, sport, and psychology, and a love of people which has guided my life.

What brought me to write this book was my **motivation to support parents** in making better decisions **'with'** their children about life and performance choices. My parents intervened at different stages of my life — often secretly — to take away my opportunities for engaging in professional sport, as well as in my chosen education and relationships. These events, amongst others, were the origins of my own 'trauma': personal disappointment, embarrassment, and humiliation, which would show themselves subconsciously in my adult life — though I was not aware of this at the time.

I've had a 'portfolio career' spanning over 30 years, involved in sport, performing arts, and working with young people and their families in both social work and psychology. These different elements finally funnelled together in 2002, during my recovery from CFS, otherwise considered to be 'burnout' from overwork.

Despite being consistently exhausted, I was persuaded by a group of painters working on my brother's house to join a local football team, St George's Easton-in-Gordano (Bristol). The lads were great, but it was hard going and exhausting but fun! Glenis Jones, the club secretary, took an interest in me and discovered I had studied psychology and had, for a time, been a youth player at Bolton Wanderers FC. In a matter of four weeks, she had enrolled me in the UEFA Level 2 football coaching course at Bristol City Football Club (BCFC) and at the same time, into BCFC's academy, all while I was studying and practising for my Diploma in Sport Psychology. My career path completely changed in just four weeks! I recovered from CFS, which I later discovered was trauma-linked. Despite the National Institute of Clinical Excellence's (NICE) view that this is not treatable, it certainly is and I demonstrate this throughout the book.

Why Focus on the Parents of Athletes and Art Performers?

I was given five young players to work with by the Academy Director at BCFC. I had just finished my job as a Training Coordinator in Mental Health Law for the London Boroughs of Camden and Islington. I thought working in sport would be a great change and contrast to mental health work. When I assessed the five players, two of them were depressed, missing their families, low in mood, and simply not performing. The other three had performance anxiety, some of which was related to parental pressure.

I realised at that moment that it would be less effective to work as a Sport Psychologist without a background in mental health. However, sport psychology training in the UK doesn't fully accommodate this yet. Only in the USA, within the Association of Applied Sport Psychology (AASP), of which I am a member, is one of the three categories 'Clinical Sport Psychologist.' That is what I am now — dually qualified as a Clinical (mental health) Psychologist, and Sport and Exercise Psychologist, Coaching Psychologist, and professional working in performance.

My deepest motivation to work with parents, though, came from my own unconscious but traumatic experience. My mother was Jewish, and my father converted from Roman Catholicism to marry her. They were both from Liverpool. In those days, to succeed in life and be Jewish, you needed to become a doctor, lawyer, or businessman. For me to be a footballer then was a non-starter in my mother's view. My dad, however, was a mad football fan on the blue side of Liverpool (yes, Everton FC) and was delighted I had signed for Bolton Wanderers FC. My two older brothers had already been pioneers in our family and gone to Leicester University. It was my mother's dream that I followed that path, and I did so by default.

When I was 18 and seeking a professional football contract, my mother persuaded my dad to write to the club, telling them not to renew my contract because I was going to university. Long before my exam results were announced, a letter arrived telling me I had been released from the club — just two lines, no explanation. I felt my world had collapsed. I was devastated; for me, at 18, the last seven years had been football, sport, and being an OK student. I hadn't realised at that moment that I had become 'traumatised,' as I now know it. I couldn't even get into the university first team and ended up just playing football for fun.

My mother only told me what she had done eight years after my father died, when I was 29. I didn't speak to her for almost a year — I was so angry — but the damage was done. That decision had severely affected my life. So, when I finally became a sport psychologist, I vowed to help prevent such situations from happening to others by fully supporting parents and their talented sons and daughters to make the best decision **with** and for their futures. Now, with every young athlete I work with, the parents are also the client, which immediately takes pressure off the child or young adult

So, what role can Clinical Sport Psychology interventions play in reversing performance loss, managing sport injury, career transitions, team communication blocks, mental health issues, rejection, bullying, or exhaustion? Are these 'presentations' something a sport psychologist can solve, and if so, how? Kaufman is concerned that sport psychology is dominated by cognitive-thinking approaches, which are limiting, and argues that it requires a biopsychosocial model of sport performance. That is: including biology, psychology, sociology.

This is what the book seeks to explain in a systemic, all-encompassing approach —helping families, coaches, teachers, and others who support athletes and performers to understand what works and what doesn't. When it's not working, why is it not working, and how can it be improved, changed, and resolved? These could well be considered **'Winning Ways' (WW)**, and throughout the book these 111 strategies are highlighted, followed by explanations and guidance on putting them into practice. It's not just about winning.

And what is this **'psychological revolution'** in the book's subtitle? In 2011, I was writing about trauma in sport with little research to go on in the UK, as this was mostly in the domain of mental health rather than sport. By good fortune, I discovered Dr Alan Goldberg and subsequently Dr David Grand in the USA, who introduced me to EMDR and taught me Brainspotting (3). This approach is trauma release from the brain and body through eye positioning. It changed my life and the lives of many people I have worked with since. It's a brain-body intervention, which is far more effective than a cognitive, talking therapy—though the latter has its benefits, especially when trauma has been released.

I will explain in the final chapters of the book how **Brainspotting** not only knows no boundaries in its ability to enable people to change their lives, but also, with athletes and families in trauma, challenges the conventions of cognitively based psychology. In essence, it turns psychology upside down — on its head, so to speak — with a focus not on thinking from the top half of the brain, the neo-cortex, but on the subcortical section below, which dominantly houses physical and emotional feelings. The brain is neuroplastic, it heals itself. "Where we look is where we feel," as David Grand said in *Brainspotting*, and "where we feel is where we look", say I.

We can heal trauma of all types, whether that trauma is in essence, personal disappointment, embarrassment, humiliation, or even physical injury. That's revolutionary —partly because psychologists are less interested in the physical body and more in how the mind works — yet 'trauma' is first and foremost physical. Later, I quote Sigmund Freud, who famously described psychology and therefore psychotherapy as occupying the middle space between philosophy and medicine. In a way, trauma is held in the midbrain mostly, yet psychology is focused on the top of the brain rather than the bottom, where trauma emerges.

This psychological revolution brings the 'whole' self together and either extends psychology or separates from it. Ultimately, what we need to do is be holistic — while psychology, as it stands, is not fully systemic.

Dr Tara Swart summarises this very well: "Physical refers to what you feel in your body; 'mental' is about what is going on in your thoughts; 'emotional' is how you are feeling; and the 'spiritual' is about how you feel deep down, at a more fundamental level, in terms of your sense of meaning, purpose, and place in the world" (4).

Multidimensional psychology recognises that human experiences and mental health are complex, influenced by multiple interconnected factors, rather than solely biological or psychological ones, and emphasises the importance of understanding these various dimensions to promote well-being. This can help us to avoid labelling persons with mental disorders (or even medical illnesses) as being due to just one cause, thereby reducing stigma (5).

Introduction to the 111 Winning Ways

The original idea for the book came in 2013 whilst working with the Monaco football team and academy to help them understand more of what sport psychology is and how it can assist and develop higher performance. These winning ways become **specific to human performance,** and have been developed by me, or recognised in my own learning and research and the practice of others. They are designed to help you take action as well as understand the ideas. Here, they are presented as a quick reference guide to the identified behaviours and distinct actions we can take to help us achieve our desired goals, performance, and life experiences. You will see the WW (Winning Ways) numbered in sequence, with reference to the chapters for further explanation. They are tried and tested.

111 WINNING WAYS

CHAPTER 1: INTRODUCTION TO WINNING WAYS

The Coach–Athlete–Parent Triad

The 'Athlete Parent'

The Contexts of Sporting and Performing Arts
Families and Parental Relationships

What to Expect Throughout the Book

111 Winning Ways / Striving for Excellence /
Chapter Guidance and Content

In 2006, whilst working with a young swimmer and his family, I recognised how much I was also supporting the parents in managing their son's sporting career. It was during the family sessions that the term **'athlete parent'** emerged, specifically to identify them in a way that was contextually different from 'normal parenting' and the parenting of a talented young person. When a couple give birth to a child or indeed adopt or foster one — whatever the situation — they may be unprepared for a son or daughter to become an elite athlete, especially in a sport or performing art in which they have little or no experience.

It has been recognised within professional football and by K. Ericsson (6) specifically, that to achieve the status of an elite player or athlete, between 7,500 and 10,000 hours of practice and competition need to have been completed by the age of 19. So, what happens to players or athletes when they spend so much of their waking life in sport, training, and competition?

It would be limiting to assume that the demands of an elite sporting lifestyle begins in adolescence. The search for 'the future elite' is now targeting ever younger individuals. In his book *Every Boy's Dream*, which focuses on English football, Chris Green says, "Sadly, it seems that coaches and scouts are either misguided or simply so focused on the task of recruiting and producing players that they fail to view them as children and boys (and girls)" (7).

One football development centre coach described a group of six-year-olds who were no longer required as "culled" (7, p9, 5, p. 9). Only 2% of 10,000 boys in football academies gain professional contracts. Imagine the extent of the disappointment amongst those thousands of players and their dedicated families. Harry Kane's story at Tottenham Hotspur is a case in point: he was rejected as an 8-year-old from Arsenal and then Spurs, and by two other clubs, but persisted and rejoined Tottenham at 13 (8). The powers that be in English football are questioning how they could nearly have missed a talent now worth over £100 million.

In the same way, young people at school might be told they are not good at maths and believe the teacher — despite their poor communication — forever limiting a child's capability! Consider the time, effort, and money parents put into their children's pursuit of happiness. If we begin to understand the impact on a family of the patience, expense, and time spent sitting in cars, driving on motorways, watching competitions in all weathers and conditions, inside or outdoors, the commitment from all concerned is phenomenal.

In my experience, there are many families where the influence of parents on their children is such that the child chooses a sport in which one or both of their parents either trained or competed in themselves or indeed became an elite athlete. However, there are many more for whom the choice of their child's sport or performing art may be completely outside of their parents' experience and knowledge base. Either way, this places responsibilities upon parents – whether they live together or are separated—that they may not have 'signed up for' when their children were born. They do this as supporting, and loving, committed parents. At least, that's the plan.

If more than one of your children happens to become an elite athlete, pursue performing arts, or have an interest or hobby that requires high levels of parental support, this may well create friction within the family. Competing needs and demands of children, available time, and travel — both inside and outside of school — may give rise to competition for limited resources. Whether there is talent or potential within their chosen sport to be nationally or professionally successful, the quest and expectations from young athletes and parents may well increase accordingly.

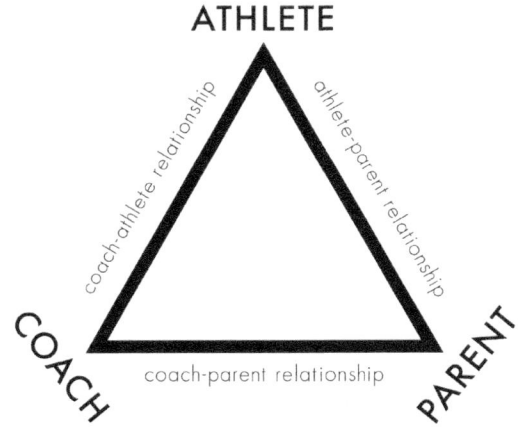

When all is well, families are happy, but the very nature of sporting competition brings additional disappointments. **Problems with coaches** may emerge; **managing injury** may become commonplace; supporting education, handling increased financial costs and making decisions about sporting **career transitions** — including the decision to stop — can all add pressure. These decisions are not always easy to make, especially when families are not fully informed.

In my first professional role as a social worker, I connected with the early developments in Systemic Family Therapy (SFT). The concept was that, with trained therapists, the whole family — or at least the 'nuclear family', which sociologists refer to as mum, dad, sons, and daughters, would meet as a group to consider the issues presented from the 'identified problem.' In other words, a child who was considered sensitive within the family would act out the felt distress within that family, often relating to something dysfunctional within parental relationships.

Within the interchanges, and dynamic of the family, the therapist would seek to take the pressure and focus away from the child as the identified problem and instead work towards finding the origin of the problem. This was often found through unclear communications within the family, particularly between parents and then with their children. Once this had been understood and clarified, interventions would start to help rebalance the **family's internal relationships,** communications, and support. Understanding would also be given to the 'identified child,' whose social isolation, inner conflict, depressed mood, or other negative experiences could often be attributed indirectly to the parents' behaviour.

When I observed and experienced how quickly, efficiently, and successfully this approach works, I realised it is a highly desirable intervention—both cost- and time-effective. In some cases, simply bringing the family together in one place, at one time, to speak and be with each other is significant. It also meant visiting the family at their home, not just in a clinic, where more insight and information could be gathered about their lived experience as a family, a rare action for psychologists who are clinic based.

I am grateful to the specialist Masters programme I attended at the University of Liverpool, where the whole social work course was centred on **'systems thinking,'** based on the book, *Integrating Social Work Methods* by Specht and Vickery (9). From that time, I became a 'systemic thinker,' with this perspective integrated into my brain patterns and in the way I viewed human behaviour—whether in couples, families, groups, teams, communities, organisations, or culture. Out of this developed the social worker role as a **'change agent'**—one who influences others within a chosen system to change their behaviour in ways that impact others within that system. It was, and still is, highly effective. It was a guiding role that gave back responsibility to the individuals involved, and with it, a greater sense of self-control and self-respect **(WW13)**.

Regardless of my past labels or status—whether policeman, social worker, developmental leader of mental health services, psychologist, football coach, ski shop owner, ski instructor, university teacher, entrepreneur, or beekeeper—the perspective remains one of observing the interactions of the group and the individuals within it and, where possible, becoming a catalyst for change.

In my role as a sports psychologist, I made it very clear that whatever issues a young and developing athlete or player may have, their **parents would also be the clients**. I viewed them as a family unit and recognised that the parents often needed support—not judgement—regardless of their son or daughter's performance in their chosen sport. Often what they need is help, advice, and an opportunity for reflection: a greater understanding of how best to communicate with their son or daughter within the context of their sport or performing art. Through these connections—with their coach, manager, physiotherapist, and sometimes even teammates—the realities begin to emerge.

There would also be times for a need to manage conflict with other parents, deal with their son's and daughter's traumatic experiences, and in some circumstances, manage their own as a result. One thing that I can assure you is that when your child experiences trauma, it's not unusual for a parent to also feel the full impact, due to the devastation it causes and the **sense of powerlessness** to stop it. Not surprisingly, many of the parents I have worked with have also had their resulting traumas desensitised independently and literally alongside their son or daughter, with me as a guide.

Parents can also be a source of pressure on their children to succeed, whether in sport, education, or performing arts. In my experience, parents do not necessarily intend to create pressure in the form of high expectations on their children but do so subconsciously or egotistically (for themselves)—what Freud referred to as 'transference,' or projection onto others. When this takes place, it becomes particularly difficult for the young athlete to challenge their parents, especially when they are investing a great deal of time and money in 'supporting' their child's elite performance.

What I know with many of these situations is that 'performance anxiety'—the main reason for referrals to me over the last 18 years—has its origin within life experience rather than just simply within the sporting context. Presentations include depression, disturbed sleep, weight loss, fatigue, dream disturbance, social withdrawal, fear of failure, suppression of anger, self-sabotage (in the kind of on-court behaviour tennis player John McEnroe made famous with adolescent bursts of racket destruction), self-abuse, and indeed "you cannot be serious."

Over the last nine years, I have become more and more involved in working within the spectrum of performing arts: musicians, orchestras, bands, opera singers, vocalists, writers, broadcasters, actors, dancers, and filmmakers. A common theme, as in sport, is performance and the expectations that surround it. I have found, especially within music, significant influences from parents and extended family. As with sport coaches, music teachers can be very harsh on their young students—unintended or otherwise—often considered to be 'old school,' such as the old maxim **"do as I say,"** rather than adopting a **cooperative coaching style** where issues are discussed together **(WW49).**

There is also a crossover from sport into performing arts, and vice versa: gymnastics, dressage, ballet, and dance, for starters. Then add music to those four! Increasingly, ballet and dance are integrated and highly respected by athletes looking to become world champions and searching for 'game inches'— incremental changes **(WW72)**. My evidence shows that parents can play a significant role in the trauma of young musicians which can continue to affect them as mature adults. Such is the strength of these subconscious behaviours that they even impact upon their children's own parenting, reinforcing intergenerational messages and passing behaviours and attitudes from parent to child—unconsciously or otherwise— throughout generations. This is even more reason for **parents to be supported** in making positive changes.

How to Use this Book: Chapter Guidance and Summaries

First and foremost, this book is intended to support parents in the complex and multitasking demands on their knowledge, drive, energy, and **love** to give their children the best opportunities they can in life. It also aims to prepare them for adulthood, which seems to be achieved around the age of 26, not 21. Throughout this process, parents can expect to have many positive shared experiences, including gains, losses, disappointments, and, in some cases, high achievement. In her song *Woodstock*, from 1970, Joni Mitchell describes the state of our "nations and our lives," still relevant 50 years later (10).

Life is for learning—something Covid-19 has further challenged us with. Parents have a huge responsibility in child-rearing, but there is no definitive manual. However, *The School of Life: Good Enough Parenting* (11) makes a more recent attempt. We tend to parent the way we were parented. In this section, I use the word 'inculcate,' a sociological term that describes this process of implanting or instilling, meaning to 'introduce' into the mind. Implant implies teaching that makes for permanence in what is taught — for example, instilling a love of reading in a student. Inculcate implies persistent or repeated efforts to impress on the mind. Instil stresses gradual, gentle imparting of knowledge over a long period of time, such as instilling traditional values in your children. This process also includes skill acquisition.

Though we seek to change some of those beliefs our parents held, that's what we knew, and it takes awareness and dedication to make changes that we believe may lead to better outcomes. Supporting parents in the development of their talented children,

I believe, requires more meaningful and practical support for an under-resourced group.

Crucial to the positive development of children are early **attachments and bonding**, which give rise to safety, security, and feelings of being loved. Disruptions to this can have strong and long-term negative consequences, but they can be resolved and healed. Another consequence for parents is what is recognised now as **'intergenerational trauma**,' described in the four phases of Brainspotting, and passed on from their own parents and grandparents. This trauma is significantly subconscious in nature and not necessarily intended. However, being aware of it and understanding it allows conscious and determined choices to be made. In turn, we may halt such unwanted feelings from being imparted onto our children and thus future generations **(WW110)**.

Much of what leads young people and young adults to seek psychological support is **'performance anxiety**,' which affects performance for reasons that are not fully understood and falls within the realm of sport and performance psychology.

In Chapter 2, I briefly introduce **Phil-osophy**: a way of looking at things, life, and performance anxiety. Entwined in performance is our **self-identity**—such as "I am a golfer," or maybe even more than that. In essence, the person as a performer. I have sought to help clarify such experiences in terms of their origins. I often say, "It's all about the golf, nothing about the golf, and all about the golf!" This comes from the context of sport and the 'stage' of performance, where this takes place under high expectation and pressure to perform, both external and internally.

It shows vulnerabilities that, for most people, originate in our life experiences rather than in the focused context of the performance itself. Hence, while the attention may be on golf, the underlying origin is something like parental pressure, which shows itself negatively in the golfing performance. These often-subconscious issues are so strong that I rank their influence to be 25% in the sport and **75% in the life experience.** This idea inspired the subtitle of the book: *Life, Art, and Sport Performance.*

We might think or believe that hitting the golf ball as we can, but not as we are, is a technical issue, when the reality is something deeper—your partner has left you, a close relative has died, or you have financial problems. This is the 'stuff' of life that interferes with our ability to perform as we are capable. When those elements of life are resolved—often needing help, support, and different perspectives—hitting the golf ball as we once did returns, free from the body tension, negative thoughts, a pounding heart, or sweating hands. Instead, we simply see the flag and the tee we aim at. In the 'present moment,' in the 'zone,' in the 'flow' of attentional focus, when we are having fun, we perform at our best.

Philosophically, it is important to recognise the person as an integrated whole, holistic, and not just as a part of that element of performance, such as a footballer or violinist, that seeks to define us solely as we are. We are much more: a parent, sister, brother, uncle, teacher, coach, friend, carpenter, gardener, or choir member.

At the 2020 Tokyo Olympics, Max Whitlock became a triple gold medallist in gymnastics on the pommel horse. He did so under remarkable pressure and expectations, at his most nervous, amidst a recent history of a range of injuries and life changes, while struggling with his mental health. Max was unable to sustain his performance with such high expectations which then materially impacted on his mental health and was unable to perform at all. "A lot of athletes talk about the low after the Olympic Games and I never could even comprehend it or even relate to it all, but now I really can. I can really relate to that feeling of being completely lost just struggling constantly" (12).

I explain **motivation, setting goals, and self-determination,** as well as the origins of self-identity and performing under pressure. From a range of negative experiences such as fear of failure, **'perfectionism'** can develop, often with significant consequences and not just in sport or music. We can develop a propensity—a strong instinct or liking for something—that is deeply ingrained and often manifests as an irresistible inclination. In such cases, we can lose control emotionally or physically and 'disconnect' from ourselves as a means of self-protection from such negative consequences. We may develop an increased tendency, alongside a 'penchant' for taking risks, which may be subconsciously driven as **self-sabotage**. For example, just one metre from touching the end of the swimming pool in a crucial race, we might suddenly seem to slow down, as though it is literally out of reach. No medal. (**WW2**)

In Chapter 3: Relationships and Performance, I draw attention to specific relationships known as the "Coach–Athlete–Parent Triad," the central theme of the book.

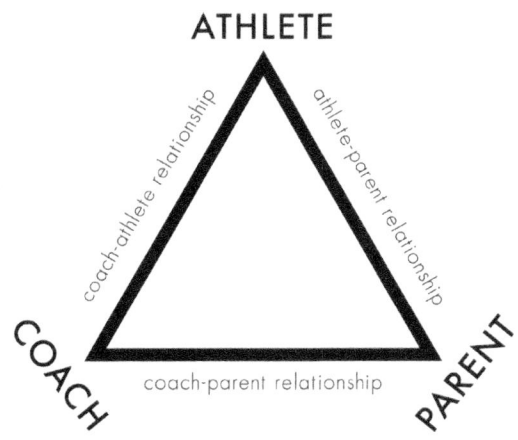

Here in the 'Triad' (triangle)—that set of **social relationships** that can allow young people to thrive in their chosen activity—the protective role of parents may not only be required but also used to seek clarity of **communication between all parties** for optimal performance and personal wellbeing. This parental 'attachment' is needed to help them feel secure. However, the Triad can also become a **power relationship**, giving rise to elements of controlling behaviours by either coaches or parents, which can negatively impact the dynamics of the relationships. Rather than the desired cooperation and awareness that gives rise to a mutual win-win scenario, it may create conflict. Recognising this dynamic provides valuable insight into how it can be managed more effectively.

In Chapter 4: Developing A Positive Identity of Self, I explain the periods of adolescence into early adult maturity, focusing on the development of a strengthened sense of **self-acceptance**. These years from 12 to 19 with the onset of puberty, bodily, hormonal, and psychological changes, require recognition, support, nurturing, and understanding, within the contexts of performance, education, art, sport, and occupation.

Over many years, my understanding of the component parts of **self-esteem** have developed robustly, giving me more ideas on how to positively influence them while also recognising difficulties with them. In this **Winning Way 1,** awareness of the link between low self-value, **limiting self-belief**, and a lack of assertiveness, gives rise to what we call 'confidence,' however that might be felt. When it is negatively interfered with through life, and sporting experiences for example, it gives rise to personal disappointment, embarrassment, and humiliation. These are the origins of personal trauma**.**

Among these developing years are various **role models** as influencers in the form of parents, siblings, teachers, friends, coaches, musicians, actors, and writers. In essence, we seek or meet with someone who inspires and supports greater competence in activity, pleasure in what they do, and fulfilment of the 'self' through the reward we call satisfaction. In such relationships, we can experience generosity, influence, and help in developing and managing our expectations and maturity. This includes creating goals for ourselves and pursuing the 'dream and ambition' to achieve or win. Understanding the dynamics, the actions of our interactions—such as those explored through **Transactional Analysis (TA)**—enables us to see our interrelationships and the dynamics between us more clearly.

In Chapter 5: Lost Adolescence and Performance Lifestyle, I explore the development of these themes by examining some of the things that go wrong, don't meet expectations, the challenges young people face and, by definition, their parents as well. One family I work with has enabled two of their talented children, aged 13 and 14, the opportunity to move to North America from the UK to be educated and play ice hockey at the highest level. This demonstrates remarkable courage from both the children and their parents, who allow and support them to be expansive in their mindsets, embrace discovery, and make bold choices.

One of the strongest emerging occurrences resulting from the Covid-19 pandemic has been young people experiencing **loneliness**. I have sought to more closely define it, to better understand it, and determine how to support those affected. This is just one of the challenges life throws at us, along with separation from family, living alone, financial worries, and uncertainty. David Grand, the developer of Brainspotting, describes the 'uncertainty principle'—which I explain further in Chapter 8—within which we work daily (13). In essence, we do not control all that we would wish and must learn to live with this reality.

There is much greater public awareness of **mental health issues**, as observed during the Tokyo Olympics in July 2021, when Simone Biles of the USA withdrew from the team gymnastics final, citing mental health concerns. A few days later, in a cricketing context, Ben Stokes—one of England's greatest cricketers—stopped immediately, overwhelmed by the pressures to perform, which were affecting his mental health and wellbeing, such as low or depressive mood, poor sleep, low energy, low self-value.

Whilst parents need to support their talented children, they can also be part of the problem they experience and therefore part of the solution. Overzealous and pressuring parents are one of the main reasons young people give up what originally inspired them and brought them joy. This happens not just in sport or the performing arts but also commonly within education. One recurring theme is a loss of belief: doubting themselves in an environment of high expectations, they lose 'faith' and motivation, driven by a fear of failure.

Managing **social media** and the internet, as technology increasingly impacts our lives, also requires education and support—especially when it is used to undermine and abuse others.

In Chapter 6: Performance Issues, I explore what can go wrong, not meeting expectations or coaching measures, and the beginnings of how these issues can be fixed and resolved. The **Four Corners Framework** is like a picture frame that contains someone's individual story. In Brainspotting, that's how we work. We are not seeking symptoms or presentations to box them into a medical or psychological label diagnosis—though these can be helpful in categorizing and understanding the current state and its history. Instead, we seek to understand (non-judgmentally), how life experiences have positively or negatively impacted the way a person feels, disconnects from, or acts as a result, and ultimately seeks change.

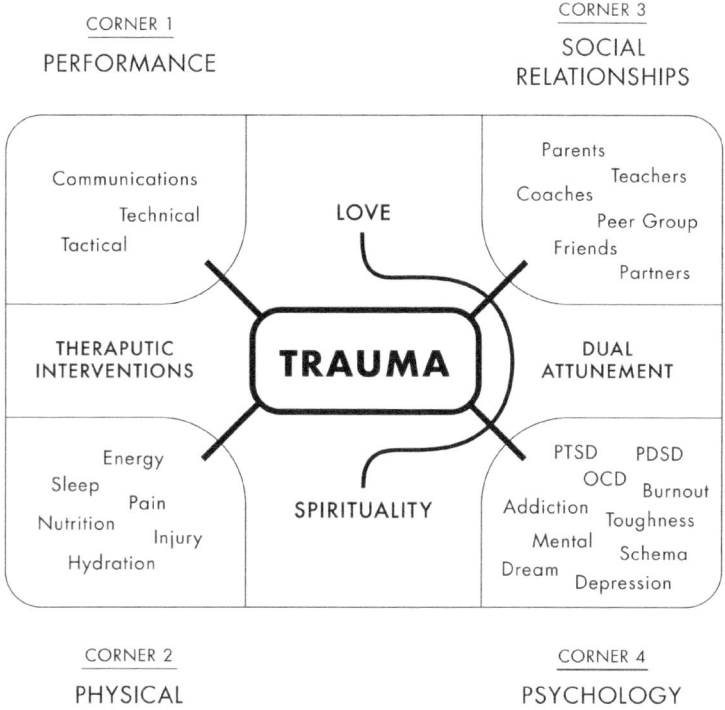

Although I refer to clinical psychology and mental health diagnoses—such as depression, addiction, eating disorders, acute anxiety, and PTSD— in my view, these are presentations of historical events and experiences based on trauma and characterised by a cluster of behaviours. This contrasts with the widely accepted **disease model**, which frames these conditions as illnesses, rather than the dis-ease of stress. When recognised as traumas they are desensitised and reprocessed. The neuroplastic, self-healing brain, changes the way we feel, think, and act! Bravo 'addiction' was really 'self-soothing behaviours'; eating disorders were loss of control, depression emerged with humiliation and dysfunctional parental attachment, chronic fatigue, deep personal trauma, and all brain-body memories.

This is the revolution: non-invasive brain-body interventions which can release and renew 'psychologically', brain-body experiences, resolving medicalised and psychiatrically driven presentations that often appear to lack an effective solution, other than pharmaceutical medicine. However, this does not take away the need for traditional medicine or surgery, which deals with the outcomes of such experiences. Instead, this approach focuses on resolution, prevention, and management in a more non-invasive and naturalistic way. This disease is resolved, by the brain, controlled by the individual.

Greek philosophers helped shape the world of knowledge, including the origins of modern medicine. Plato associates physical and mental health with virtues, particularly the virtue of temperance (*sophrosyne*, meaning "healthy mindedness"). Aristotle relates health with the Supreme Good for 'man.' This Supreme Good, he says, is 'eudaimonia,' a philosophical term loosely translated as "happiness," but perhaps best translated as "human flourishing," according to Neil Burton. As Socrates states in the *Lesser Hippias*, "You will do me a much greater benefit if you were to cure my soul of ignorance, than you would if you were to cure my body of disease" (14).

My point here is that, for the last 30+ years, I have worked alternatively alongside the **'medical model,'** demonstrating—through close to 2,000 clients and patients—that disease, as Socrates first considered, is **dis-ease**. In other words, what we call stress affects the 'mind and body,' beginning with the body then impacting the mind.

Within the work of Brainspotting—a brain-body intervention—and the science of the brain, 'trauma' is held in the low, subcortical, and midbrain regions, connected by the brainstem to the spinal cord. The spinal cord comprises bundles of nerve axons forming pathways that carry incoming and outgoing messages between the brain and the rest of the body, and it is connected to the 'second brain,' the stomach.

We also refer to this as the gut, hence the term **'gut-feeling'**—our instinct. Such information reaches the brainstem, vagus nerve, amygdala, hypothalamus, and thalamus (our limbic system), half a second before visual information from our eyes (processed by the visual cortex) reaches the same areas! As we breathe, this additional second allows emotional intelligence to develop by combining the information from both hemispheres of the brain, leading to better decision-making and improved outcomes.

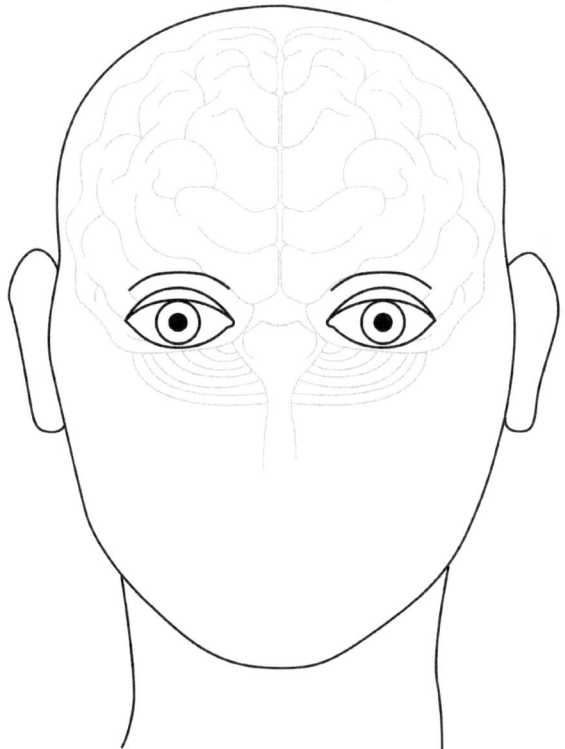

This image shows the two hemispheres / sides of the brain, and how they connect to the eyes and each other. The brain is further subdivided whereby the top of the brain on both hemispheres is where the story dominantly resides.

The subcortical brain is where the trauma is and the psychology needs to be.

UPSIDE DOWN BRAIN:

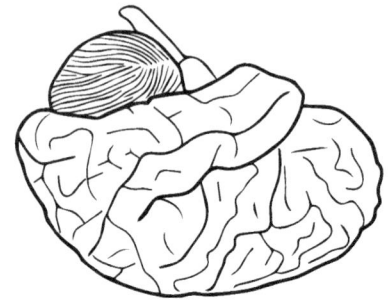

NEW NEURAL PATHWAYS:

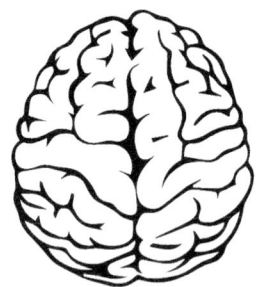

In *Be Good to Your Gut* (15), Eve Kalinik describes the enteric nervous system (ENS) as part of the peripheral nervous system (PNS), which directly controls the gastrointestinal system. The ENS communicates with the vagus nerve inside the brainstem, delivering our fight–flight–freeze responses through the sympathetic nervous system (SNS). Trauma can be held in an immobilised state as memory within the SNS, not discharged or released to the parasympathetic nervous system (PSNS), where it can be deactivated.

One of the neurotransmitters created in the ENS is serotonin, which Kalinik describes as the 'happy hormone.' When serotonin is depleted, it can give rise to depressive feelings, as can dopamine depletion. Approximately 90% of serotonin is manufactured in the gut. Serotonin-specific reuptake inhibitors (SSRIs), a major component of antidepressants, work by increasing serotonin availability in the brain.

This is why I observe the direct relationship between energy, mood, motivation, and performance (EMMP). Alongside this, our stress hormones—noradrenaline and adrenaline—are generated through the SNS, triggering our fight–flight–freeze responses. When these hormones overload in highly stressful situations, the left hemisphere of the brain becomes overloaded by the right hemisphere through hyperarousal, pushing too much stimulus. As a result, we panic in fear, freeze, avoid, and even develop phobias, such as those of space and spiders. **This is trauma**, which the brain remembers and triggers. Kalinik, a nutritionist, advocates the importance of gut health as part of a holistic approach.

This leads me to the creation of my **Four Corners Framework,** a system that considers the different elements of someone's life: performance, physicality, social relationships, and psychological components, including trauma histories. These are the stops and blocks to performance enhancement. In doing so, I trust it provides a wealth of information that supports understanding and recognising both positive and dysfunctional behaviours. This understanding enables the development of life and performance skills, as well as the capability to develop successfully. This process, which we call 'nurture,' builds on our genetically predisposed curiosity and the mind's cognitive (thinking) nature.

Psychology is the scientific study of the mind and how it dictates and influences our behaviour, from communication and memory to thought and emotion (16). Psychologists are less focused on physiology and, as a result, may miss critical information—especially as trauma is defined as physiologically based.

Given that almost a third of the population suffers from sleep problems, many people are unaware of the importance of **electrolyte replacement** and its impact on hydration and nutrition. This represents a missed opportunity **(WW55)**. Approximately 70% of my clients, upon assessment, are found to be electrolyte deficient and thus dehydrated. This affects sleep, either due to dehydration itself or because drinking two litres of water before bedtime doesn't quench thirst but leads to waking at 4 a.m. to release it!

The Four Corners Framework enables professionals, parents, athletes, and coaches to assess what is working and what isn't. Teaching nutrition and exercise physiology taught me how significantly these are intertwined with psychology.

In supporting parents with talented children—and that can be all children—I would say that the section on social relationships is a critical element. Hence the **Coach–Athlete–Parent Triad** plays a central role. Leadership is another topic I raise with young athletes and performers, as they often exhibit these traits and behaviours seemingly naturally, or they may not be aware of how they already lead. This requires support, encouragement, and the permission to express these abilities.

Engaging in activities outside of their primary performance focus helps develop more of a balance, offering opportunities to connect with different groups of people beyond sport, dance, or music. For example, Scottish country dancing, suitable for ages 3 to 100, is one of the most **inclusive social activities** I've ever witnessed—or taken part in—especially on the Scottish island of Colonsay.

The **psychology corner** looks at a simple view of **Mental Toughness**, which is self-measured and can be useful to gain insight into your son or daughter's perception—and how it compares to your own! It is so important to have clear definitions of such topics, especially considering the 2020 –2021 lockdowns, during which there was a notable rise in young people feeling they had major anxiety or clinical depression. Often, however, this was not critical but rather indicative of a 'depressed mood.'

It can sometimes involve 'catastrophizing'—thinking the worst—and feeling unsupported. While there is always a genuine worry around suicidal ideation that may emerge from feeling isolated and lonely (and this is important to always follow up and fully understand), it may not be clinical depression. The Covid-19 pandemic separated a lot of young people from 'normalised' social connection, leading to isolation, and the consequences of this separation are still being felt two years later.

I reference **The Four Agreements** by Don Miguel Ruiz (17), as they give us a simple and important guide on how to be **respectful** with each other—and indeed, in **a kind of loving way**. Making **assumptions** is a daily occurrence, and I champion the stopping of the words '**obviously**' and 'of course' used so much by politicians and broadcasters when things are not 'obvious' to us at all.

The concept of '**comfort zones**' is something we refer to without clarity about when and how we regulate within and outside of them. I trust that the work and research in this area is more than helpful; in essence, it emphasises the importance of support during transition as the key message.

The identification of clinical mental health issues—ranging from **depression and addiction to PTSD** and **eating disorders**—is crucial for understanding the need for secure attachment and the emergence of 'self-soothing behaviours' alongside the need for feeling **safe**. Recently, sport psychologists have begun paying more attention to mental health, increasing their understanding and exploring some forms of intervention.

Clinical Sport Psychologists, as such, do not exist under this title in the UK, though clinical psychologists may work in sport. The title, however, is recognised in the USA, where I am a member of the professional group. I am duly qualified in both disciplines—mental health and sport and exercise psychology—as well as in sport science. The connection between the two disciplines needs to be much closer and also improved significantly.

In Chapter 7: Psychological Approaches and Interventions, I share a **parental guide** to sport and performance, especially during stages of change and transitions. This chapter also addresses how parents are significantly affected by what happens to their children, sometimes leaving parents with a sense of powerlessness—or, in some cases, even traumatised themselves.

Giving feedback is a major issue for parents, for their talented children, as well as for coaches, who also need to be skilled in giving feedback. However, some—perhaps many—are not skilled in this, even to the point of not giving feedback at all.

The **cooperative coach** is such a valuable asset in nurturing talent, whether in sport or in teaching—such as the teaching of maths. You could say they are worth their weight in 'Gold medals'. The **'gift relationship'** is not simply about generosity, though for me this is a key element of being a good person. It is also about the act of communication and intention.

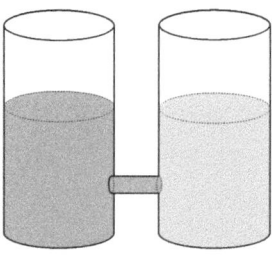
UNCONDITIONAL GIVING AND RECEIVING

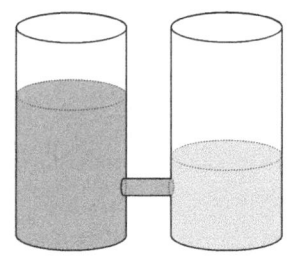
CONDITIONAL GIVING

The Gift relationship and the Love Bank Account. In the gift relationship is the giving and the receiving. The unconditional giving of 'love', is dependent on giving from surplus volume without needing a return. Where 'love' and self worth is low, giving and loving is likely to be conditional of a return. When we have little left, we borrow from the bank with interest. And so what we give then is not our own but belongs to the bank until we can repay it, with self deposits of love, and love received from others – this increases value.

In Chapter 8: A Psychological Revolution, I share a true game-changer in the realm of psychology. Brainspotting is the most successful intervention I have ever come across—it has **changed my life**, and I have supported hundreds of others to do the same, through both direct interventions and training others in over 5,000 hours of interventions.

Understanding that some of the negative behaviours we have, or the frustrations we feel, are **not our fault** is critical. These issues are rooted physiologically in the body, where a capsule of memory in the subcortical/lower brain is triggered by activated memories, causing disproportionate reactions in the present moment. Trauma blocks the two hemispheres of the brain from connecting and communicating at the point of its occurrence. To disable this blockage, and allow the brain to automatically recalibrate the connection, is truly amazing. The brain is not only self-healing and neuroplastic but also deeply subconscious in dominantly driving our actions and behaviours.

When we understand that **trauma** can manifest as **personal disappointment, embarrassment, and humiliation,** we see how it affects so many people in vastly different ways. Resolving trauma through Brainspotting interventions is transformative. The beauty of this approach is that it is a brain-body intervention, using eye positioning and is not **a 'talking therapy'**—making it particularly useful for less communicative adolescents.

The use of **bilateral sounds** (moving from one side to another repetitively) enhances the process by speeding up both release and reprocessing by around 25%. This technique helps calm the individual and supports the transfer to deactivation within the PSNS, promoting relaxation.

The nature of **trauma is physiological**; it causes us to **disconnect and dissociate** emotionally at the point of the event. Through interventions, the reconnection of physiological sensations (feelings), and linked emotions takes place. In the UK, we often refer to feelings as being emotional. It is key to resolving and understanding trauma that we disconnect and reconnect both physiologically and emotionally. As such, I encourage awareness of both!

I describe the **Four Phases of Brainspotting**: these phases can be felt and observed as examples of change, encompassing felt experiences, cognitive shifts, and mental expressions.

In Chapter 9: Brainspotting in Practice, I share a diverse collection of the kind of presentations that come to me on a regular basis and highlight their complexity. The systemic assessment using the Four Corners Framework, enables greater curiosity and understanding, combined with a trauma history. This approach helps us identify what needs to be resolved and changed without relying heavily on diagnostic labels. The 'client' has control of their own process. There is **no judgement**; **the brain does all the work**. Yes, all you need to do is remember, feel, and look—your brain remembers where you 'looked'!

All the presentations are real, but the clients' names remain anonymous and are shared with their permission. I hope these examples give a broad range of real-life scenarios and experiences across different sports and performing arts settings, while also significantly illustrating the vital role parents play in these processes.

There are a variety of resources for you to use, including the Burnout and Overtraining Scales, tools for measuring your Mental Toughness, recognising your Comfort Zones, understanding Pacing in Energy Management, and positive strategies for managing sleep. Additional resources include recipes for electrolyte replacement, insights into understanding momentum in sport, tackling perfectionism, and adopting the concept of '**Striving for Excellence'**! These resources are part of the **111 Winning Ways.**

In Chapter 10: Developing Excellence, I share an overarching theme through the book, and through life, which is 'Love'. I believe the word 'love' is often employed in various contexts without clarity about its true meaning and intended purpose. I view love as a fundamental component of human connection, something not always fully acknowledged within therapeutic relationships between professionals and their clients or patients. This **goes beyond romantic love** and is clearly defined as authentic human connection. It's crucial to recognize how 'present' in the moment this love is, and how it manifests and projects within therapeutic connections and relationships as an essential element of the healing journey.

There exists natural evolutions and nurturing of love within ourselves, which then find expression in relationships of all kinds, and further in the development of intimacy between two individuals. As intimacy deepens and becomes more profound, we can transcend ourselves through spiritual means into an elevated state of being, experiencing heightened feelings that contribute to excellence in our lives. A more recent development in therapy has been professionals expressing love as part of their caring for clients as human beings, fostering their safety and sense of secure attachment, which is vital for healing and growth.

There is also greater recognition of the spiritual dimensions of our existence, without necessarily connecting to organized religion. This is masterfully demonstrated by the Brainspotting community and others, and consistently documented by leaders in this field, emphatically recorded in the *Power of Brainspotting* book, and certainly evident in my own practice. Ultimately, our own **self-acceptance** becomes the foundation of our being, purpose, and life directions, along with some conception of connection to the 'universe' and its inherent energy, and a reverence for humanity and the earth upon which it exists.

Summary: Conclusions and Realisations

This book, I recognise now, is part of my legacy. It has taken decades to understand all of this, and I will be forever grateful to Dr Alan Goldberg, sport psychologist from Amhurst, Massachusetts, USA, for introducing me to Somatic Experience, EMDR, and Brainspotting, as well as to Dr David Grand, New York, USA, the developer of Brainspotting, for their inspiration and humanity (18).

In ***The Rise of the Meritocracy***, sociologist Michael Young wrote, "Were we to evaluate people, not only according to their intelligence and their education, their occupation, and their power, but according to their kindliness and their courage, their imagination and sensitivity, their sympathy and generosity, there could be no classes" (19, p. 31). I am deeply moved by this quote from my studies in sociology. In other words, this is **love in action**—a theme that begins to weave through this book as we understand the importance of the therapeutic relationship and Dual-Attunement used in Brainspotting therapy.

In time, there will be an interactive web platform to enable parents to connect with each other, share resources and experiences, and participate in workshops for parents, coaches, and educators.

Thank you for taking the opportunity to read this book. I hope that, in some way, it becomes life-changing for you, your talented child, or someone that you coach, or teach.

I have had the privilege of working with some of the most famous athletes and well-known parents. However, regardless of age or status, the principles are no different—whether for a 12-year-old gymnast, a Premier League footballer, or an F1 driver.

Enjoy the journey; there will be twists and turns, the occasional 'chicane', but you will reach the finish line.

CHAPTER 2: PHIL-OSOPHY

The Person as the Performer

The Humanistic Perspective
Philosophical and Psychological Frameworks of Understanding

Systems Thinking, Schemas, Guided and
Unguided Imagery, Self-Identity

Perfection, Excellence, Attentional Focus, and Trauma Defined

"People may be understandably confused about what philosophy is," wrote Alain de Botton, a somewhat modern philosopher leading the School of Life, and the emotional education, in his book *The Consolations of Philosophy* (20). I was surprised to discover that my perceptions of philosophy did not align with its definitions! From a distance, de Botton observes, "it seems weird, irrelevant, boring and yet also—just a little—intriguing, who, what and why have we developed a topic philosophy." Are those who seek fundamental questions about existence, reason, values, the mind, language and knowledge self-appointed philosophers, or otherwise? (Note the play on 'other' – 'wise.') The word philosophy itself is derived from *Philo-Sophia*. In Greek, *'philo'* means love—or devotion—and *'sophia'* means wisdom. Thus, philosophers are people devoted to the love of wisdom, which can also be framed as 'knowledge.'

The view of the School of Life is that "being wise means attempting to live and die well, leading as good a life as possible within the troubled conditions of existence. The goal of wisdom is fulfilment, compatible with a lot of pain and suffering, which every decent life must by necessity have." Thus, a philosopher—or 'person devoted to wisdom'—is someone who strives for systematic expertise in working out how one may best find individual and collective fulfilment. In their pursuit of wisdom, philosophers have developed a very specific skill set over centuries.

Socrates developed an open-questioning approach in the search for answers to his enlightened curiosity—an approach by which we can establish clarity by playing devil's advocate with any idea. In other words, this involves examining others' perspectives to generate debate, allowing new ideas to form and, ultimately, fostering some sense of realisation. This process enables a change or adaptation within ourselves and serves as a test as to whether the ideas guiding our lives are sound.

The Humanistic Perspective

The focus then, appears to be on the individual, and less so the communities we live and act within. In this **'context'** (context is key to the framework of psychology), my focus is on performers and the environments, stages, and arenas in which they literally and metaphorically 'act,' appear, and perform. To reflect on and understand our actions—and how we might change them to be 'wiser' or improve—we need to engage in a process of adaptation. I see philosophy—indeed, my own Phil-osophy—as the overarching framework for a 'systematic' understanding of ourselves within the context of 'life.' It is about knowing what works for us and others, why it works, and how, through reflection and the perspectives of others (wise), we might enable adaptations and transitions in our performance of life, art, and sport. Our relationship—'to be or not be'—is an enhanced version of what we already are in terms of our time on this planet. Discover more in Chapter 6: The Four Corners Framework, where I explore tools for self-reflection and adaptation in life, art, and sport.

The **humanistic perspective** is a way of evaluating an individual as a whole, rather than looking at them through a single lens or focusing on smaller aspect of their person. It is a branch of psychology that relates to the idea of being entirely unique and your own individual. This relatively new theory looks at the way the hierarchy of needs impacts what you do in your life and what you want for your future. It also intersects with the realms of manifestation, in other words asking for what you want, if indeed you know.

For both you and me, having a framework for understanding—a systematic assessment process of presenting current and historical issues—allows for practical approaches (interventions) to support positive change. For the past 20 years or so, cognitive thinking and problem-solving approaches have been the central psychological focus, and considered economical, alongside the emergence of a **bio-psycho-social model** within a **'systems' framework**. In other words, it's about putting it all together to understand what makes us tick, identifying what goes wrong when things don't work, and, crucially, determining how that can be changed!

To explain more simply how the brain works, consider **'schemas'**—the collections of memories stored in organised forms held in the brain's long-term memory. These are central to the working of 'cognition,' our thinking processes. Think of schemas as 'folders' on a computer, where memories are stored like 'Word' documents. The brain searches for these schemas (folders), within which sub-schemas (sub-folders) exist, to check what we know from the past to help us make decisions in the present. These decisions are based on our consciously accessed memories and the meanings we have attached to them. For example, imagine a schema (folder) containing all the restaurants you've been to. If someone suggests going to a specific restaurant where you once had coffee spilled all over you, your subconscious brain might immediately say, "No, not there!"

With the use of **guided imagery**, we can change negative or limiting schematic memories, neutralising them or transforming them into more positive ones **(WW102)**. As you will see later, there are specific places in the subcortical (lower) parts of the brain where these memories are stored. When we access them, release them, and desensitise their negative thoughts and feelings—by connecting them with their specific eye positions (even with our eyes closed)—those feelings seem to disappear, as if by magic! More on this later. For now, let's better understand how we—and our children—develop, especially when and where 'performance' is deemed so important.

With this in mind, and the premise of **Self-Determination Theory** by Deci and Ryan (21), consider the consequences of athletes developing their identity solely based on their performance in their chosen sport. For example, John the footballer, rather than John the person who also happens to be a talented player. Given what we know about career-threatening injury, negative coach-athlete relationships, failures, and other challenges, there is significant vulnerability when our **self-identity** is entirely reliant upon good performance. Shifting the perspective to view sport performance as only part of who we are can, for some, represent a positive change in thinking and self-perception. This mindset acknowledges that they are a whole person first and a sport performer second; they are more than just an athlete or team player.

Mental health issues can arise from deep disappointments, embarrassments, and humiliations, considered traumatic. These can lead to conditions such as depression, increased anxiety, obsessive-compulsive disorder (OCD), eating disorders, addictive **'self-soothing behaviours,'** and even physical injury. These challenges often extend beyond the scope of current training and knowledge for sport psychologists, as they are more the focus of clinical psychologists who specialize in mental health.

Such a view is reaffirmed by Gardner and Moore in their book *Clinical Sport Psychology,* where they state: "The clinical sport psychologist is strongly encouraged to guard against immediately focusing on performance concerns at the expense of the overall psycho-social considerations of the client. The result is a greater understanding of the athlete, and overall enhancement in all life domains" (22, p. 196).

I have extensive experience working with athletes, players, teams, musicians, and others in performing arts who identify themselves, both subconsciously and consciously, solely with their performance. Jason isn't seen as a person—he is a footballer! His performances in training and in matches are one measure of success, but whether the team wins or loses is another. If he plays well in the matches, despite the team losing, it's "OK"; however, if he plays poorly, this is precisely how he then measures himself. When poor performance happens, it is all too easy to become self-critical, perfectionistic, socially and emotionally withdrawn, and, crucially, emotionally and physiologically disassociated — disconnected. "I'm not good enough," he tells himself, not just as an athlete, but as a person.

Why is there a loss of personal identity? Strong negative emotional experiences— are what we identify as trauma—show us that personal disappointment, embarrassment, and humiliation are major sources of this loss. These experiences may be 'projected' onto young people by coaches, teachers, fellow athletes and players, or even parents, often in the form of emotional and physical abuse, manipulation, or even ignorance. However, it is the individual's capability to manage such situations that ultimately determines their reactions and response.

What we know about performing under pressure is that it reveals our vulnerability. The origins of that vulnerability lie within our personal experiences and memories, especially where these include traumatic events—ranging from car accidents, illness, and serious injury to disappointments and embarrassments. This is why our brains react in a particular way, triggering responses to past events. These reactions keep us disconnected from our feelings, preventing us from being 'in the moment'—not present, frozen, choked, panicked, angry, frightened, and often alone. The brain does not differentiate between a life-threatening trauma, such as a car accident, and a humiliation in the classroom. More on vulnerability and **Mental Toughness** is explored in Chapter 4, including tools to better understand and manage these responses.

This disconnected or dissociative part of ourselves, where we separate from ourselves and our emotions, can be numbing, like a suppression of unwanted negative feelings. It often arises in our primary activity, whether it be a sport, education, work, or another form of performance. We may even disconnect from the very support network that tries to sustain our connection—parents, coaches, teammates, and friends. When we remain emotionally attached primarily to our performance, disappointment and self-criticism inevitably follow. This is particularly pronounced in individual sports like tennis, swimming, or trampoline, where being out on your own makes you more vulnerable compared to the relative 'protection' provided by being part of a team.

In psychology, **perfectionism** is considered a personality trait, characterised by a person's striving for flawlessness and setting the highest performance standards, accompanied by a critical self-evaluation and concerns regarding others' evaluations, opinions, and influences. It is a state where whatever we do, however well we may do it, is very rarely good enough! While perfection is possible, it is often transient. Striving toward it can be positive, but perfectionism is frequently marked by two key characteristics: 1. A tendency to be consistently self-critical when making mistakes or errors, rejecting the idea that mistakes are a crucial part of learning and performance development. In essence, this mindset sets us up to fail. 2. There is no or limited satisfaction, as the underlying belief persists that whatever is achieved is not 'good enough,' reflecting a diminished sense of self-value.

In my long experience, perfectionism often develops out of a need for self-control, which tends to be trauma-based. This usually relates to early childhood experience, dysfunctional attachment issues with parents—the mother in particular—that give rise to a sense of insecurity and doubt. It may also stem from significant events where control was lost or taken away. In other situations, individuals have been overpowered or overwhelmed by someone or something, leaving them with a sense of powerlessness or helplessness.

Developing perfectionism can create a belief that this gives rise to control and power. However, it is often a form of **self-sabotage**, driven by its inherently self-critical nature. This mindset guarantees a sense of failure, a lack of satisfaction, and rigidity in both the body and thinking. Perfectionism becomes a default template, that ultimately fails to deliver any benefit! Its subconscious construct fosters a tunnel-vision approach, enabling intense concentration on one thing while blocking out external factors that could interfere with the desired focus or an ability to manage unwanted feelings.

The tunnel image frames the separation from intrusive thoughts and activities, whilst showing the straight tracks and light at the end of the tunnel.

In the sporting context, the overall direction of the mind is described as concentration, defined as "the ability to think carefully about something you are doing and nothing else" (Cambridge Dictionary). This gives rise to the concept of **attentional focus**—a state that initiates entry into the zone of performance by cutting out external interferences and enabling us to be 'present.' Thinking about the past or the future moves us away from the present. Staying present requires consistent levels of concentration in the form of attention and focus **(WW2)**.

Our eyes act like a video camera: scanning replicates concentration, stopping at a certain point is attention, while zooming in represents focus. Maintaining attentional-focus is a dynamic, ongoing active state that can be disrupted or consciously changed **(WW3)**. This is where the tunnel-vision approach can be helpful. However, it is often subconsciously driven by the need to create some level of control in situations where control was historically taken away or given up—contexts where there appeared no choice, leaving a sense of hopelessness and powerlessness. Bullying is an example. This can otherwise be known as abuse, controlling behaviour, incidents or trauma. It is important to note that 'tunnel vision' can also be a result of perfectionism. In these cases, we cut out the external 'noise' and follow the light, but never get there, as the light moves further away, setting us up to fail or become dispirited and exhausted.

The creation of '**Striving for Excellence**' **(WW4)** gives a new window into the mind, as well as our beliefs and actions. In schools, colleges, and universities, an essay given a mark of 70% is considered 1st Class. The same designation applies to scores of 85%, 95%, or even 100%. This creates a 30% range of performance that is 1st Class and, as such, excellent. A chef creating a spectacular dish of food engaging all the modalities of taste, smell, vision, touch, and even hearing, can be excellent, as can a painting on canvas. As such 'excellence' becomes both **quantitative and qualitatively measured**. In addition, a score of 68% is not so disappointing, it borders on excellence, and gives rise to the notion of progress, development, and learning. It also helps navigate the line between **novice and expert**, showing potential for our progress. We allow ourselves to respect what we know more than others, especially novices, without feeling we must be 'expert.' This is more 'expertise,' which is developmental and dynamic, in action **(WW5)**.

One major issue for parents is when their sons or daughters become disconnected and dissociated—they feel as though they cannot 'reach' their child. Despite the **love** and support given to them, this is neither felt nor often understood by the child, who may be constrained by the narrowness of their perception within their own self-experience. **Parents** often seek some form of external help, only to find limited resources at their disposal. In my experience working with families with elite athletes, there is often a sense of powerlessness. This dynamic is explored further in relation to the Coach–Athlete–Parent Triad in Chapter 3, as well as other situations where power, authority, money, and career are at stake.

It is with the reconnection of ourselves, emotionally and physiologically, that we become able to be cognitively 'present' in the moment, in flow, or in "the zone," allowing our own self-acknowledgement as an individual. This may also align with Maslow's concept **self-actualisation**. For me, this is the greatest challenge in life: achieving our own self-acceptance**.** That's my Phil-osophy. When we reach this state, we can become happier members of the family, team, class, hobby group, choir, church, or volunteer organisation. In essence, we become whole individuals, rather than fragmented beings defined solely by the performance of a sport or other single primary activity.

While many coaches, players, and athletes around the world consider their sport paramount, it is often their families who provide the stability and sense of purpose that underpin their success. Families are there to celebrate with them during winning moments and ceremonies, offering a positive lifestyle that supports not only their achievements but also helps define them during and beyond their athletic careers.

Consider examples such as Sir Mo Farrah, Sir Steve Redgrave, Sir David Beckham, Sir Chris Hoyle, Sir Paul McCartney, Sir Andy Murray, Karen Carney MBE, and Jenny Jones OBE, who have all celebrated alongside family, coaches, and close supporters. It's a team effort— even for those in individual sports, such as singles tennis players or motor racing drivers.

In Chapter 9, I demonstrate how the reintegration of 'self'— by **releasing the trauma history**, building self-value, **modifying limiting self-beliefs**, and fostering assertiveness with a stronger sense of boundaries—often leads to performance levels never before achieved.

CHAPTER 3: RELATIONSHIPS AND PERFORMANCE

The Coach–Athlete–Parent Triad

The Influence of Teachers in Education

Coaching, Peer Group Relationships, and Youth Culture

Coaching Relationships

While sport psychology research has focused a great deal on the coach–athlete (dyad) relationship, less attention has been given to the often most difficult relationship between parents, coaches, and their talented athletic sons and daughters. Dr. Misia Gervais wrote, **"The details of this triangular relationship, this 'Triad,'** demonstrates the very extremes of the relationship in terms of closeness, high performance and success, contrasted with devastation, bullying, and even sexual abuse" (23).

The primary issue, as I see it, lies in the **quality of communication**—in the intention, understanding, perception, and the ability of all parties to be mutually heard and respected. In my experience, as well as what others have reported to me, a significant proportion of sport coaches across the sporting spectrum often struggle with this. Their ability to communicate

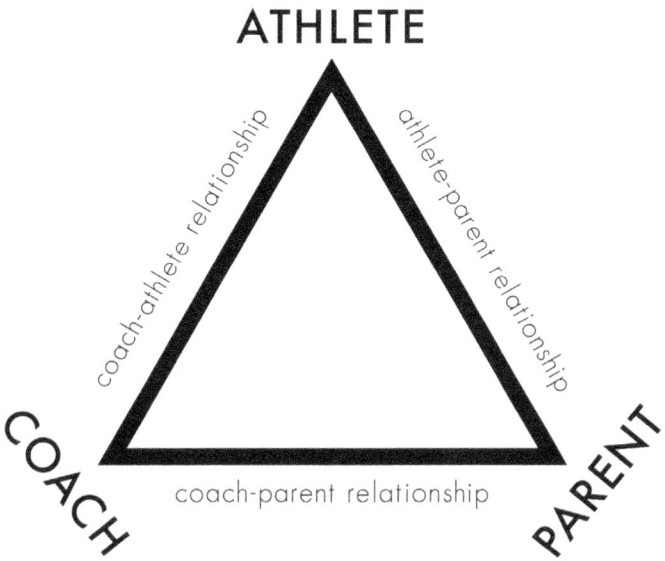

with athletes effectively—with clarity and good intention—is now recognised by me through a wealth of observations and feedback. This presents a substantial issue.

We consider the concept of '**feedback**' on performance fundamental to supporting development and success, whether in sport, art, business, families, or education **(WW6)**. Ample evidence suggests that some coaches and teachers, knowingly or otherwise, may unconsciously damage young people psychologically. This is also key in relationships, as mastered by Dr Harville Hendrix and Alain De Botton. This concept will be explained in more detail later.

The Influence of Teachers in Education

One of the activities that stands out most clearly among the hundreds of young athletes and performing artists I have worked with over a 20+ year period is the importance and impact of teachers and their influence. Teachers, like their students, are individuals with their own emotional experiences, which often find expression in their teaching and how they relate to their students. I often hear of the life-changing impact **inspired by a teacher**, who may also be a sport coach. It seems that it takes just one person outside of the family group to **inspire a young person**, and that alone can be transformative **(WW7).**

If this is the case, then a teacher who is either consciously or unconsciously negative, unenthusiastic, distracted, or **bullying** in any way can disappoint, embarrass, or humiliate their students, too. In contrast to inspiring teachers, those who create strong negative experiences for their students can leave them traumatised—immobilised, disconnected, and disheartened. Some of these events may appear at the time to be unimportant. However, when the trauma history is investigated using the lens of personal disappointment, embarrassment, and humiliation, their impact can prove devastating and long-lasting.

A common example is one where a teacher identifies a particular student and consciously places them under pressure to answer questions (to perform). As a result, the student not only struggles to provide the correct answer or gets it wrong but also outwardly displays embarrassment. This can give rise to taunts of humour and ridicule from fellow classmates, which only adds insult to injury on an emotional level. Depending on the teacher's own predisposition, they may further humiliate the student by making derogatory remarks about their competence, such as labelling them 'stupid.' Such actions are devastating and deeply humiliating.

In these situations, the student may already have low confidence in themselves or in a specific subject. The teacher may also know this but nevertheless continues to expose an already vulnerable member of the class. This can demotivate a student, leading them to avoid the teacher, and avoid answering future questions in front of their peers. Such experiences remain subconsciously in the subcortical brain, waiting to be triggered into a 'fight, flight, or freeze' response—without permission or control from the conscious self. This is particularly impactful for young students with neurodivergent learning issues, such as attention-deficit/hyperactivity disorder (ADHD), or who are on the autistic spectrum, and for those studying maths, and dyslexia. Poor performance in maths sends the brain an unconscious message that it is less capable of problem-solving in certain areas of life. These experiences are also known to affect global self-esteem—a conclusion supported both by research and my first-hand experience.

It is widely considered by professionals in both teaching and sport that feedback of this nature weakens an individual's capacity to cope. Many of the athletes and students I have spoken with not only experience humiliation and embarrassment, but these experiences can be life-changing, particularly in relation to the four elements of trauma: hyper-arousal, numbing, intrusive thoughts, and avoidance of a person, place, situation, or event. These experiences often form the cornerstone of poor performance not only in the academic subject where the event took place, but also in other subjects, sometimes culminating in school refusal.

Even in adulthood and higher education, the same triggered experiences create those avoiding behaviours. They manifest as bowing one's head to avoid the teacher's gaze, hiding behind a fellow student to escape attention, avoiding colourful clothing to remain unnoticed, and becoming extremely anxious simply at the possibility of being asked a question—even when the answer is known. Such behaviours are not only energy-draining but also give rise to cognitive impairment, a sense of overload, and diminished understanding.

Teachers and lecturers may be completely unaware of the impact they have on their students and may wonder why one of their students is so hesitant to answer what might appear to be a simple and straightforward question.

Some mental health issues are considered particularly challenging because, unlike an injury to a leg or arm that can be plastered and protected—and thus observed—humiliation is often deeply internalised and unseen. The **command style of coaching** or teaching, the 'do as I say' approach, is further compounded by personal dislikes of individual students, who may be consciously or unconsciously targeted to demonstrate the teacher's sense of authority. This is especially true when the student is perceived as particularly bright, behaviourally difficult, or challenging. Commonly referred to as being 'put down,' this behaviour is frequently described to me by individuals in the context of marriage relationships or employment, where a partner or boss seeks to overpower rather than assert and balance control.

Such controlling mechanisms in the teacher–student, coach–athlete, and sometimes parent–child relationships serve to undermine confidence, keeping individuals 'in their place' to prevent them from becoming problematic for reasons that may vary within the given context. These behaviours fall into the category of emotional abuse, manipulation, passive-aggression, anger, and overt victimisation.

When such experiences happen to young people, my observations suggest that these patterns continue into adulthood, shaping individuals who become angry and defensive. They may struggle to understand why they were targeted, why no one helped them, and why they now spend time, effort, and energy trying to suppress the feelings that get triggered when they find themselves in similar situations.

Thus, in my definition of 'trauma' within Brainspotting interventions, this process helps young people and others understand what has happened to them. They also start to recognise the underlying dynamics of their experiences, often realising what occurred for the first time. After all, teachers and coaches should be socially responsible and interested in the welfare of their students— so why would they do such a thing? The answer is often that they too were **bullied**, manipulated, undermined in some way, frequently by a person in authority. These events and their resolutions are explored in greater detail in Chapters 7, 8, and 9.

These experiences often lead a young person to 'disconnect' from unpleasant events, such as bullying. In this dissociative state, their normal functioning is disrupted, prompting avoidance of people, places, situations, and events that serve as reminders. This avoidance affects relationships by numbing emotional responses and fosters a **fear of intimacy**.

Peer Group Relationships

The term 'peer group' emerged from studies by sociologists, of which I was one for a time, on the impact of groups of children on each other, particularly during adolescence (primarily ages 12– 16). Sociologists also researched 'youth culture,' the framework within which these influences occur.

In sociology, a **peer group** refers to both a social group and a primary group of people who have similar interests, ages, backgrounds, or social statuses. Members of such groups often exert significant influence on one another's beliefs and behaviour.

Understanding peer influence of similar aged people, and social dynamics within peer groups is vital for emerging leaders aiming to navigate and excel in complex social structures. (https://www. jointhecollective.com/article/understanding-what-is-a-peer-group-in-sociology-a-key-to-empowering-emerging-leaders/) **Youth culture** encompasses the collective ways of living among adolescents, including the norms, values, and practices they recognise and share as appropriate guides for behaviour within their society. This concept includes two elements. The first is culture, which refers to the symbolic systems and the processes through which these systems are organised, maintained, and transformed by the people who share them. The second part is that youth culture is specific to adolescents and differs, at least partially, from the culture of older generations **(WW6)**.

Elements of youth culture include beliefs, behaviours, styles, and interests. Emphasis on clothing fashions, popular music, sports, vocabulary and dating, sets adolescents apart from other age groups, giving them what many believe is a distinct culture of their own. Within youth culture, there are many distinct and constantly changing youth subcultures. The norms, values, behaviours, and styles of these subcultures vary widely and may differ from the general youth culture as perhaps adults see it.

Despite the efforts of parents, coaches, teachers, and other support networks, peer groups can be fantastically **inclusive**, supportive, creative, trusting, and cohesive. However, they can also become sources of friction, conflict, bullying, undermining, **isolation**, and alienation, often stemming from **'peer pressure,'** which can be life-changing and destructive. What we might call 'banter' in the sports dressing room can, for some players and athletes, feel demeaning and become a source of anxiety, avoidance, and even performance loss. After all, these environments are inherently competitive—even within the same team—but they are also where mental toughness is developed, alongside leadership, cooperation, and a sense of group cohesion.

Ken Robinson discusses the concept of **'Group Think'** and while recognising the powerful influence of parents and families, argues that the peer group is even stronger (24). At this point, parents may feel disempowered by their inability to be heard or to exert influence, even as they observe the distress that arises from these dynamics.

CHAPTER 4:
DEVELOPING A POSITIVE
IDENTITY OF SELF

Social and Individual Identity

The Process of Maturation and Self-Responsibility

Cognitive Brain Development and Motivational Types

Understanding Self-Esteem and Intergenerational Trauma

**Managing Elite Status and Self-Acceptance /
Performance Anxiety and the Gift Relationship**

**Overtraining / Burnout and Transactional Analysis (TA) /
Who Am I – The Total Person**

From birth to approximately nine years of age, humans are physically dependent on their parents for food, shelter, warmth, and emotionally for **love**. As infants, we are the most vulnerable of any species for the longest period of time. This period of growth is primarily supported by mothers and, where fathers are present, by them as well. However, this model is increasingly influenced by factors such as the high percentage of marriage and relationship breakdowns (30% in 2019). Changes to family structure can also arise from an absent parent due to work, illness, or other forms of separation and divorce, resulting in single parenting and shared caregiving arrangements.

From the age of 7 to 11, children begin to develop greater awareness of themselves and different ways of thinking about the world in which they live. Jean Piaget refers to this as the 'concrete operational stage' of **cognitive brain development.** This stage leads naturally into puberty, where physiological, cognitive, and emotional changes become apparent.

The fourth and final stage of Piagetian cognitive brain development, known as the '**formal operational stage**,' begins at approximately age 11 and lasts into adulthood. During this stage, individuals develop the ability to think about abstract concepts and to logically test hypotheses, theories, and ideas. This period corresponds to adolescence, and the onset of puberty—defined as "the period at the beginning of adolescence when the sex glands become functional and the secondary sexual characteristics emerge" (Collins Dictionary).

PIAGET'S PERIODS OF COGNITIVE DEVELOPMENT			
Birth to 2 years	Sensori-motor	Uses senses and motor skills, items known by use	Object permanence learned
2-6 years	Pre-operational	Symbolic thinking language used; ergocentric thinking	Imagination/experience grow, child de-centers
7-11 years	Concrete operational	Logic applied, has objective/rational interpretations	Conservation, numbers, ideas, classifications
12 years to adulthood	Formal operational	Thinks abstractly, hypothetical ideas (broader issues)	Ethics, politics, social/moral issues explored

In many cultures, societies have symbolically recognized the transition from childhood to adulthood through '**rites of passage**.' These rituals are universal to the adolescent experience and represent a cross-cultural phenomenon. While the specifics of such ceremonies are based on tradition, they are often adapted to make them relevant to contemporary, modern culture. Rites of passage have existed throughout human history and may play a significant role in shaping the stability of the adult personality (25). Examples may include the practices of Indigenous communities and Jewish religious traditions, such as the Bar/Bat Mitzvah. A 'rite of passage' is both a **spiritual and psychological** undertaking **(WW7)**.

During the period of maturity from birth to the teenage years, we observe a slow yet definite **shift in 'power and influence'** from the parents to the child as they progress toward adulthood. In healthy and functional families, parents gradually reduce their control over their children, acknowledging and respecting their children's growth toward adult maturity. They begin to treat their sons and daughters with greater **independence**, encouraging them to make their own decisions. This naturally leads into the realms of intrinsic and extrinsic motivation.

In 2008, I conducted research under the auspices of decision-making in pursuit of a professional football career, together with one of my students. The findings clearly demonstrated that for boys between the ages of 15 and 16, the vast majority decided either to continue playing football purely for personal satisfaction, to stop playing altogether, or to pursue the possibility of a professional career. What significantly influenced these choices in the earlier stages was what psychologists refer to as **'extrinsic motivation'** **(WW8)**, where the desire to engage in an activity is heavily shaped by external factors, particularly the influence of teachers, coaches, and parents.

The critical shift in decision-making occurs when an individual's transition is through '**intrinsic motivation' (WW9)**, meaning they pursue an activity for their own satisfaction. This shift coincides with continued brain development, particularly between the ages of 15 and 18, as physical and emotional maturity progresses. When asked who had most influenced them in their choice of sport and their decision to continue participation, **parents consistently ranked highest (WW10)**. This indicates a balance between both intrinsic and extrinsic motivation at this stage of development (50:50), and later (75:25) intrinsically for the young footballer. Good news for parents.

The way we interact and connect with young people as adults, and with each other as young people especially teenagers is a **'dynamic', of actions between us.** When these ways of communicating are unclear or misunderstood, what are we to do? These issues are considered within the framework of **Transactional Analysis (TA) (WW11)**. This means the 'transaction' is a connection with another person, and we do this showing one of the three types of behaviour, which can be more clearly identified to further understand the meanings of these communications.

Transactional Analysis is a psychological theory developed by Eric Berne in the 1950s. It helps people understand their interactions and communication patterns with others.

Key Concepts: Ideas

1. **Ego States:** We have three 'ego states' that influence how we think, feel, and behave:
   - **Parent:** Behaviours and attitudes we learned from authority figures.
   - **Adult:** Objective and rational thinking.
   - **Child:** Emotions and behaviours from childhood.

2. **Transactions:** The way we communicate with others, which can be complementary, smooth and easy interactions, or crossed and miscommunications.

3. **Life Scripts:** The unconscious life plan we develop in childhood, influenced by our interactions with parents and society. Otherwise known as beliefs.

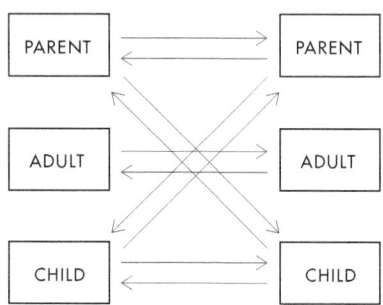

For example, an appropriate and balanced adult-to-adult transaction, communication, might well represent a mature and responsible interchange, and conversation. This represents an ideal and balanced, equal, interchange. This is one of three **states**—Parent, Adult, and Child (PAC)—that are present in a dynamic action of the inter-change between two or more people at any given time, in the way we behave. A parent-to-child transaction demonstrates authority and power in the interaction, someone seeking to use authority, such as a teacher or coach towards another. TA provides a framework to recognise and adapt to changes within these dynamics. For example, in a peer group one teenager of 15 years maybe trying to boss a 14-year-old to do something because they are older. The influence may not be in keeping with equality and taking advantage of the younger person. In such a situation the 15-year-old is being parental in nature, and the 14-year-old, unconsciously acts as a child. If the 14-year-old resists this behaviour and states their own view, rejecting the 15-year-old, the 15-year-old needs to change! If the 15-year-old does, adult style behaviour to adult style behaviour, creates balance and equality, and they get along better.

In this mutual state of respect and acceptance, parents sometimes find the 18 to 21 age range difficult to manage. In my experience, some parents may struggle to move beyond the 'child' perspective of their children as emerging adults. **Moving away from home—** often for further education—naturally facilitates physical, emotional, and financial separation. However, more recent research (26) suggests that the relative point of **adult maturity** is closer to the age of 26, yet young people become adults 'officially in law' from 18!

Parents who struggle to 'let go' of their 'child' may well have experienced something similar within their own family. When this happens, it is often subconscious rather than a conscious decision. In the same way, we tend to parent in the way that we were parented— despite our desire for it to be otherwise or by deliberately choosing to do the opposite. Part of the role of the sport psychologist in this context is to enhance parents' awareness, helping them move towards an adult-to-adult state **(WW12)**.

Key characteristics of maturity include:

1. Maintaining long-term relationships
2. Remaining unshaken by flattery or criticism
3. Demonstrating a spirit of humility
4. Exhibiting emotional intelligence
5. Expressing gratitude consistently
6. Appropriately prioritising others before themselves
7. Seeking wisdom before acting

Boys may have a particularly close relationship with their mothers, just as girls may tend to have a unique relationship with their fathers. While this is an overgeneralisation, it may well be part of the experience of developing both the masculine and feminine elements of these archetype behaviours of both, and vice versa, learning the 'traits 'of each. These early experiences are key to future adult behaviours and mutual respect. I demonstrate later how the horse can symbolise traditional masculine features of power and strength, and unconditional love to a female teenager, especially when they have an 'absent father'. This is because the horse does not judge but accepts the loving attention of the teenager regardless of the sex of the horse.

Although Freud has faced significant criticism over the years for his portrayal of the masculine and feminine, it is important to make allowances for the Victorian era in which he lived, and the current culture. I believe his work has contributed greatly to our understanding of ourselves, particularly in how we cope with growing up, maturing, and managing the powerful influences of our parents. Freud's view that we must, at some point, let go of the images and voices of our parents that shape our actions and behaviours holds some merit. These influences can sometimes be restrictive, limiting, or indeed abusive. Perhaps in the same way, when individuals become parents themselves, they often identify aspects of their own upbringing they wish to avoid repeating, particularly behaviours they found unsatisfactory or unwelcome.

At the same time, parents also provide positive resources, which we need to assess and intentionally cultivate. The process of physically—and symbolically—**separating from parents** is essential for developing a stronger sense of self-identity. Without this separation, we risk remaining in their shadow, constantly seeking their approval (whether they are present or not) or adhering to what they might think to be 'good enough.' Such thoughts, even when consciously addressed, are more likely to subconsciously prevent action, activity, or the ability to engage meaningfully in relationships.

During a placement in the Probation Service on the Wirral, I asked my supervisor why it seemed that men stopped offending around the age of 28, often without explanation. The answer was striking; they meet someone who loves them, find purpose, and develop a stronger sense of self, which is a positive incentive to stop criminality.

In separating from our parents, we do not necessarily seek to reject them. Rather, we aim to finally cut the psychological umbilical cord—to free ourselves to act, think, and behave in ways that are not parent-driven. This separation allows us to form thoughts, make independent decisions, and experiment in ways we may not have previously allowed ourselves. The word that comes to mind is 'freedom,' the basis of Freudian thinking.

An Active Framework of Understanding Self-Esteem

In person-centred counselling, Carl Rogers refers to the perceptions and values that characterise the 'self' (27). Depending on experience, these perceptions will have either a positive or negative impact on self-value, which is a key determinant of our overall self-esteem. Carl Rogers also developed the concept of 'congruence,' defined as authenticity and genuineness in alignment. This concept is illustrated by the 'dissonance' or tension between the perceived concept of self (for example, as a footballer) and the true experience (how it feels). When these differ, they are considered incongruent. For example, an athlete might say, "everything is fine" after losing a game, while their physical 'affect'—eyes down, head bowed, and a low voice—suggests otherwise.

Rogers emphasised the importance of a therapist's deep and genuine care for the client. In chapter 10, I consider this as also a demonstration of 'love'. While the therapist may not approve of some of the client's actions, they must fully accept the client as a person, that is without judgement. In essence, the therapist needs an attitude of "I accept you as you are." A therapist's ability to be authentic and transparent with their client is considered the most important attribute, often used interchangeably with the term 'genuineness.' This principle is the foundation of dual-attunement, as demonstrated by Brainspotting Therapists in particular – both 'love', and spiritually attuned.

Self-esteem serves as an index of emotional stability and adjustment to life's demands and is positively associated with several desirable qualities, including life satisfaction, vitality, psychological adjustment, functionality, integration, leadership, and resilience to stress according to Deci and Ryan (28). They also write that "Low self-esteem can initiate self-destructive behaviours, and drug use is one of these. It's a fundamental need to have a good sense of self. Without it, people may become pathologically unhappy with themselves, and that can lead to some very serious problems." These issues often manifest as depression, feelings of helplessness, suicidal thoughts, and high levels of anxiety—a pattern frequently observed in my practice. (See also the section on addiction in Chapter 6.)

For the athletes I support, particularly those facing mental health challenges, I have devised a model through decades of practice, research, and observation to help both myself and my clients focus on the measurable increase of **'authentic self-esteem'** (humanistic). I have termed this model the **'Configuration of Self-Esteem,'** which comprises, **self-value, self-belief, and assertiveness.** In my view, these components are key to developing self-confidence and performance across all areas of life, particularly in sporting and performance contexts. Each component serves as a definable building block for enhancing self-esteem, which underpins self-confidence and ultimately contributes to **'Mental Toughness,'** as developed by Jones and Moorhouse (29). This model will be further demonstrated and illustrated in Chapters 7 and 8, along with interviews.

In practice, my experience shows that we are more likely to question the expression of our self-esteem when it is under pressure; otherwise, it tends to be 'assumed' as positive during periods of sustained successful performance. In contrast, positive self-esteem can decline during periods of underperformance, revealing its lack of robustness and susceptibility to frequent change. I consider assertiveness to be a more stable measure of self-esteem—tangible, measurable, and consistent over time **(WW14)**. Proactively and practically, assertiveness can be developed to support maturity in young athletes, aid coach development, and provide the measure of positive self-regard that Carl Rogers intended to support. The act of positively representing ourselves in the world.

Self-Value

The concept of **'acceptance of self'** is central to the approach taken in mindfulness and acceptance-based therapies, a more recent development in cognitive therapy. "Rather than controlling or inducing internal experiences, mindfulness (thinking) and acceptance-based interventions, emphasise the development of a mindful, non-judging awareness, and acceptance of in the moment, cognitive affective, and sensory experiences" (19, p. 100 ??).

The **concept of relatedness** is also important: "The need for competence pertains to the human desire to produce desired outcomes. Autonomy is the origin of one's behaviour, and relatedness a desire to be connected to significant individuals" (30, p. 211). In my view, the increase in self-value is key to the development of assertiveness, which in turn is a behaviour where confidence is demonstrated in measurable ways. Tafarodi and Swann Jr state, "Rather than experiencing ourselves as simply positive or negative, we experience ourselves as globally 'acceptable or unacceptable' (self-liking) and globally 'strong or weak' (self-competence). Together these dimensions are held to constitute global self-esteem" (31, p. 324) **(WW15)**.

Self-Belief

Self-belief is widely regarded as an integral part of self-esteem and the development of confidence, often linked to positive and negative 'self-talk.' Jones and Moorhouse assert that "Self-belief is an essential part of the make-up of the very best performers" (29, p. 79) **(WW16).** Among the elements that support self-belief are the ability to accept criticism without personalising it, engage in more rational analysis, and, as part of the second pillar of mental toughness, recover effectively from setbacks.

From the perspective of the person first and athlete second, self-belief—primarily linked to sporting prowess—is subject to great variability and change, being directly dependent on performance achievements. Similarly, Vallerand (27) argues that motivation and self-belief are both shaped by our perception of self and the world around us. Michael Martin from the Australian Institute of Sport says, "having a high degree of self-belief is critical to optimising technical and tactical performance."

Low self-belief and self-value can discourage individuals from asking for what they want or striving for their goals, often resulting in a lack of assertiveness. According to Dr Clint Rogers, only 1% of the population has a clear understanding of what they truly want in their lives (32). Similar, Jones and Moorhouse describes assertiveness as "the ability to believe that you are equal with others and have the same basic rights" (29 p. 68).

With these insights, I developed the 'Configuration of Self-Esteem,' which highlights self-value, self-belief, and assertiveness as critical to building both inner and outward demonstrations of self-confidence and performance. Conversely, negative states of self-esteem contribute to challenges such as depression, anxiety, eating disorders, hindered rehabilitation, overtraining, dysfunction within teams, isolation, and avoidance behaviours.

Our **trauma history**, whether developed in sport or not, limits and even prevents the development of positive self-value and self-belief because the brain literally blocks them. This is due to the memory-specific disconnections between the right hemisphere of the brain, which predominantly deals with physical and emotional responses, and the left hemisphere, where information processing predominates. It doesn't happen unless we release it. This, and **Brainspotting**, represent the **Psychological Revolution, moving beyond talking therapies.**

So why is self-belief so important**,** and how are these beliefs developed? As children, we begin to trust—and indeed believe—what parents and adults tell us as absolute truth and reality. This corresponds to Piaget's pre-operational and concrete operational stages. Through the myriad of experiences that shape us, parents pass on not only what they know but also what they believe. These beliefs are shaped by the stories and experiences of their own families, the influence of their parents, and their interactions through education, work, and relationships. Another crucial element about beliefs is that they shape and determine the way that we react, respond and behave, often subconsciously. In essence beliefs are the major drivers of our actions and are subconsciously generated **(WW17)**.

Self-Acceptance

In my experience, one of the **biggest challenges for any individual in life** is, at some point, to recognise and accept the beliefs they have developed about themselves and/or others **(WW18)**. When tested, these beliefs may prove to be erroneous, untrue, or perhaps never validated. They remain internal constructs that shape how we perceive ourselves, view the world, and interact with the people in it, dominantly driving our behaviours—positively or otherwise.

Therapeutically, I've been working with a particular approach for two decades in which I recognise how parents and grandparents pass on to their children, traumatic memories they themselves have experienced, or that they too have absorbed from their own parents and passed down further to their own children. This is known as **'intergenerational trauma' (WW19)**, a term coined by Dr Roby Abeles, based on her experiences working with Indigenous American communities. Dr Abeles is a fellow Brainspotting trainer in the USA, where I also engaged in her training. Mostly, this transmission happens subconsciously. When young people have the benefit of knowing their grandparents, they can observe for themselves what Freud refers to as **'transference'**—in other words, the projection of personal issues onto others without recognising, owning, or taking responsibility for them. The result is that young people either unknowingly, unwillingly, or unconsciously take on a responsibility for something that does not belong to them. The consequence is that these adopted burdens become part of their own belief system, which can, in turn, limit their capacity and capability to perform.

One compelling example of intergenerational trauma stands out to me from my work with a talented artist, athlete, and musician whose self-identity had strongly become performance-related, resulting in depression. Her **performance anxiety**, deep sadness, and disconnection from herself and those close to her persisted despite public appearances, where she presented herself as happy, content, and successful. After working together for eight months on a particular issue, I asked if she experienced any pain or discomfort in her back. She replied, "All over." When I clarified if she meant all over her back, she said, "No, all over my body." I then asked how long she had experienced this pain and discomfort, and to my great surprise, she told me that she'd experienced it for 10 years!

I questioned why she hadn't mentioned this pain before, and she explained that she had become so used to the pain that she didn't notice it much anymore, though it was always present. (See Natalie's story in Chapter 9.) **Pain and discomfort** of this nature are physiologically and emotionally draining, but she and her brain had adapted to it, believing there was nothing she could do to alleviate it, especially as she did not understand its origins.

It so happened that during our previous work, I recalled an event from 10 years earlier involving her father. When I asked about it, she described how, in her early teenage years, she had become very sad. Although she hadn't fully understood why, she realised that as an active, high-performing athlete, dancer, and musician, she had begun to absorb the pain and sadness of her father's physical disability and increasing immobility. Not only did she feel his pain, but she also constructed a limiting belief about herself— that she could not achieve high levels of success and enjoyment in her chosen pathways due to the guilt she experienced knowing her father's physical and mental limitations.

This limiting self-belief caused her deep sadness, frustration, anger, fear, emotional disconnection, and social withdrawal from her family and friends, leading her to retreat further into herself. It also manifested in developing an eating disorder and struggling with **learning difficulties**, especially in music. Through work addressing this brain-body memory, we identified the appropriate eye positions connected to these feelings. Within 30 minutes, the pains and discomfort she had endured for the past 10 years were desensitised and dissipated—and have never returned. See **WW20**: *The Body Keeps the Score* by Bessel Van de Kolk (33)—essential reading!

This is an example of intergenerational trauma that was unconsciously and undesirably absorbed. The shock of recognising that she had limited herself for many years, believing that she could not achieve the level of performance she desired—nor the associated satisfaction—was powerful. She discovered that her successes had, in fact, brought her father great pleasure and joy, something she had unconsciously denied to both of them.

I have observed many times in the sporting context, particularly at a football game or on the side of a ski slope, where a parent is trying to teach their son or daughter to play better (in their view), or ski more proficiently. For background, I am a coach in both sports. I am a ski teacher, but with very different techniques.

In 1988, I created and founded a ski shop, The Ski Exchange in Cambridge, England, which, to my delight, is now in its 36th season, ably owned and run now by Simon Elliot. I became a ski technician and then ski teacher while developing an encyclopaedic knowledge of skiing. I have also conducted skiing workshops focused on the mental performance and learning aspects of skiing—commonly known as skill acquisition—before heading out onto the snow. These workshops involved small groups practising this 'learning 'on the slopes, resulting in resounding positive changes for participants in just four hours. One major reason people struggle to learn to ski well and quickly is that instructors rarely explain **how the skis** they are using are **designed or how they work (WW21).**

A Skiing Demonstration

In 2018, while spending two days on the mountain in a small ski area in Austria and beginning the first chapter of this book, I observed three sets of parents **modelling** their own skiing style to their young children—with strong negative consequences! There are common technical elements in skiing that developing skiers struggle with, often based out of fear, limited knowledge, and poor role modelling by an 'instructor-parent or friend.'

As a result, developing skiers often:

1. Rotate their upper body left and right, believing this helps them turn.
2. Exhibit a fear of falling or heights, which leads them to avoid looking down the mountain to see where they are going—two issues that are inextricably linked.
3. Fail to understand the fundamental design of the ski. Skis are arc-shaped, and when pressure is applied to the inside edge of the ski, it initiates a turn in an arc, known as a radius-turn. Pressure-Edge-Turn.

If the ski is allowed to complete a full radius turn, it naturally springs back, a design feature that dynamically helps the initiation of the next turn in the opposite direction. This creates an energetic 'bouncing back' or 'spring' motion, visually represented as the 'S' turn **(WW22).**

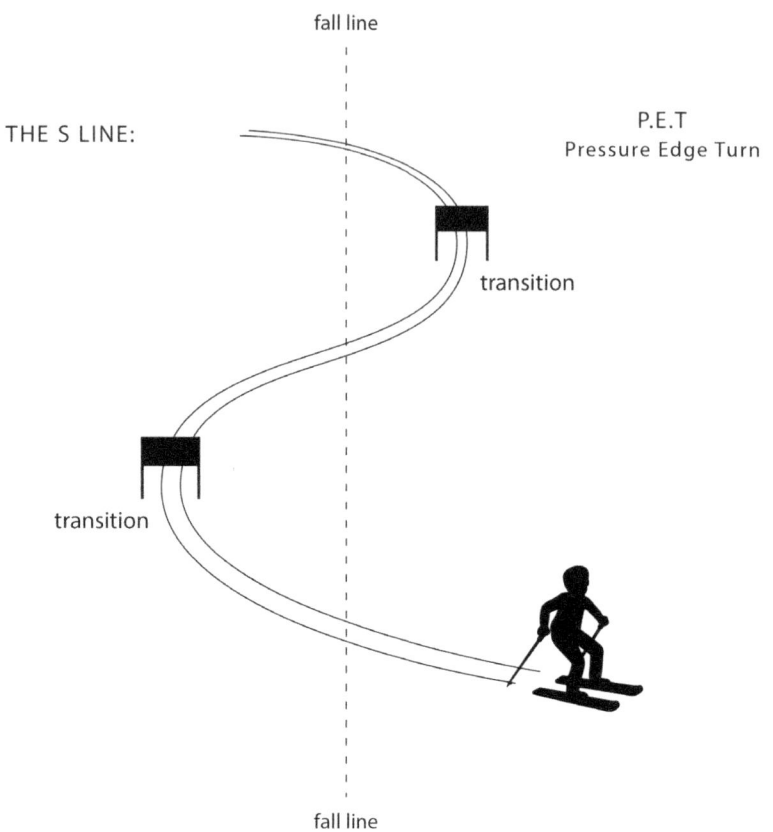

THE S LINE:

fall line

P.E.T
Pressure Edge Turn

transition

transition

fall line

To my knowledge, many skiers at the beginning and intermediate stages rarely experience this phenomenon. Technically, the ski turns under pressure applied through the leg into the ski boot, causing the ski to manoeuvre in a chosen direction. Central to the competence of secure and accurate turns is the technical and psychological ability to look straight down the mountain during this process. This approach ensures proper balance and dynamic control of the turn while avoiding the **upper body rotation, which removes pressure from the ski.**

For many developing skiers, however, looking down the mountain introduces a significant fear factor. The technical term for looking down the mountain is the 'fall line,' referring to the direct fall of the slope of the mountain—not the skier! Looking down the fall line significantly reduces the upper body rotation left and right, allowing the legs alone to move. There is a common misconception that upper body rotation is what causes the ski to turn. Through my observations and discussions with numerous skiers, this misconception seems almost universal!

To succeed in turning the skis and creating the 'S' turns, the planting of the ski pole becomes a psychological cue to mentally initiate a turn. This action facilitates the downward and upward movement of the whole body, changing the pressure on the upper ski edge through the transfer of weight via the ski boot. This weight then shifts to the lower ski, onto which new 'balance' is sustained. Allowing the ski to complete the full radius of its turn sets the stage for it to begin turning in the opposite direction. In this process, **the skier discovers 'flow'** and security—the performance element that all athletes seek, often described as being 'in the moment.' Pointing out these elements has often transformed skiers within an hour, a process further enabled by addressing the original traumatic experiences through Brainspotting.

When a **parent models** or demonstrates incorrect technical methods while trying to get down a mountain on skis, these are the methods their children learn. I see the distress, fear, and loss of confidence in novice skiers who are eager to understand what they need to do to ski properly! In such moments, we see **intergenerational transference of memory**, knowledge, and behaviour—including fear. This transference operates both consciously and subconsciously and becomes embedded in a belief system. When tested against reality, these beliefs often prove dysfunctional.

Despite recognising the ineffectiveness of these patterns, they persist because it's what the individuals know—it forms a default template that they revert to under pressure, as the brain's dedicated response to fear and panic. In such situations, the immobilising fear can be released.

On one day in Austria, I was able to assist two sets of parents and three children! While there were some linguistic challenges, I role-modelled proper technique for the parents, helping them adjust their methods. We then worked together with the children, ensuring that the parents' authority was not undermined **(WW23)**. The changes were dramatic.

What struck me most was that neither the parents nor the children had ever had a ski lesson. They were learning through trial and error, unaware of what they didn't know. Where is the message in that?

Assertiveness

Assertiveness is defined as "the insistence on one's rights or opinions or beliefs" (Oxford Dictionary). Joseph Wolpe, in his 1958 book *Psychotherapy by Reciprocal Inhibition,* stated, "As a communication style and strategy, assertiveness is distinguished from aggression and passivity. How people deal with personal boundaries; their own and those of other people, helps to distinguish between these three concepts" (34, p. 53). Wolpe and others have observed that anxiety and assertiveness do not coexist and, as such, saw the development of assertion as a cognitive behavioural approach to managing anxiety. Wolpe referred to this process as 'reciprocal inhibition'—a method of relearning in which, in the presence of a stimulus, a non-anxiety-producing response is continually repeated until the old, undesirable response is extinguished.

Nicholson and Bayne define assertiveness as "expressing and acting on your rights as a person, whilst respecting the rights of other people" (35, p. 51). Importantly, in describing the therapeutic process, they identify skills such as giving and receiving compliments, (reciprocity) and making requests as fundamental to assertiveness. In essence, the right to say 'No.'

Later, I describe **'The Gift Relationship' (WW24),** first developed by Bronisław Malinowki according to *The SAGE Dictionary of Sociology* (36), and **'The Love Bank Account' (WW25)**, a concept I developed to literally build self-value and self-acceptance. These concepts align closely with Rogerian Humanistic, Person-Centred approaches in therapy. This is particularly relevant within the athlete–coach relationship, as discussed in Chapter 6 on athlete abuse, which explores these notions in the context of both children and adults.

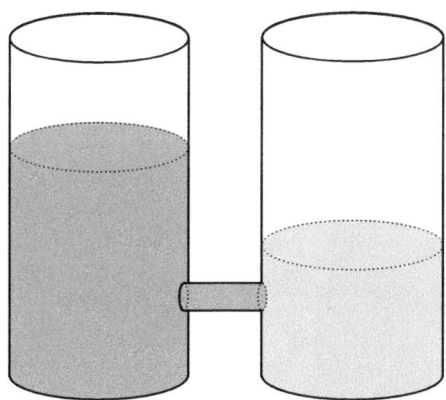

Assertiveness is not just a skill for athletes to develop, but also one for **sport psychologists to role model**. The ability to challenge abuse, dishonesty, and overpowering relationships on behalf of athletes is both a professional and ethical responsibility, as outlined by the British Psychological Society (BPS) and the American Psychological Association (APA). Additionally, sport psychologists must manage their own behaviour as professionals and promote their science and practice. In this respect, we are no different from our athletes or coaches, who seek to assert themselves, represent their skills, and adhere to the codes of conduct they trust—and which we must also uphold.

It is, therefore, essential that sport psychologists are not only able to observe low self-esteem, low self-value, and limiting self-belief but are also able to assist their clients in reconstructing these within a secure and supportive environment. From this develops the necessary concept of **'boundary' (WW26),** within which we personally set parameters for behaviour, such as personal space. Concepts such as **'The Locus of Control' (WW27)** and **'The Circle of Influence' (WW28)** are essential tools in this process. **Together this forms a matrix for The Hula-Hoop** personal boundary system **(WW97)**.

The Hula Hoop creates personal space, and a 360 degree sense of boundary.

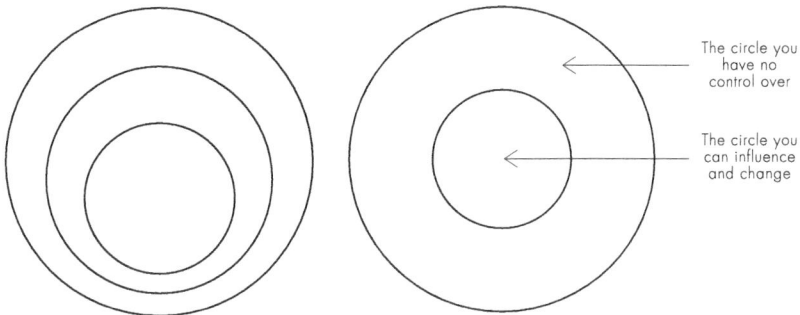

The circle you have no control over

The circle you can influence and change

The Circle of influence allows thoughts and ideas from others to be considered by us, whilst the Locus of Control clarifies what it is we can control, and that which we are unable to, such as the weather! Together with the Hula Hoop, this creates a matrix of personal boundary.

Self-Confidence

Self-confidence is defined as "a sense of self-reliance and assuredness" (Oxford Dictionary). Working on self-esteem naturally supports and strengthens self-confidence, making it robust and stable over time, though it can still be changed or modified. Here, I consider several elements and perspectives of confidence that not only underpin high performance but also contribute to strong mental health. These factors are often closely related but are also context-driven, depending on where you are and with whom you interact.

Jones and Moorhouse (29), consider **confidence** to be associated with recent accomplishments, and guides future intention, reflected in goal setting and developing positive self-talk associated with positive mental skills. A **feedback loop** in performance psychology refers to a cyclical process in which information about a person's performance is gathered, evaluated, and then used to adjust future behaviour or strategies to improve outcomes. This loop involves receiving feedback (from self, coaches, or the environment), interpreting it, making adjustments, and then performing again—continuously refining skills and mental processes over time. Control Theory by C. S.Carver and M. F. Scheier (1982) Psychological Bulletin 92(1) 111–135.

In my view, language serves as a 'window into the mind.'

Highlighting the sport performance link, Zinsser, Bunker, and Williams (38, pp. 349–360), identify the most consistent finding in **peak performance** literature as the direct correlation between self-confidence and success. While self-efficacy (capability) can be considered a very specific form of self-confidence, Harwood's Five 'C's model of confidence—which includes **C**onfidence as an overarching concept supported by **C**ommitment, **C**ommunication, **C**oncentration and **C**ontrol—provides further tangibility to the concept (39) **(WW29)**. Confidence is a central theme in sport psychology literature, as evidenced by Weinberg and Gould (40).

Who am I? Athlete-Performer-Person?

What I've discovered over time about **performance loss in athletes** is that when sport is played competitively in the public domain, there are added expectations that come externally from spectators, coaches, support staff, parents, friends, teammates, and a range of other influences. These external pressures combine with the athlete's desire and expectation to perform in the public arena, where individual vulnerabilities of any type may appear. These vulnerabilities are tested daily and weekly.

Professional and elite athletes face even greater pressure due to higher expectations, often tied to financial stakes. When their performance lacks strength or consistency, they may begin to make errors far more frequently than they would hope, particularly under the scrutiny of selectors and the sporting press.

My observations from practice indicates that reduced performance shows itself in the public arena, where players and athletes feel more vulnerable due to heightened expectations and pressures to perform. What commonly happens to individual athletes, and those in teams, is there is a tendency to respond simply by 'trying harder'—a directive often given by coaches or parents. This approach stems partly from not knowing how to fix the problem, or from a lack of understanding about what to do, and sometimes there is no one available to support them through the process.

As a result, athletes expend more energy and effort, often relying on the same levels of nutrition—or even less—to reach a higher level of performance. While there may be minor initial improvements, it's not long before performance begins to decline. In some cases, signs of overtraining emerge, eventually escalating into the potential for burnout, regardless of whether the pressures are external or internally driven. In such situations, the person begins to equate their identity solely with their performance, losing touch with the broader sense of self that extends beyond sport. For further insight, explore the **Overtraining and Burnout Scale** in Chapter 5.

How and Why Self-Identity Diminishes, and How to Manage It: The Role of Transactional Analysis (TA) in Communication

Transactional Analysis (TA) is a therapeutic intervention model that, in my view, provides a simplistic and practical approach to acting appropriately within social interactions and understanding the behaviour of others in relation to oneself. It enables us to observe and determine the dynamics of interactions within relationships to others, fostering the development of assertiveness, a **stronger sense of boundaries,** and self-responsibility. Introduction first explained on Page 49.

TA is particularly effective for adolescents, as it helps them begin to understand the dynamics of relationships and differentiate between Parent, Adult, and Child roles. Without a strong sense of boundaries and clarity about what is right and wrong, individuals may struggle to recognise abuse—an intrusion, both physical and emotional, into their personal 'space.' TA also helps to describe the process of 'separation' from parents for adolescents and young adults.

First developed by Berne (41), TA provides a simplistic yet effective model and approach for understanding 'ego states' (how we feel about ourselves, derived from Freudian perspectives), relationship dynamics, and assertiveness (how we represent ourselves positively in the world). Harris describes the unit of social intercourse as a 'transaction,' where the speaker or main communicator provides a 'Transactional Stimulus,' which is met by a 'Transactional Response' (42). TA helps us to examine these transactions and identify which part of the 'multiple natures' (states) are being portrayed and translated. The multiple ego states are Parent, Adult, and Child. This framework provides a method of organising and interpreting behavioural information and language—the critical elements of the TA approach.

What is also important in TA, in my view, is the simultaneous changes in facial expressions, vocabulary, gestures, posture, and body functions—such as rapid breathing or heart rate— which are observable. Parent, Adult, and Child states are **phenomenological** realities; that is, they are directly experienced.

Parents impart rules and hold ascribed, inherited, accrued, and allocated authority. **Parents set rules and boundaries** for behaviour, facilitating protection, social norms, and opportunities for learning and maturation during early years of dependency and reliance. The 'Adult' acts as the decision-maker, relying on an objective appraisal of reality, while the 'Child' is the dependent and learner.

There are four life positions in TA:

1. I'm OK – You're <u>Not</u> OK
2. I'm <u>Not</u> OK – You're OK
3. I'm <u>Not</u> OK – You're <u>Not</u> OK
4. I'm OK – You're OK

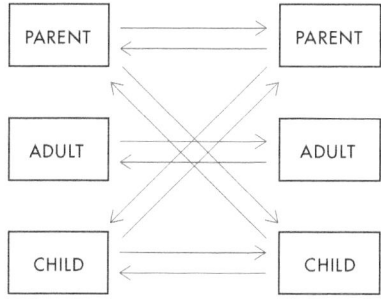

The goal of TA is emancipation—**to give freedom of choice** while representing what we believe to be good for ourselves. Harris identifies three key factors that drive people to change: They hurt, they are ready to change, and they want to change (42, p. 56).

TA Parent-Adult-Child Dynamics (WW30)

Parent Clues:

- (Physical) Finger wagging, pointing, head wagging, surprised look, foot tapping, hands on hips, arms folded, wringing hands, patting head(s), sighing.
- (Verbal) Stopping, closed questions, "should" and "ought."

Child Cues:
- (Physical) Quivering lip, pouting, temper tantrums, shrugging, whining, eye-rolling, downcast posture, nail-biting.
- (Verbal) Use of superlatives: "better," "bigger," "greater," and questions such as "what," "where," "why," "how," "who," and "when."

Adult Cues:
- (Physical) Straight forward, non-movement, listening, showing curiosity.
- (Verbal) Open questioning, such as "How much?" or "In what way?"

TA provides a clear mechanism for understanding behaviour in a dynamic form, highlighting how changes occur. However, it requires contextual interpretation—that is, an explanation of the circumstances surrounding the behaviour.

TA works particularly well with prepubescent young people who have not yet undergone significant physical, emotional, and conceptual changes. It allows them to develop an understanding of themselves and others without the added complexity that emerges in later adolescence and early adulthood.

In my practice, I find that TA it is an excellent paradigm **or framework that older teenagers** and young adults can relate to and practice **(WW31)**. It helps them develop knowledge and skills in recognising symbolic and social cues, enabling a better understanding of others and how to respond effectively.

This is particularly pertinent to elite athletes, whose drive for excellence often involves opting out of the 'normalisation of experiences' typically associated with childhood and teenage years. As a result, their confidence in specific areas related to sport may be well-developed, but this often proves inadequate and even disabling in other social and relational contexts. This is a significant issue for many athletes and, as Sport Psychologist David Alcock and I have observed, is a consequence of what we term **'lost adolescence.'** This refers to the missed opportunities for more non-sporting experiences during critical teenage developmental years.

TA allows this group to:

- Categorise styles and types of behaviour.
- Develop a greater understanding of verbal and non-verbal cues.
- Experiment with Parent, Adult, and Child states to determine better outcomes for themselves.

In psychology, **context is everything**, as it determines how behaviour can be accurately understood within its specific environment **(WW32)**. Body Dysmorphia – altered perception see also p96.

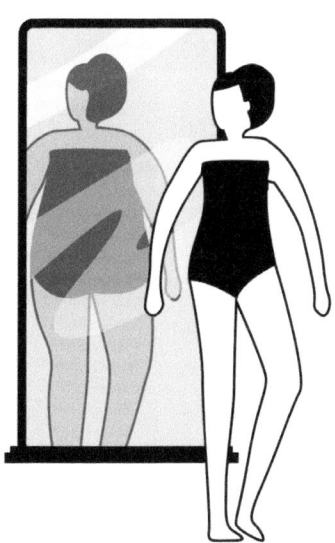

CHAPTER 5:
LOST ADOLESCENCE AND
PERFORMANCE LIFESTYLE

What Is Lost Adolescence and How Does It Affect Athlete and Performing Arts Development?

Living in Academies: Living Away from Family, 'Surrogate Parents,' and Loneliness

Attachment Issues and Early Trauma: Feeling Safe, Secure, and Loved

Parental and Family Influences: The Good, The Bad, and The Ugly

Coping With and Understanding Loneliness, Family Pressures, and Social Media

Lost Adolescence

Lost adolescence is the term I developed with David Alcock, a sport psychologist at the University of the West of England, Bristol. He and I collaborated in 2011 to deepen our understanding of what is known as **Clinical Sport Psychology**. We were particularly mindful of the demands placed on young people who show sporting and artistic talent, as well as the high levels of commitment required to achieve and sustain elite performance. We believe these demands often deny young people in elite sport the ordinary, desirable experiences necessary for broader self-development and social inclusion outside the context of sport. In essence, it represents a lost opportunity for wider personal development that supports positive self-identity. One of the consequences is an over-reliance on sport performance to strengthen this sense of identity—a strategy that works well, but only when everything is going right.

What is Lost Adolescence?

The period of adolescence encompasses a range of significant life events and processes, marked by biological, sociological, and psychological changes. Byrne, Davenport, and Mazanov describe adolescence as arguably the one life-stage most "marked by rapid and potentially tumultuous transition, including biological, social, and psychological changes, as well as shifting self-concepts" (43).

From a cognitive perspective, Jean Piaget highlights the emergence of **'formal operational thought,'** a way of thinking characterized by the ability to analyse problems from multiple perspectives, consider issues hypothetically and conceptually, and evaluate possible outcomes and the consequences of given actions.

This leads to the question: Are the lifestyle and psychological demands of becoming and maintaining an elite athlete status different from the norm in terms of the experience of adolescence, and if so, what are the differences? Understanding these differences requires examining how these biological, psychological, and social transitions intersect with the unique pressures faced by elite athletes. The biopsychosocial approach.

From a **social perspective**, adolescence marks the **transition from childhood** to adulthood and is widely regarded as a critical period for establishing the foundations of adult identity. From a **biological perspective**, the physical changes associated with puberty have psychological and emotional consequences. Hormonal changes can have a notable impact on both mood and behaviour, and the age at which young people experience puberty can also play an important role. From a **sporting perspective**, adolescence is often the time when an athletic identity begins to emerge or becomes more **concrete and defined**. This occurs both within the individual and in their relationships with the sporting organisations they are involved with.

Tanti et al. (44, p. 2) note that "early adolescents are exposed to the **transition** from primary school to secondary school, and late adolescents experience the transition from secondary school to further and higher education, or work."

In sport, career transitions are more commonly framed in terms of progression through academy systems, reserve teams, high-performance programmes, podium pathways, professional squads, World Class Performance programmes, and international competition. However, within the field of sport psychology, it is perhaps surprising how little attention has been given to understanding **"the experience of adolescence"** in the context of athletic development. A lifespan developmental perspective has yet to be fully embraced by researchers and practitioners in sport and exercise psychology. References to "young athletes" often lack clarity, with no consistent indication of the ages being referred to. This issue has become more prominent in recent years, partly due to the need to address problems as they arise and the increasing focus on **age-specific coaching (WW33).**

Elite Athletes and Performance Lifestyle

Over a decade ago, the English Institute of Sport (EIS), established a support system for elite athletes known as Performance Lifestyle Advisors. Their roles include assisting athletes with education, fitness, nutrition, physical and mental health, travel, managing training programmes and competitions, as well as financial management. These athletes are often part of specialised groups such as World Class Performance or Podium programmes. In team sports, similar support systems are typically integrated within academies, with musicians and dancers much the same form. Regardless of the structure, living away from home and family is often one of the trade-offs for pursuing elite performance. This separation has emotional impacts on both athletes and their parents.

Athletes **living in academies** face unique challenges, including shared accommodation —sometimes even shared rooms— communal living, eating, and training, as well as competing against each other. In these environments, parents lose much of their effective control and influence, though they remain a crucial emotional support.

Athletes and team players in such settings can be challenged with educational demands, conflictual relationships with other team members, coaches, or teachers, or may simply struggle with homesickness. Within the high-pressure dynamics of a **performance environment,** expressing feelings or knowing whom to trust can be difficult. Not all academies provide access to a psychologist, Performance Lifestyle Advisor, or tutor. One of the first signs of stress in such situations is **performance loss**, though the origins of this stress are not always recognised or communicated **(WW34)**. For more insights, explore more about overtraining on p 81–85.

For those in further education, particular at universities, the combination of higher academic demands and high-performance expectations within their chosen sport creates significant challenges. Academic teachers often require peak performance from students and may overlook additional sporting pressures from coaches. Some universities address this by offering **four-year programmes** instead of the traditional three, allowing for a more balanced schedule **(WW35)**.

The level of competition and the locations of events, which can sometimes be thousands of miles away, add further complexity and require cooperation and understanding from academic staff. As elite performers gain public recognition, they also attract media attention. To navigate this, **media training** becomes essential, equipping athletes with the skills to handle press interactions and conduct radio and television interviews effectively **(WW36)**.

Having worked in several environments where young athletes and players achieve high levels of success, I have observed the need to protect them from external pressures to allow normal growth and development. During my time at Monaco Football Club (FC), we had five players under the age of 24 sold for over €25 million each, including James Rodríguez, who transferred to Real Madrid for €109 million. The football world has seen the amazing rise of Kylian Mbappé, who moved from Monaco FC to Paris Saint-Germain for £164 million at just 18 years old. While Kylian was a happy and well-adjusted young man, this is not always the case. Even so, it took him time to adjust to playing in front of 50,000 fans at the Stade de France, compared to the Stade Louis II, which has a capacity of 18,500 and an average crowd of 10,000; and now he is playing at the Santiago Bernabéu, with a capacity of 78,000 (in 2025).

One of the more recent challenges—and a significant source of attention—is the use of social media platforms such as Facebook,

Twitter-X, Instagram, and Snapchat. While these platforms are often managed by sporting organisations as part of an athlete's contract, they also come with uncontrollable and unpredictable elements. Issues arise when athletes post comments, controversial or otherwise, or when members of the public or the press make unsubstantiated remarks about individuals, which can harm the performance of those involved.

Living in Academies and Living Away from Family

Depending on the art or sport that a young person pursues, their level of performance and potential may lead to an opportunity to join an elite group, with or without education running alongside, after the age of 16. Joining an academy linked to a professional team is usually a highly organised process and often requires further education, but it may also involve relocating far away from the athlete's home.

In such cases, families face decisions about relocating—whether the entire family moves, one parent accompanies the athlete, or the young person joins a residential facility to pursue their goal of a professional career in sport or the performing arts. Some schools with extremely high sporting profiles draw students and their families, either as boarders or as full-time residents following a family move.

In my first week at Bristol City FC Academy, it became abundantly clear that teenagers aged 16 or 17 often face significant challenges when separated from their families for the first time. Depending on the support they receive, the adjustments they need to make, and how they manage setbacks in their sporting performance, this experience can be overwhelming and negatively impactful. Some young people struggle to adapt and ultimately give up their academy opportunity to return home.

Schools often have pastoral systems where trained staff members act as counsellors or surrogate parents to support such **transitions.** Part of their role involves maintaining regular contact with parents to keep them informed about their children's progress. For parents who are distanced, this communication is crucial— though, unfortunately, it is often neglected by many establishments. My research strongly indicates **the positive impact that parents have on their children's performance (WW37)**.

It's not simply the adjustment of being away from family; it also includes parting from close attachments to siblings, particularly older siblings who may have played a significant role in the care and wellbeing of their younger brothers and sisters. The pursuit of performance success often drives these decisions, with the opportunity to perform in their chosen sport or art form on a full time, fully paid basis. As reflected in the title of Chris Green's book, this is *Every Boy's Dream*—and for many girls too.

Relationships with teachers can offer some degree of independence from the sporting context, but often, the studies themselves are sport-science focused. Teachers expect commitment, effort, and high-performance from their students— expectations that can conflict with the similar demand from performance coaches, as mentioned earlier. Problems arise when the athletes become overtrained, whether through injury and/or low performance levels. If those close to the athlete fail to recognise these issues, they can and often do lead to burnout.

Recognising the signs of overtraining and burnout is a critical way for teachers, coaches, and parents to become alert to changes in an athlete's behaviour and performance, which often reflect the pressures they face. Below is a checklist and measurement tool that I have been using and adapting for many years. Note that burnout is almost exclusively psychological in nature.

This draws on the work of Hackney, Perlman, and Nowacki (45), as adapted by Weinberg and Gould (40, p. 504). And further amended by me.

How to Use the Assessment Scales

These scales consists of 15 questions each, with each question scored from 1 to 6.5. The maximum total score is 98% (rather than 100% as you might expect).

The scoring works as follows:

- Higher scores indicate more severe problems
- For example, severely disturbed sleep would score 5, 5.5, or even 6.5
- A total score of 60% or more indicates the person is moving toward significant overtraining or burnout

The key benefit of this assessment isn't just the total percentage but identifying which specific elements received high scores. This information reveals exactly what aspects need to be addressed or changed in the training or recovery program.

Overtraining and Burnout Scale

Overtraining: Self-Rating 1 to 6.5

1 **Loss of performance**: In sport, work, and activity
2 **Apathy**: Lack or suppression of feelings of emotion, interest, or concern
3 **Lethargy**: A state of tiredness, weariness, fatigue, or lack of energy
4 **Sleep disturbance**: Disordered sleep patterns, insomnia, early morning wakening
5 **Weight loss**: In last three months
6 **Elevated resting heart rate**: An inability to create calm despite rest
7 **Muscle pain or soreness**: On a sustained basis 2–8+ weeks duration

8 **Mood changes**: A state of mind or emotion that fluctuates with worry or stress

9 **Elevated resting blood pressure**: Higher than 135/85

10 **Gastrointestinal disturbances**: Constipation, irritable bowel, heartburn, or reflux

11 **Retarded recovery from exertion**: Delayed refreshing of energy beyond 24 hours

12 **Appetite loss**: Missing meals or a reduced desire for food

13 **Overuse injuries**: Repeated small injuries, ongoing wear and tear of the body

14 **Immune system deficiency**: The body's main ability to fight infection

15 **Concentration loss**: A reduced ability to continue to pay attention and focus

Burnout

1 **Low energy, fatigue.**

2 **Concentration problems**: A reduced ability to pay attention and focus

3 **Loss of desire**: To play sport, or participate in activities, reduced motivation

4 **Lack of caring**: Ability to take proper care of eating, sleeping, and grooming

5 **Sleep disturbance**: Disordered sleep patterns, insomnia, early morning wakening

6 **Physical and mental exhaustion**: Severe lack of ability to perform tasks

7 **Lowered self-esteem**: Feeling negative about oneself, low value, limiting beliefs

8 **Negative affect**: Negative outward expression of feelings and emotion

9 **Mood changes**: A state of mind or emotion that fluctuates with worry or stress

10 **Substance abuse**: A pattern of harmful use for mood-altering purposes

11 **Changes in values/beliefs**: A rapid change in emotions, beliefs, and behaviours in daily life, including suicidal ideas.

12 **Emotional isolation**: Lack of connection to self or others, often avoiding people

13 **Increased anxiety**: Recurring intrusive thoughts with heightened reactions

14 **Highs and lows**: Mood variability, depressed and elated feelings

15 **Loss of pleasure**: With self, others, and activities, that previously brought pleasure

TOTAL present Score 0-6.5 to give a max of 98% All good =0

Another version will be shown on the website

As a guideline, scores up to 30% indicate the early stages of overtraining and burnout, while scores above 50% suggest that daily living is directly affected. Individuals experiencing full burnout typically have a minimum score of 85%, and often as high as 95%, based on my experience.

Once high scores of **5–6.5** are identified and highlighted, patterns often emerge, revealing **links between those high-scoring elements (WW38)**. Brainspotting interventions focus on these high-scoring elements first, and reduction in burnout of up to 60% can be achieved within four sessions. There are also 111 Winning Ways in this book to help.

The concept of the three R's—**Rest, Recovery, and Relaxation (WW39)**—may be foreign to athletes and performers who habitually 'push' themselves not just to their limits, but beyond what is considered normal. This pattern is one I have consistently observed in cases of Chronic Fatigue Syndrome CFS / ME.

Weinberg and Gould acknowledge that there is no universally accepted definition of athletic burnout but describe it as: "**A physical, emotional, and social withdrawal** from a formerly enjoyable sport activity. This withdrawal is characterised by emotional and physical exhaustion, reduced sense of accomplishments, and sport devaluation. Moreover, burnout occurs because of chronic stress, considered a perceived or actual imbalance between what is expected of an athlete physically, psychologically, and socially and his or her response capabilities, and motivational orientations and changes in the athlete" (40).

I have developed my own version of this definition for greater consistency and accuracy. In my view, when burnout is analysed, it is predominantly psychological—approximately 95%—with brain-body reactions playing a significant role in its production **(WW40)**.

Below, I provide a table offering guidance for both parents and performers in understanding the distinctions between overtraining and burnout. Overtraining is characterised by a relatively equal balance of physiological and psychological causes, while burnout is predominantly mental, with 95% of its origins being psychological. The people who 'burnout' are not the people who **push themselves to the limit, but they go beyond it**.

The emergence of overtraining often results from pressures applied not only by coaches, teachers, trainers, and parents but also by the performers and athletes themselves. Over the last 15 years —particularly the last 12 years since I began teaching nutrition and exercise physiology—I have observed that when 'performance decrement' occurs (a downward spiral in performance), the instinct is to **'try harder'** and exert even more effort. This often leads to the realisation that **"it's not about the effort, but how you use it" (WW41)**.

The table below draws on the work of Hackney, Perlman, and Nowacki (45), as adapted by Weinberg and Gould (40, p. 504).

Overtraining	Burnout
Loss of performance	Low motivation and energy
Apathy	Concentration problems
Lethargy	Loss of desire
Sleep disturbance	Lack of caring
Weight loss	Sleep disturbance
Elevated resting heart rate	Physical and mental exhaustion
Muscle pain or soreness	Lowered self-esteem
Mood changes	Negative affect

Elevated resting blood pressure	Mood changes
Gastrointestinal disturbances	Substance abuse
Retarded recovery from exertion	Changes in values/beliefs
Appetite loss	Emotional isolation
Overuse injuries	Increased anxiety
Immune system deficiency	Highs and lows (variable mood)
Concentration loss	Loss of pleasure

When athletes try harder, they often fail to support these efforts with adequate increases in nutrition (food as fuel), hydration, or rest and recovery. While they may experience a short-term benefit, the body becomes progressively fatigued and more susceptible to injury. Eventually, performance loss declines again, and additional efforts to improve only exacerbate the stress. This cycle becomes the source of overtraining, marked by the onset of small injuries, pain, muscle soreness, and sleep disturbances. Overtraining is often the precursor to burnout. **Pacing** is a concept used in energy management for chronic fatigue, but certainly benefits athletes and performers especially where a great deal of travel and changing time zones are involved.

Coping with Loneliness: Intimacy / Internet and Sexually Explicit Material / Social Media Influences / Suicidal Ideation. The Dark Side of Success...

Loneliness is a mind, body, and emotional state. Emotionally, we may lack connection to another person, or someone closely attached to us. Physically, we may feel distanced from others, and even in a room full of people, we can experience a sense of energetic disconnection. This often leads to withdrawal and a diminished sense of self-worth. As humans we are inherently designed for connection and to live in close-knit communities and families. We can also still use the word 'tribe'. At the same time, we can be content in our own alone space. Friendships and shared interests serve as vital points of connection, particularly in sport and the performing arts. However, coping with silence and separation can be a real challenge.

John Capaccio describes loneliness as being "related to an increase in egocentrism, where your sense of self depends more on your attention to your outcomes when you're lonely than when you have lots of connections. Egoism is that central focus on yourself to the exclusion of others" (46). It is important to distinguish egoism from egotism, in which the latter refers to an overvaluation of one's own importance or activities.

For example, consider a lonely person who talks incessantly, leaving you feeling unable to interrupt or disengage. How can such interactions become mutual rather than one-sided? As John Capaccio explains, "It's about interactions, it's about synergy, it's about mutuality."

Interestingly, loneliness is not exclusive to those lacking resources; millionaires and billionaires often feel lonely, as do many athletes and musicians in my experience. While many people may want to be their friend, there is often the underlying perception that these friendships are motivated by material or social benefits rather than genuine connection. This has certainly been my experience in the high-glitz environment of Monaco. For one young millionaire we had to work out storylines to avoid his wealth and position being revealed, simply so he could socialise more normally with people, until he felt 'safe' to do so.

It may seem strange to consider loneliness when you're surrounded by many people, but loneliness is an internalised experience often hidden, particularly among young male athletes. While females are often encouraged from an early age to **express their feelings** in safe environments, boys tend to avoid verbalising negative feelings, instead using diversions like sport. This behaviour is often reinforced by male role models who also suppress emotional expression, whether consciously or unconsciously.

American counselling sport psychologist Jim Mastrich states "Historically, masculinity too greatly constrains boys into preordained social roles, for instance, sensitivity and vulnerability are not considered experiences that a 'real' man has, but athleticism and aggression are seen as outdated, and have little relevance in today's world" (47, p. 3). Two decades later, some changes in that perspective are finally taking place, with sports media increasingly highlighting examples of athlete mental health issues.

Later in life, "The **shame of vulnerability** is one of the reasons why so many overtly depressed men 'don't want to talk about it,' finding their vulnerability of depression unacceptable," writes Terrence Real (48, p. 148).

Only more recently, in 2020, has the Minister for Sport in England called for mental health issues to be considered a higher priority. Now, Premier League footballers are being hospitalised under the Mental Health Act 1983, and Princes Harry and William have spoken openly about their own depression following the death of their mother, Princess Diana, placing depression and mental health firmly in the public conscience and on the national agenda (BBC, 7.8.2020).

Even now, I work with many people and clubs as a 'secret psychologist' with top athletes, because of the potential stigma attached to mental health issues such as performance anxiety; depression, addiction, and eating disorders. They fear these issues could affect their selection to play or lead to misrepresentation in the media.

Loneliness arises not just from a sense of human isolation but also an emotional disconnection from oneself. According to Dr Barbara Markway (49), "Men may convert stereotypically feminine feelings, such as sadness or vulnerability, into feelings like anger or pride to be far more socially acceptable for them to experience."

The issues of **mental health and indeed loneliness** are explored more in greater depth in the next two chapters, particularly within the global context of the Covid-19 pandemic and the enforced isolation it brought. Sadly, this has left an unwelcome legacy, especially for our younger generation.

Intimacy

Intimacy is defined in the Collins Dictionary as:

1. The state of being intimate.
2. A close, familiar, and usually affectionate or loving personal relationship with another person or group.
3. A close association with or detailed knowledge or deep understanding of a place, subject, period of history.

It is most associated with an intimate sexual relationship.

Intimacy is defined by the American Psychological Association (APA) as an interpersonal state of extreme emotional closeness such that each party's personal space can be entered by any of the other parties without causing discomfort to that person. It characterises close, familiar, and usually affectionate or **loving personal relationships,** requiring the parties to have a detailed knowledge or deep understanding of each other.

From a sociological perspective, humans inherently seek connections with individuals, groups, family, and communities.

The close grouping in which we live is referred to as the **'nuclear family,'** while the wider grouping is known as the **'extended family.'** Breakdowns in intimacy occur, causing for example, a third of marriages to end in divorce, leading to single-parent situations or children placed in the care of the local authorities. Whilst leaving home is a natural progression as adolescents transition into adulthood, it also changes the way we experience intimacy. It is important for parents to understand that the age of 26 is approximately when young people reach established maturity, as supported by intensive research. Maintaining affection is a key human need.

Our sense of intimacy begins at birth through the attachment to the mother, breastfeeding, and subsequently being cared for in what is hoped to be a safe, secure, and **loving** or affectionate relationship with parents and others. When this attachment breaks down, temporarily or otherwise, some sense of intimacy or closeness may be lost, potentially leading to early experiences of **separation anxiety**—essentially, a loss of 'safe' intimacy. Moving away from home can intensify this feeling, often subconsciously, and it is important for supporting professionals to recognise and address it.

Parental and Family Influences

"The Good, The Bad and The Ugly" is the title of an old Clint Eastwood cowboy movie. The **'good'** refers to the many ways parents encourage, support**, love, and nurture their children.** However, sometimes parents make unintentional mistakes, misjudging a situation either consciously or unconsciously. Consequently, their son or daughter may find themselves disadvantaged in their respective sport or performance context, given the strength of influence. The same can be true for siblings or even cousins, who, in their enthusiasm or **sibling rivalry**, can negatively impact their brother or sister.

The **'bad'** arises when parents create situations where they seek to motivate high performance by offering monetary or similar **incentives.** While these reward mechanisms may seem logical, they can undermine the quality of the parent–child relationship, making the child feel they are only **loved** and appreciated when they perform well. In such cases, **fear of failure** and performance anxiety often result from the young person's self-talk, convincing them that if their performance is substandard, their parents will be angry and less loving—whether this is done unwittingly or consciously.

Pressure from parents is often a matter of interpreting the purpose and intention behind the support they offer. Through basic questioning of young athletes and performers, I have discovered that many feel their high-level activity is reliant on 'paying back' their parents for the time, effort, and financial support provided. However, what parents often genuinely want is simply for their children to be happy!

This miscommunication frequently gets 'lost in translation' and rarely emerges in family communications, as both sides make 'assumptions' about the other without clarifying them. Such situations reflect a self-esteem issue for young people, interfering with their ability to 'accept' not only the 'gift' from their parents being 'unconditional' but also placing a limit on their 'self-acceptance' and their sense of who they are. This challenge relates to the concept of self-esteem and highlights a potential warning signal—a 'red light'— that has already missed the 'amber' phase of the 'traffic lights'.

Another key feature is that young athletes may begin to feel uncomfortable when they feel they have less control over their activities, leading to tensions within the family. For example, setting up a gymnasium in the garage without consulting their son or daughter may not only be misplaced but also create high expectation for its use, especially given the expense involved. At these ages up to 16, even 18 the concept of unconditional love may not be understood or recognised.

Overzealous parents, whether through enthusiasm or direct interventions in training or performance, cannot only be unhelpful but also deeply embarrassing for young athletes or performers. This phenomenon has long been recognised in the USA, where workshops and specific guidelines for parents of elite athletes have been developed since the late 1990s.

One such message, recorded by the European Federation of Sport Psychology in 1996, stated "Those involved in children's sports should understand that children are **not mini adults**," emphasizing the need for **age-appropriate** activities. An important element of this involves recognising the cognitive development of young people to determine at what ages they cannot only absorb information purposefully but also understand concepts that adults might mistakenly assume are comprehensible to them **(WW42)**.

In their efforts to develop their identity, children may feel the need to pursue non-sport activities**,** risking disappointment from their parents. In such situations, the child may ultimately drop out of sport entirely, despite their talent.

This is particularly prevalent in equestrianism, where significant financial investment is required—not only for owning a horse or pony but also for purchasing tack and saddlery, as well as covering livery costs. Over an eight-year period, I saw a great deal of this first hand as the partner of a riding centre and later as an equestrian psychologist. Many of my students reported encountering similar situations.

When it comes to **'ugly,'** one of the most **embarrassing and humiliating situations** for young athletes and performers arises when parents are not only highly visible but also extremely loud in coaching their children. This can occur from the stands, the sidelines, behind the goal, or even during public confrontations with the coach, opposing players, or other parents.

This behaviour is particularly well-known in English football, where many parents have invested significantly in their children's potential success as professional footballers. The vast sums of money their children could potentially earn, coupled with the parents' own disappointments as young players who didn't make it, often drive a desire for reflective glory. This ambition is further linked to the parents' sense of higher status through their children's achievements in sport.

This perfectly illustrates how the parent–child relationship in the context of sport or performance changes the family dynamic. It can disrupt the natural feelings that might otherwise exist between them, as weekly competition performances become the central focus for discussions and analyses—vastly out of proportion to a 'normal' family life.

In such situations, children may feel their parents only love them when they perform well, leading to significant feelings of insecurity and vulnerability. As documented earlier, this can have a lasting negative impact on adulthood. Andre Agassi's autobiography *Open* (50) provides a sensational example of this, illustrating an extreme version of **a father transitioning into a coach**, much like how parents successful in business find themselves being the Chief Executive Officer rather than as a dad or mum—it's a must read **(WW43)**.

Another aspect of this occurs when children and young people in sporting performance contexts are humiliated, unequally treated, or unfavoured by coaches. Parents often feel a sense of powerlessness to stop this, prioritising the goal of their child becoming a professional. In such circumstances, not only is the young person traumatised, even bullied, but one or both parents may also experience feelings of disempowerment and become unconsciously traumatised. I have encountered many examples of this in practice.

Social Media, Internet Use, Technology, and Loneliness

The use of the internet and new technology has revolutionised our lives. Over the past decade, young people have experienced an explosion of applications (apps), websites, gaming, social media, and smartphones, which have significantly absorbed their attention, often to the detriment of their mental and emotional wellbeing, and connectedness.

The untimely death of elite snowboarder Ellie Soutter in July 2018 symbolises the loneliness experienced by some athletes and highlights how social media can become **intrusive and traumatising for young people**—sometimes to the point of either considering ending their lives, or worse, fatally acting on it. In a BBC South-East interview, her father, Tony, described how Ellie missed a flight to join Team GB training in the Alps. Seemingly distraught, he said, "She felt she'd let them down, felt she'd let me down, and just tragically it takes one silly little thing like that to tip someone over the edge, because there's a lot of pressure on children. "

The use of social media to stay in contact and connect intimately with 'friends' on platforms like Facebook, visually through Snap-Chat and Instagram, or with followers on Twitter-X, also exposes young people to negative public comments. These often come from individuals who may be jealous, angry, or disrespectful, and such negativity can be destructive to young people as they develop their self-identity. It can create states of severe anxiety, depressed mood, and negative self-perceptions of their body shape, leading to dysmorphia, disordered eating, and a distorted belief that they must strive for what might be considered perfection.

Now an advocate for supporting mental health and wellbeing in sport, Olympian and Football Hall of Fame member Karen Carney MBE has transitioned into a prominent role as a football commentator on TV and radio. A sport psychologist and trained in managing trauma, Carney built a stunningly successful football career with Birmingham, Arsenal, and Chelsea, winning 144 caps for England. In 2017, she spoke openly and courageously about her mental health challenges during her career. Her experience highlights the internal and external pressures of performing at the highest levels, coping with career-threatening injuries, and feeling desperately lonely at times, despite being surrounded by people. She has become a beacon of openness in managing mental health issues within the sporting context, particularly for women. As a true leader of human spirit, she now serves as a Government Advisor and continues to inspire others with her advocacy and leadership.

Training is essential for sports psychologists and coaches to become more aware of behaviours that may indicate a risk of self-harm or self-destruction. Additionally, the curriculum for training sports psychologists needs to place greater emphasis on mental health issues. In 2011, I highlighted this need while drafting *Applied Clinical Sport Psychology,* elements of which are included in this edition.

The Internet and Sexually Explicit Material

The expansion of the internet since 2000, along with the ability to act anonymously within it, has exposed young people—and adults—

to sexually explicit material, often below the legal age of 18. Among athletes and performers, issues arise concerning how people engage sexually, the creation of images, and the popularisation of perfectionism in such encounters. These are often artificial 'performances' that lead to unrealistic expectations for men and women to look and present themselves in highly sexualised or 'ideal' ways, particularly regarding body shape and attractiveness. As a result, individuals may feel pressured to conform to such role models, perhaps believing that these standards are 'normal,' desirable, and achievable. This can further contribute to misunderstandings about the true nature of intimacy.

Research by Yaniv Efrati in 2019, involving 600 adolescents, identified indicators of social isolation, difficulties with intimacy, and variable levels of social anxiety, highlighting issues of attachment—typically formed with parents in early life (51). A key concern considered in 'Lost Adolescence' is that commitment to sport and performing arts can affect normalised elements of social interactions with peer groups, particularly those outside of sport. This can lead to challenges in successfully 'connecting' and developing healthy intimate relationships later in adolescence and early adulthood. The accessibility of the internet, coupled with the availability of sexually explicit material and 'live connections' to virtual sexualised relationships, further alters the ability to develop close and intimate relationships in real-life. These behaviours, often conducted in secrecy and isolation, can exacerbate feelings of disconnection. Help is available—seek it.

Sport can often provide the perfect 'cover' for someone developing **disordered eating**, as many behaviours associated with eating disorders are also considered highly desirable within a sporting context. I recall one athlete suffering from an eating disorder who was praised as the 'perfect professional' because of her total commitment to training and maintenance of body shape. In reality, she was battling something very different— she was 'exercise addicted,' a common comorbidity of anorexia, and regularly purging to control her weight.

The influence of sexually explicit imagery can further compound low self-value and limiting self-beliefs, particularly concerning body shape and sense of attractiveness. These perceptions are shaped not only by sport but also by broader media influences and resulting in body dysmorphia as one outcome.

For further reading, see *Eating Disorders in Sport* by Thompson and Sherman (52), and *Exercise and Eating Disorders* by Simona Giordano (53).

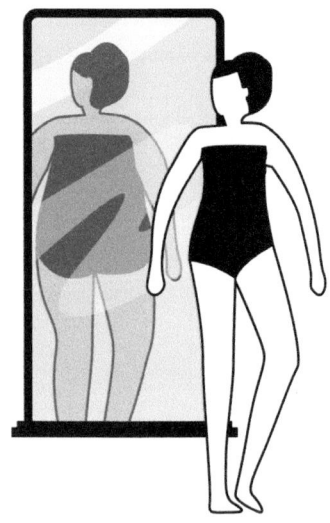

Body Dysmorphia:
We perceive that we are fat when this is not the reality.

We can feel a sense of shame about ourselves, given to very low self-value.

CHAPTER 6:
PERFORMANCE ISSUES

The Four Corners Framework:
1. Performance 2. Physical 3. Social 4. Psychological

Systemic (Whole-Person) Assessment and Understanding

When, What, and Why Things Go Wrong

Barriers to High Performance and Excellence

My approach has been systematic ever since my social work training at Liverpool University, where I learned to examine all elements of the 'big picture' to understand the origins of a problem and address both current and earlier life experiences, covering all elements. Predominantly in sport, when things go wrong, that do not meet expectation or measurement, my consistent observation is that **approximately 75% of the problem's origins** are not rooted in the sport or performance context itself, but in other aspects of our life experience which influence them **(WW44)**. So, what is the problem? It often stems from being children in families; being educated in schools; trained by coaches; participating as members of teams; navigating friendships, relationships, marriages and so on, **life**. In other words, the problems we encounter are shaped by our life experiences, which also help to create the very beliefs we hold about ourselves and others—beliefs that impact our performance in artistic or sporting environment, as well as in occupational work.

Philosophy: What Is It, and Why Is It Important?

What are philosophers? The answer lies in the word *philosophy* itself. In Greek, *'philo'* means love—or devotion—and *'sophia'* means wisdom. Philosophers are people devoted to wisdom (17). I'm not sure how much my mother realised this at the time of my birth!

My Phil-osophy is that I'm not just looking at a 'footballer,' for example, ensuring he or she passes the ball accurately and knows the game plan; I'm interested in the 'person first' and foremost— the whole person. Whether you are a son, daughter, brother, sister, friend, chess player, stamp collector, musician, or someone who supports a charity, these aspects contribute to your identity as a **'total,' whole person** who happens to have a significant talent in football or acting. According to *The School of Life* (54), "Being wise means attempting to live and die well, leading as good a life as possible within the troubled conditions of existence. The goal of wisdom is fulfilment, a means of satisfaction within ourselves, and with our lives as we live them."

A philosopher is someone who strives for 'systematic expertise' in working out how one may best find individual and collective fulfilment. Understanding the problem is the first step in solving it. The original Greek philosopher Socrates encouraged us to be **curious** about ourselves and others and to play 'devil's advocate'— to look at things in different ways. This approach increases our knowledge and enables better choices and decisions.

I encourage you, as parents, to adopt a Socratic approach, using open questioning with yourselves, your children, coaches, and teachers **(WW45)**. Through this sense of inquiry, we become less directive or oppressive, allowing respondents to be more open in how they react, and respond.

This principle forms the basis of '**Motivational Interviewing,**' a method initially developed to support individuals with addictive behaviours who were in denial about their condition. This book intends to support these **processes of enlightenment and discovery**.

If we take a purely psychological or cognitive perspective, it has, in my experience, some limitations. I quickly realised this teaching nutrition and exercise physiology, where I observed how much of what happens in the body also affects emotional responses and thought processes—and vice versa.

Brainspotting, as a brain-body intervention, differs significantly from a 'cognitive' thinking or talking therapy, especially at the beginning of the process. David Grand, its developer, states "Brainspotting is a physiological approach with psychological consequences" (3) a majority of my referrals, often self-referrals, over the last 15 years have been as a result of **lost performance**, **panic attacks**, and recovering from injury. While psychology and psychologists are still regarded with suspicion in some quarters, this often stems from a lack of understanding about their role. In many sports—and as my professional colleagues also experience—connecting with a psychologist can still be seen as a sign of weakness, being vulnerable, not being quite 'right in the head'.

Parents frequently refer their children when they have run out of ideas on how to stop the downward spiral of performance and the accompanying angst. This can be frustrating for parents and, with some, a suggestion that they are not good enough to solve the problem themselves.

This is the essence of the book: information is power! Assessment and understanding what is wrong is the first step. **Structured interventions** that follow are the key to progression toward positively desired goals.

Systemic (Whole-Person) Assessment and Understanding the Four Corners Framework:
1. Performance 2. Physical 3. Social 4. Psychological

I discovered several years ago the direct relationship between Performance, Energy (Physical), Mood (Psychological), and Motivation (Social and Psychological) **(WW45).**

The four corners in brief.

The origin of the idea was developed out of the football coaching model, developed by The England and Wales Football Association's coaching module in 2002. The original 'four corners' were: **technical, tactical, physical, psychological.** In further developing the model, I recognised the significant absence of social relationships. The technical and tactical offer essential elements of performance, but they rely upon good communication between team members, coaches, support staff, as well as players' own internal communications. What follows is the full development of this as a framework for action, which forms the basis for understanding problems such as loss of performance, recovery from injury, performance anxiety, addiction, depression, and so on.

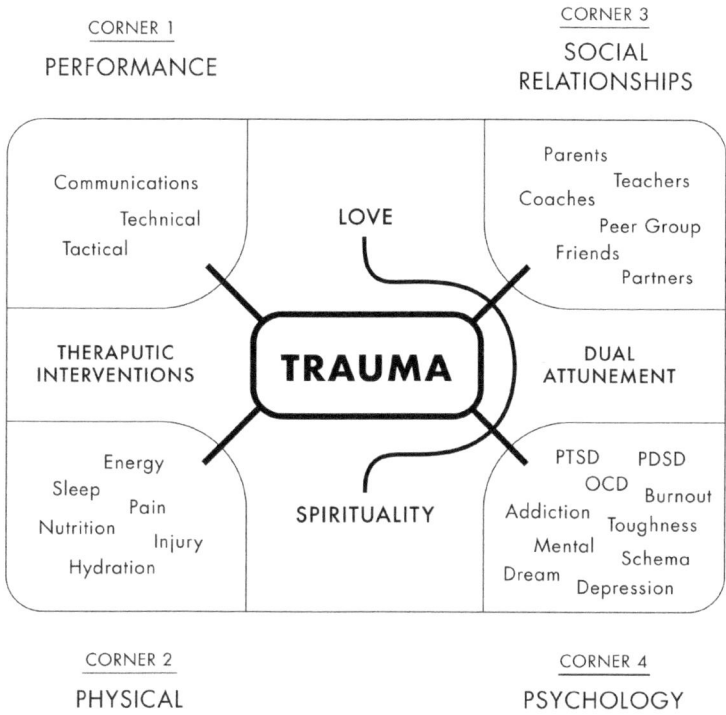

CORNER 1
PERFORMANCE

CORNER 3
SOCIAL
RELATIONSHIPS

Communications
Technical
Tactical

LOVE

Parents
Teachers
Coaches
Peer Group
Friends
Partners

THERAPUTIC
INTERVENTIONS

TRAUMA

DUAL
ATTUNEMENT

Energy
Sleep
Pain
Nutrition
Injury
Hydration

SPIRITUALITY

PTSD   PDSD
OCD
Burnout
Addiction
Toughness
Mental
Schema
Dream
Depression

CORNER 2
PHYSICAL

CORNER 4
PSYCHOLOGY

Corner 1: Performance

Technical

Technical elements in the original design were focused on **skill acquisition and performance development** within football, such as passing, first touch, moving into spaces, dribbling skills, tackling, keeping possession, defending, and, finally, shooting on goal—if only! This also includes taking penalties (think England football teams—though it is improving!). The technical development of skills in other sports is, in essence, the foundation required to achieve high performance within the specifics of their sport or performing art. In this sense, my mantra is: "**Do the basics well**, **and you will always perform well**" **(WW46).**

The question then is: **'What are the basics'?** Surprisingly, many athletes, even at the highest levels, struggle to have a clear view of what these are until prompted, which often highlights a deficit in their foundational knowledge. Knowing the basics helps to establish the **cornerstones of performance**, enabling coaches to identify gaps, a lack of, or loss of skill. This allows them to consider immediate development tasks to help the player improve.

At this stage, the issue of **communication** becomes critical, particularly the quality of communication and connections between the coach and player, athlete, or artist. Effective communication creates clarity about what is expected to change and, importantly, how it can be achieved. The key word in the communication is the 'intent'. This process alone is often a major obstacle in coach–athlete, teacher–student, and parent–child interactions.

Within psychological approaches, also known as interventions, therapists seek **clarification** both in their own communication and in that of their clients by **'checking out'** what they mean **(WW47).** This concept is demonstrated clearly by Harville Hendrix in his book *Getting the Love You Want* (55). While the book is aimed specifically at couples, clarity of understanding is the cornerstone of all healthy communications.

The process begins with the intention behind the initial communication**,** where the recipient seeks to clarify the accuracy of the message by paraphrasing it in their own words. The initial speaker then has an opportunity to confirm whether their intended message has been accurately received and understood. This process ensures that the speaker feels validated and heard—not only through the content of what they have said but also through the attention and active listening demonstrated by the recipient. In turn, the recipient is granted the same level of respect when it is their time to speak. This reciprocal process fosters mutual respect and, over time, builds **trust** within the relationship **(WW48)**.

In my experience, and that of many of my clients, a large proportion of coaches underperform in their communication and often fail to 'check out' or seek clarification. This aligns with the **command-style** approach of coaching, characterized by the directive, "do as I say." For me, the 'art of coaching'—and ultimately, its success—is based on the quality of the communication and the personalised connection coaches establish with their players, athletes, teams, and artists. This naturally leads into the crucial elements of **'performance feedback' and self-analysis.**

Skill acquisition and skill development are gradual, automated processes that are age dependent. One of the challenges for coaches and parents is consistently observing such interactions to ensure that coaching remains age appropriate. Perhaps even more challenging for coaches is the language they use with athletes— ensuring it aligns with the sport but also with the athlete's capability and understanding according to their age. As noted earlier, coaches often have a tendency to treat younger people like adults, using adult-oriented language because it's easier for them or because no one has given them feedback on their coaching performance! For instance, how many 5- or 6- years-olds are expected to kick a full-size football instead of a more appropriate mini ball?

As I work with athletes to understand their **barriers to performance**, they often seek, through their parents, ways of trying to understand what their coaches are telling them. They frequently become frustrated by not knowing how to improve, despite their coaches constantly requesting it. These situations develop through a lack of good role modelling and a need for positive visualisation— 'pictures 'and direct demonstrations to help them 'see' how it works. In education and psychology, this relates to the 'dominant modalities' of learning: visual, auditory, and kinaesthetic (feeling).

When coaches or teachers tell a young person that they are not good enough, it affects them emotionally and can become a source of trauma and limiting self-belief, weakening their mental strength. At this point, I work with the athlete to help them recognise where their skills and movements are below par, understand why, and determine how they might be resolved and improved. This **cooperative approach—working together** to understand and improve—is the desired coaching model **(WW49)**.

Ideally, a coach would help set short-term goals for the player to work through over a two-week cycle and focus on these developments. In my view, what is also important—and often not discussed with athletes or players—is simply identifying what they do well. When this is positively reinforced, it enables new neural pathways to develop in the brain. Once established, this foundation supports increased confidence and improved concentration. This is the essence of encouraging a positive and developmental training plan. It's Socratic. I mentioned this once to a world-famous football coach. He was so impressed I thought he was joking with me. The reality was that he rarely encouraged players he simply told them what to do. On following this the players produce their best performance of the season. Did he continue? No. Why? Because it wasn't his idea.

Much like learning to drive a car, the brain cannot process all the new information at once and needs it to be **'chunked' into smaller parts** so it can more easily process it. Eventually, clutch actions and gear changing become automated, freeing the brain's working memory to attend to other tasks. Unfortunately, coaches and teachers often give several instructions at once, overloading the brain's working or short-term memory. This can leave the athlete feeling uncertain, embarrassed, stupid, and anxious because they didn't understand. It's not their fault the brain can only process 3–7 units of information in **short-term or working memory** at any one time **(WW50)**. This is vital for those who are Neuro Diverse.

While **verbal feedback** from coaches is essential, it must be performance-led and not personalised. Statements such as, "You did this; you were stupid" or "Your performance was rubbish today; if you continue to play like that, don't bother turning up next week" constitute **emotional abuse** in my view. These 'put-downs' not only undermine confidence and destabilise the athlete but also cause embarrassment to both the athlete and their parents, and teammates. When a coach focuses their analysis on what works, what requires development, and what went wrong in a particular situation, the athlete, player, or artist can receive this feedback constructively and with a determination to improve. This is the essence of **cooperative coaching** and the foundation of good quality **feedback**.

When using **video analysis**—which I highly recommend and believe is incredibly under-utilised (especially in swimming)—it's important for the athlete to review it not solely on their own. Watching alone often leads to overly critical self-assessment without a balanced external perspective—parents, take note. Imagine doing this with a violinist or cellist, whose posture is cumbersome, and becoming painful. They and others can then observe the ergonomic movements and retrain the positioning. **(WW51)**.

Video analysis offers a valuable opportunity for both the coach and the athlete to observe the same performance and discuss differing interpretations or viewpoints. This collaborative approach fosters understanding of both the observed behaviour and the athlete's internal experience of their actions. This is cooperative coaching in action, and in my experience, brings out the best for all concerned—a true win-win.

Parents can also play a constructive role by sitting with their children, offering considered feedback that is thoughtful, encouraging, and supportive. However, it's important to avoid exaggeration—remember, these are your children! This approach aligns with how we work in Brainspotting, where feedback is constructive and growth-focused, and expansive.

Ultimately, these measures pave the way for adapting to new training methods with the goal of achieving sustained and measurably improved performance.

Tactical Thinking and Communication

Tactics for a game, match, training session, or performance are often created by a collective of coaches, team managers, and **performance analysts**, in conjunction with the understanding and technical skills of the athletes or performers involved. When working as part of a team, these considerations can become more complex, as individual expectations must align with the overarching team goals—both literally and metaphorically. This leads to the fundamental question: What is your role?

Most of my experience has been in team sports, particularly in football and rugby. One specific set of events illustrates this communication concept well. While observing a team manager and privately listening to his spoken thoughts, ideas, and tactical approaches, I started to realise that he delivered substantial amounts of information that the players were not fully absorbing. This was evident through their body language and other behavioural cues, which signalled overload. Before one game, I watched him speak to the team for 30 minutes. When the players returned at half-time, trailing 0-3, he was furious. Despite showing his frustration, anger, and a desire to inspire better performance, the team ultimately lost 2-3— a pattern I saw repeatedly. Recognising this, I proposed a change to the style, quality, and **pacing of the information** he delivered to the players. My plan included introducing a new approach: **asking the players questions** to confirm their understanding (or 'checking out') of his instructions **(WW52)**. The results were illuminating! Sounds simple does it not, but it was not 'obvious' to him.

During the week leading up to the next home game, I worked with the manager to help him understand the player's perspectives. While he was highly self-competent as a former international player, he was now managing a team performing at a level below the professional football he had played. This required him to adjust for their age, experience, and ability to understand his concepts and ideas. I also explained how the brain processes information, highlighting the limitations of **short-term memory** (STM), which can only handle a maximum of 6–7 units of information at any one time.

Given the speed and complexity of his information, there was a high risk of overload, where no information was effectively processed or absorbed. I introduced the concept of 'chunking' information into smaller parts with deliberate pauses to allow players time to process. I likened it to a parent asking their child to go upstairs, brush their teeth, wash behind their ears, and grab their schoolbook—only to hear the reply, "What was that you said?"

Before my interventions, I suggested that the manager ask players **to clarify their tasks and roles** after delivering instructions. He was shocked to discover their lack of understanding and limited ability to retain information. In essence, his game plan wasn't being effectively communicated, leading to underperformance and costly mistakes that kept the team stuck in the relegation zone.

My intervention with him was to **'chunk' his information** into smaller, manageable pieces. After delivering each instruction, he would ask the player in question to describe back (feedback) to him the role they were expected to perform during the match **(WW53)**. Additionally, four leaders in the team were selected to provide feedback at half-time, sharing their perspectives—an approach that was seen as revolutionary at the time!

As an example of 'chunking,' a sequence like 1 9 4 5 2 0 1 2 1 0 6 6 can feel overwhelming as a string of 12 digits. However, breaking it into meaningful groups—1945, 2012, 1066—reduces the cognitive load, transforming it into three easily remembered chunks. Similarly, breaking down instructions into smaller parts allows players to process and retain critical information more effectively.

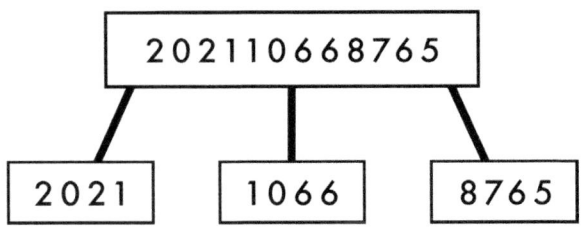

Initially, the players were very nervous, partly because they had never experienced a 'culture' where they were asked questions about their role and performance. As a result, they were somewhat hesitant at first. However, through this process, the manager was able to clarify their understanding. As the players gained a clearer grasp of their roles, their confidence improved, and they began delivering what was expected of them. I call that a **win-win scenario**—and they did win!

Once we established improved communication between the manager and the players, it became necessary to enhance communication within the team during training and matches.

This effort required effective **leadership**. In football teams, I favour a particular leadership strategy—now adopted by Gareth Southgate with the England World Cup team—that ensures the team game plan is understood and implemented through key players, coordinated by the captain. Football captains tend to come from central defender roles, partly because they are in the centre of the team play, but it's not unusual for the captain to be a goalkeeper or even a striker. I encourage managers and coaches to select players in strategic positions on the field to support the captain, ensuring effective communication across all areas. These key players relay instructions from the captain to those in their immediate vicinity, creating a well-coordinated team dynamic.

For the captain, strategically placed support leaders help distribute his responsibility across the team, reducing the captain's overall burden in conveying the coach's messages. This communication system relies on these additional leaders to relay instructions effectively, especially when adjustments to the game plan are needed.

The football team went on a streak of six wins, but not before implementing my enhanced physical recovery programme from training and matches. This included the use of electrolyte replacement drinks and consuming carbohydrates and protein within 90 minutes of intensive exercise, facilitating recovery within 24 hours. These improvements played a crucial role in helping the team avoid what had seemed to be almost certain relegation.

Within the **technical and tactical** elements of performance, effective communication plays a crucial role, particularly in team settings. Regardless of the context—whether it be sport, work, an organisation, an orchestra, or TV production—knowing the game plan, backup strategies, individual roles within the team, and having a shared sense of clarity are key to success.

While internal, self-communication is explored in more detail within the psychological corner, the quality of communication during training and competition is not only decisive for performance but also serves as an external measure of confidence and a hallmark of strong leadership.

Momentum Analysis: Changing the Game (WW54)

Momentum is "the force that dictates the flow of a match, a hidden force. It is invisible because it comes from a flow of energy between competitors, and who holds the balance of power at key moments" (36). The concept was originally developed by Alistair Higham, a national English tennis coach, in collaboration with Chris Harwood, through observing the dynamics and shifts in tennis matches. Momentum becomes highly visible in players' attitudes, emotions, speed, flow, and immediacy of scoring. A striking example of this was Emma Raducanu's groundbreaking success in her 2021 US Open Final, where momentum visibly shifted and switched between points, particularly during moments of high tension, such as at Deuce. The concept was later adapted into the first-ever Diploma in Psychology in Football, offered by the Football Association in 2003–2004, in which I was among the first group of participants, and where we were introduced to momentum analysis through tennis.

Momentum builds on itself, much like a snowball rolling down a hill. We can see how the ball seems to fall perfectly for one player, while another struggles with a touch that is just too strong—both scenarios can shift momentum or amplify strength and power. The essence of momentum analysis and its application lies in the ability to change and control it. Considering a national football team like England, as spectators we often witness missed scoring opportunities, goals scored against the run of play, negative refereeing [including video assistant referee (VAR) decisions], injuries, treatments, and fatigue —all of which can dramatically influence momentum.

There are three phases of momentum:

1. Momentum for the team.
2. Momentum in the balance.
3. Momentum against the team.

"Momentum is the force that dictates the flow of a match, a hidden force because it is not always reflected in the score. It flows between competitors, and it changes, there is a sense of holding the balance of power" (36). As such, momentum is understood and observed by individuals, such as coaches or spectators, and can be perceived differently by each person, even at the same time! In football, possession of the ball may dictate momentum, whereas in tennis, momentum might be present even when chasing a ball to return a hit. Recognising momentum is therefore vital for coaches, players, and athletes to effectively influence performance and outcomes.

The next element is recognising which stage of momentum you are in—whether you are sustaining it, trying to gain more of it, or recovering it after losing it.

When You Have It: Momentum is with You

Momentum brings control, 'luck,' good decisions, ease of movement, strong positioning, and effective communication within yourself and with others. Within the game, you feel a sense of ascendancy. In team sports, this often translates to cohesion, being all together in the flow of the game, and greater composure, where everyone is working seamlessly together.

When Momentum is in Balance:

In this stage, the game feels evenly matched. For example, in football, neither team maintains possession for long, and both sides keep hustling without any one team taking clear control. In tennis, this is akin to a state of 'deuce' with one set all—everything is balanced, and the outcome could tip either way.

When Momentum is Against You:

Play feels unsettled, and efforts seem to yield little reward. Despite trying harder, physical energy drains, team energy dissipates, and there may even be a growing sense of hopelessness. This shift becomes noticeable to the opposition, bolstering their confidence as they sense the momentum not only favouring them but also gaining strength.

How Momentum Switches:

Momentum in sports can shift dramatically due to various factors, often described as 'game changers.' In football, these shifts may result from goals, controversial refereeing decisions, tactical substitutions, or moments of brilliance by the opposition. Other influences, such as spectator noise, weather conditions, or time-wasting tactics, can also tip the balance. Specific incidents, like a penalty decision—whether pre-VAR or influenced by VAR— are often described as game changers. These changes can occur outside the control of an individual or team, but intrinsic factors such as strong leadership, strategic substitutions, and heightened focus during vulnerable moments (like the last five minutes of play) can also drive momentum shifts.

In tennis, momentum changes are even more noticeable due to the structured environment, with clear boundaries like the net and lines. Consider a player serving for the match at 5-4 in the final set:

the first serve lands in the net, trying for power. The next serve is too long due to overcorrection. The opponent capitalises, wins the game, and then carries the momentum to take the next two games and the match. Such scenarios were famously part of Andy Murray's early career struggles before his rise to dominance.

These examples highlight the importance of recognising and managing momentum. In your sport or performance, consider identifying these elements of momentum. Focus on strategies to force change, sustain positive momentum, and use it to your advantage to achieve victory.

Corner 2: Physical

When we feel fatigue—tired, drained, or exhausted—our mood is inevitably affected. **Mood** is defined as a "conscious state of mind or predominant emotion" (Oxford Dictionary), and is, therefore, subject to variability. It can shift depending on circumstances, context, time of day, relationships, emotional reactions, and other factors. Our energy levels significantly influence our mood. When energy is high, we tend to feel more positive, motivated to take action, and decisive, which shows itself in our performance. Thus, maintaining good energy levels is crucial!

This brings us to the importance of understanding our physiology and ensuring our bodies function well so we can perform effectively in our chosen domains—whether in life, sport or the performing arts. Hence, **Corner 2 is Physical**. Taking care of the athlete's body involves a deliberate approach to nutrition, hydration, exercise physiology, basic biomechanics, pain management, supportive orthotics, and good posture. These are all critical elements of performance.

If we consider that cars cannot drive without a functioning engine, it becomes clear that we cannot play sports or perform a dance without the strength, flexibility, energy, and fitness of our bodies. Yet, we do not always look after them enough to maintain consistent high performance. Modern tennis provides a striking example: world-class players such as Federer, Murray, Djokovic, and Nadal, have all experienced significant breaks in their careers due to overtraining, and burnout, in addition to major injuries.

While many professional academies teach sport science in their programmes, not all do, and parents may not be fully informed about what is required for their children's development, particularly in elite sport. Here's some guidance to help!

Electrolyte Replacement and Recovery

Electrolyte replacement drinks are essential for maintaining hydration, yet they are often overlooked or not widely understood **(WW55)**. Electrolytes are body salts—potassium, sodium, calcium, and magnesium. The body is unable to replace them naturally, so we need to do so with foods and fluids. Failure to do so can result in feelings of constant thirst, even with as little as a 2% reduction in hydration. This often results in increased fluid intake, which is not effectively absorbed into the bloodstream. Consequently, frequent urination occurs, flushing out vital existing nutrients and contributing to fatigue.

Similarly, inadequate electrolyte levels can prevent proper nutrient absorption from food. To counteract this, taking an electrolyte drink within 30 minutes of intense exercise is most important. Dehydration, coupled with excessive fluid intake, can also disrupt sleep, as frequent waking to urinate becomes necessary. It affects problem solving capacity too.

In my experience, electrolyte recovery has become a significant issue **(WW56)**. As an example, during the Covid-19 pandemic, one Further Education College interviewed 50 staff members and

4 students and revealed that all were chronically dehydrated and failing to replace electrolytes. This had a notable impact on their sleep, either because they were dehydrated or because they drank copious amounts of water, leading to frequent trips to the toilet—sometimes two or three times per night.

Why does this happen? When electrolytes are depleted, the body is not capable of regeneration. Potassium, sodium, calcium, and magnesium can only be replaced through specific drinks or foods. Without this replenishment, persistent thirst (even at just 2% dehydration) prevents water we ingest from being absorbed into the bloodstream. Instead, the kidneys excrete this water, depleting the body of nutrients and causing greater energy loss. Additionally, poor electrolyte levels hinder nutrient absorption from food, preventing these nutrients from being converted into energy and effectively wasting them. Approximately 70% of the clients I have worked with are electrolyte depleted. However, psychologists—and even sport psychologists—may not recognise the symptoms of electrolyte imbalance. Fatigue, poor motivation, sleep problems, and diminished focus and concentration are all commonly affected by this overlooked issue.

A 19-year-old rugby player I worked with was encouraged to drink more fluids. A week later, however, he appeared exhausted and foggy in his thinking. He then admitted to drinking six litres of water per night, which disrupted his sleep. When I asked about electrolytes, he confessed he had forgotten to replenish them. After 48 hours of restoring his electrolyte balance, his sleep returned to normal, and his water intake reduced to a healthy two litres per night.

Electrolytes—potassium, sodium, calcium, and magnesium—must be replenished through drinks containing these essential minerals. Additionally, consuming carbohydrates and proteins within the critical 60–90-minute window after exercise is vital. Failing to do so can delay recovery by up to 24 hours for each hour that passes beyond this window, potentially extending the recovery period to as long as 72 hours.

Sleep and Sleep Disturbance

Good-quality sleep is fundamental to wellbeing and performance for everyone, yet it can be troublesome at some point of our lives due to a variety of reasons, including emotional stress **(WW57)**. Studies suggest that up to 35% of the adult population have sleep issues, with the figure rising to 42% among young people. These sleep disturbances affect both mental and physical health, as highlighted in the same study.

Young people may try to hide sleep deprivation caused by late-night gaming, internet use, movie-watching, or texting friends. These activities stimulate them physically and mentally, making it difficult to fall asleep. This is known as hyper-arousal and is driven by the sympathetic nervous system (SNS). Over time, the brain and body may adapt to a disrupted sleep pattern, resulting in frequent awakenings between 2–5 a.m. and a persistent sense of fatigue and unrefreshing sleep upon waking.

And it's not just the kids! Parents often face their own sleep challenges due to work pressures, childcare responsibilities, full- or part-time jobs, commuting, and financial stress—all of which contribute to a hectic lifestyle and disturbed sleep.

Initial insomnia refers to difficulties in falling sleep. This often leads to insufficient sleep, resulting in fatigue and reduced concentration during the day. A major cause of initial insomnia is the stress response to everyday issues, where we tend to overthink, worry, or feel anxious. During these moments, the brain signals the 'fight' (anger) or 'flight' (fear) response, releasing hormones such as adrenaline and cortisol into the bloodstream. These hormones stimulate the body, making relaxation and restful sleep difficult to achieve. This, in turn, impairs the brain's ability to filter and process information during sleep, which is essential for memory recall and skill acquisition.

Younger people require longer periods of sleep than their adult parents, particularly during adolescence. While they may be secretive about not going to sleep as expected, the effects eventually manifest physiologically. These include changes in physical appearance, sluggish movement, low mood, anger, poor concentration, forgetfulness, avoidance of social contact, and reduced appetite. Notably, these behaviours can also be early signs of depression, which will be discussed later.

What can you do? Firstly, it's important to recognise that this is happening to your son or daughter. They may feel embarrassed to discuss it, but their thoughts that are stopping them from sleeping could range from academic performance, interactions with fellow pupils, teachers, or coaches, to bullying, relationship issues, sexuality, or self-image issues.

Sleep apnoea (also spelled sleep apnea) is a sleep disorder characterised by frequent pauses in breathing or periods of shallow breathing during sleep. According to the Sleep Apnoea Trust, 25% of the UK population suffer from some form of sleep disorder that results in excessive daytime sleepiness (56)**. Early morning wakening** is the 3rd element affecting sleep.

Energy

Energy drives our activities and influences our mood, how we feel, and our motivation to do things **(WW39)**. While sleep disturbance has a major impact, other factors also contribute, including overtraining, injury, illness, travel, and the competing demands of academics, sport, and performance. These pressures can lead to overtraining and burnout.

Consistent evidence of the importance of rest has been highlighted in *The Times* (57), emphasising the significance of Rest, Recovery, and Relaxation—the three 'R's. These elements are critical to high performance yet are often neglected by athletes who simply don't know how to rest or relax, as their lives are so heavily focused on training, practice, and competition.

Coaches often feel that they are only doing their job when they are actively coaching and in the public eye. As a result, they may overtrain athletes and interfere with their necessary rest and recovery times. Similarly, athletes—and musicians, for example—often feel driven to practise constantly, experiencing 'guilt' if they take time to rest.

For me, **'guilt'** has never served a beneficial purpose. On the contrary, it often forms the foundation of limiting self-beliefs, regardless of religious or spiritual contexts. So, let go of 'guilt' if you can—it's not yours to carry **(WW59)**!

Athletes not only require the 3 'R's but also need to gradually taper off from intensive exercise to maximise its benefits. Allowing the body to naturally adapt over a 24-hour period ensures optimal gains. This highlights the importance of physiological recovery after intensive exercise or practice, particularly following heavy sweating. Meditation.

Body Issues

Delayed-onset muscle soreness (DOMS) can be reduced—or even avoided—through proper nutrition, warm-down exercises, massage, and adequate sleep **(WW60)**. It's astonishing how many elite athletes I encounter who neither don't know or choose to ignore these fundamental principles. During the Covid-19 pandemic,

I observed many individuals suffering unnecessarily simply because they failed to follow the same advice.

One often overlooked factor is sweating during sleep, which can result from worry, dreams, restlessness, or illness. The same principles of recovery apply here. In fact, much of the 'sleep' work I do in my practice reveals that poor sleep is often caused by dehydration due to depleted electrolytes—a condition that is frequently chronic. Unfortunately, in my experience, many General Practitioners fail to ask their patients about this key factor.

Body dysmorphia disorder (BDD) is a mental health condition characterised by an obsessive preoccupation with perceived flaws in one's appearance, often leading to extreme measures to hide or fix them. **Eating disorders** are frequently linked to BDD, and these issues are not exclusive to girls and young women. There is strong evidence that boys and young men are equally affected. Sports such as gymnastics, swimming, athletics, and football are disproportionately associated with these conditions in my observations **(WW58)**.

Clinical psychologists suggest that a loss of self-control is a central factor driving the controlling behaviours associated with these disorders. From my experience, I would also add that this loss of control, coupled with feelings of powerlessness, can contribute to the development of perfectionism, and 'tunnel vision' to block things out.

To address these challenges, it is important to identify the underlying stressors. Simply expressing these stressors can be beneficial and determining how to intervene—whether by speaking with teachers, coaches, or seeking professional advice—is crucial. Tackling the source of stress can help reduce its impact and improve management.

Practical techniques with proven outcomes include breathing exercises, body relaxation methods, visualisations, mindfulness, meditation, and soothing or bilateral sounds. In cases where there is intrusion in the form of flashbacks, dreams, or negative thoughts, these may be linked to trauma and are addressed in the 4th Corner focused on Psychology.

Injury and Medical History

While overtraining is a common cause of injury, repeated injuries, and slow recovery, injury is also a natural part of being an athlete. **Injury prevention** requires a balanced approach that includes high-quality training, adequate rest and recovery, and effective coaching. When the body is not overstressed, the likelihood of injury decreases significantly. Practices such as yoga, meditation, massage, acupuncture, osteopathy, Qi Gong, and chiropractic care are well-established approaches to support a healthy body. These approaches are beneficial not only for young athletes but also for their parents, helping to promote overall wellbeing and resilience. Fear of injury tenses the body.

There is a considerable psychological component to injuries and there are a range of interventions to work with conscious and unconscious limiting factors in recovery and post injury memory, which are explained more thoroughly in Chapter 9. Below is a detailed description of head injury and concussion.

Head injuries are most common among children and young people but are often underestimated, overlooked, or forgotten. Everyday accidents, such as falling off bicycles or walking into glass doors and windows, contribute to the list of head injuries. In sport, activities like rugby, football, diving, equestrian sports, ice hockey, field hockey, and American football carry an even greater risk.

While many head injuries are considered to be resolved to a degree, specialist assessment and intervention is often necessary. One particularly effective approach is Brainspotting, which has shown significant experienced change in addressing the issues associated with **concussion,** the interventions created and developed by me. These problems are discussed further below and in Chapters 8 and 9, where the involvement of Brainspotting interventions is explored. However, it should be noted that these interventions are not yet widely practised, nor have I trained others in the approach yet.

Injury is not simply a physical issue; it often has a profound emotional impact on young and mature athletes, preventing them from participation not only in sport but sometimes in education as well. When an athlete's self-esteem is heavily reliant on their sporting performance, injury can lead to depressed mood, sleep disturbances, and a lack of motivation. A significant concern arises when athletes attempt to return to training and competition too early, risking further damage and prolonged recovery times. Ideally, the process of returning after injury should be carefully managed through a gradual progression back to fitness and competition.

This approach is most effective when guided by experienced professionals, such as physiotherapists, strength and conditioning coaches, osteopaths or chiropractors, and practitioners of Pilates.

Concussion: issues of Diagnosis, Post-Concussion Syndrome, injury Rehabilitation-, Treatment, Brainspotting

The Australian Institute of Sport defines concussion as a Traumatic Brain Injury (TBI), caused by biomechanical forces to the head or to other parts of the body that transmit an impulsive force to the head. It results in short-lived neurological impairment, with symptoms that may develop over the hours or days following the injury (58). Further, Bloom and Caron (2020) add "the impact created by these forces causes brain tissues to deform due to increased intracranial pressure, which can lead to metabolic dysregulation, and other conditions", relating to changes in the way the body functions, and cognitive, psychological impairments (p84).

These hematomas are bleeding in and around the brain caused by a burst blood vessel. Contusions are bruising and swelling caused by bleeding into brain tissue. Evidence from animal studies and functional imaging suggests that concussion triggers a series of interrelated biochemical and physiological changes that impair neuronal function. Typically, symptoms resolve without the need for medical intervention. The primary treatment involves rest, followed by a gradual return to activity. There are contrasting views on this statement.

Recognising concussion can be difficult, as its symptoms and signs are variable, non-specific, and often subtle. Concussion should be suspected whenever an injury involves a knock to the head or body that transmits force to the head. Importantly, a hard knock is not required to generate concussion, it can occur even from minor impacts.

Some signs of concussion are more obvious, such as loss of consciousness, brief convulsions, or difficulty with balance and walking. However, the signs can also be much more subtle, requiring careful observation. The Sport Concussion Assessment Tool (SCAT5) is a valuable resource for identifying and assessing concussion symptoms.

Concussion Diagram · · · · · · · · · · · · · Eyes Forward, Concussion

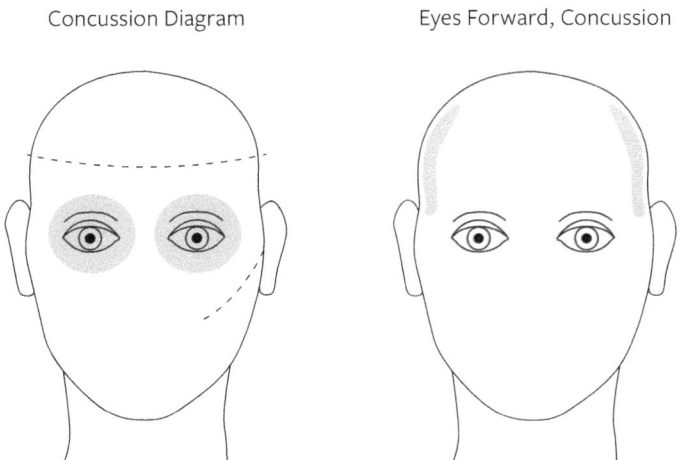

Possible Symptoms of Concussion (WW62)

1. Headache
2. 'Don't feel right'.
3. 'Pressure in the head'
4. Difficulty concentrating
5. Neck pain
6. Difficulty remembering
7. Nausea or vomiting
8. Fatigue or low energy
9. Dizziness or confusion

10. Blurred vision
11. Drowsiness
12. Balance problems
13. Sensitivity to light
14. More emotional
15. Sensitive to noise
16. Irritability
17. Feeling slowed down.
18. Sadness
19. Feeling like 'in a fog'
20. Nervousness
21. Anxiety
22. Trouble falling asleep (if applicable)

Recognising concussion is critical to ensuring correct management and preventing further injury. The Concussion Recognition Tool (CRT5), developed by the Concussion in Sport Group UK, provides valuable guidance for identifying concussion. When an athlete is suspected of having a concussion, first aid principles should always apply. A systematic approach to assessing airway, breathing, circulation, disability, and exposure (ABCDE) is essential in all situations. Cervical spine injuries should be suspected if the athlete has experienced any loss of consciousness, reports neck pain, or has been involved in a mechanism that could lead to spinal injury. In such cases, manual in-line stabilisation should be undertaken, and a hard collar applied until a cervical spine injury has been ruled out.

A medical practitioner should review any athlete with a suspected concussion. In situations where access to a medical practitioner is not available, the athlete must not return to sport on the same day. If there is any doubt about whether an athlete is concussed, they should not be allowed to return to sport that day.

An athlete with suspected concussion should be reassessed for developing symptoms and must be cleared by a medical practitioner before returning to play. Due to the evolving nature of concussion and the possibility of delayed symptom onset, athletes suspected of concussion should be closely monitored during the game or competition. If symptoms or signs develop, the athlete should be immediately removed from sport.

Sometimes there are clear signs that an athlete has sustained a concussion. Athletes displaying any of the following clinical features should be immediately removed from sport:

1. Loss of consciousness
2. No protective action taken by the athlete during a fall to the ground (observed directly or on video)
3. Impact seizure or tonic posturing, a stiffening of the body posture
4. Confusion or disorientation
5. Memory impairment
6. Balance disturbance or motor incoordination (e.g., ataxia)
7. Athlete reports significant, new, or progressive concussion symptoms
8. Dazed, blank, or vacant stare
9. Behaviour changes that are atypical for the athlete

Some features may suggest a more serious injury. Athletes displaying any of the following signs should be immediately referred to the nearest emergency department:

1. Neck pain
2. Increasing confusion, agitation, or irritability
3. Repeated vomiting
4. Seizure or convulsion

5. Weakness or tingling/burning in the arms or legs
6. Deteriorating conscious state
7. Severe or increasing headache
8. Unusual behavioural changes
9. Double vision

Diagnosing Concussion

Concussion diagnosis should always be conducted by a qualified medical practitioner. This process involves taking a detailed clinical history and performing a comprehensive examination. Key areas to evaluate include the mechanism of injury, presenting symptoms and signs, cognitive function, and neurological health, which may include balance testing.

The internationally recognised SCAT5 is a valuable resource for evaluating concussion. While it covers the essential areas mentioned above, it should not be used as a standalone diagnostic tool but rather as part of a broader clinical assessment. Additionally, computerised neurocognitive testing can complement the assessment but, like the SCAT5, should never be relied upon in isolation. Preseason baseline neurocognitive testing can provide a useful point of comparison for post-injury evaluations. In the absence of baseline testing, many programmes offer reference ranges for interpretation.

Currently, there are no reliable serum biomarkers or genetic tests available for diagnosing concussion. Routine blood tests are unnecessary for uncomplicated cases, and medical imaging is generally not required unless there is a concern about more severe head or brain injuries.

Where resources permit, sports organisations may consider incorporating modern technology, such as instant video review at pitch-side, to improve the detection and management of concussion during games or competitions. (Australian Institute of Sport)

According to Kontos (p46 Bloom and Caron) "There are relatively few empirically (by means of observation or experience rather than theory or pure logic) supported therapeutic approaches to treating psychological issues following concussion." I **discovered** the capacity of Brainspotting to release concussion from the brain in 2013 whilst working with footballers with historical and current concussions at AS Monaco FC, initially demonstrated by a fear of heading the ball. I learnt that when questioned about head or facial injury retrospectively, players demonstrated features of concussion at the time of impact and day later.

One player in particular had experienced serious facial and head injuries, and I noticed 9 times in his next game, he pulled his head away from the ball. As I desensitised the trauma of the injury with Brainspotting, a cluster of unusual activity took place, and the player reported significant relief, improved concentration, clearer thinking, and better sleep. In the next match he headed his first goal in 2 years and went on to be player of the year.

In practice, it could take up to between 8–13 minutes of having remembered a concussion event, before 'symptoms', would show themselves. There is no judgement in this process. The brain and body have the memory. If symptoms of the original injury do not surface, there is no concussion to resolve. Acute pain, and heavy, dull feelings in the head causing fatigue, were common, but it was the pressure around the eyes that appeared to be key to its diagnosis, and release. I also discovered that during the fixed eye positioning required to release the trauma, ongoing silence was important, as it was essential to allow the sub-cortical brain to continue to unconsciously release brain / body sensations without the 'interruption' from spoken sentences or words, language, which would take the client into the conscious, thinking, neo-cortex, and away from lower brain for healing. There are a number of indicators that the brain is changing, and ultimately the client experiences a loss of 'fogging', a clarity of thinking, and relief, loss of triggered nausea, and postural changes to the upper body, enabled by the release of body tension. **Concussions are accumulative**, and build one on top of the other, and I have been able to detect through observations, and knowing sporting histories, how other concussions through facial expressions, activated blinking, twitching, neck and shoulder jolts, acute pain, eye rolling, amongst others, show themselves, backed up by reported but forgotten conscious memory.

How it works: Imagine a motorway with 3 carriageways as a symbol of how information is transferred between the two hemispheres of the brain. At the point of impact on the head, and the subsequent bruising, and subcutaneous bleeding, two of the 'carriageways' are blocked with 'crashed cars' / bleeding. Whilst traffic 'information' can use the one lane that remains open, inevitably there develops a backlog of other vehicles/data, and so they seek to leave from the motorway at the nearest exit to an A road, to circumvent the 'crash site'. But then the A road might also become congested, and so some of the cars might use a B road, and then come back on to the A road, to return to the motorway further on.

This in my view is what happens within the brain, that the messaging system which had been direct, is blocked, and forced to find another route, and with the capacity for neuroplasticity, it can do this automatically. However, a consequence is it takes longer to get from A to B, in essence the messaging system within the brain is slowed down. This is experienced as 'fogging', a lack of clarity in thinking, and an unrecognised tension they carry around the neck and shoulders. It seems that when the concussion is released, the blockages on the two carriageways are cleared, and normal functioning and data messaging can resume. These are the new neural pathways (motorway carriageways) that become possible once the blockage is released by both the sympathetic nervous system and the two hemispheres of the brain itself reconnecting, automatically. The amygdala is positioned across both hemispheres.

I have worked with well over 200 concussions since 2013 and have built up a detailed and graphical illustration of what takes place within the process. Some of these examples are shown in Chapter 9 and further demonstrated in some of the client and athlete stories relating to their trauma history. In 2016 whilst completing the Brainspotting training for trainers in New York with David Grand, I met a colleague from Colorado, Dr Pie Frey, who had discovered the removal of concussion through Brainspotting 2 years earlier and independently. When we compared our notes, approaches, and techniques, we had a 90% correlation. Since then, I've become able to recognise concussion with minimal symptomatic presentation, developed through experience and observation. It is my intention to train others to use this method, and for researchers to audit both quantitatively and qualitatively, how it works, why it works, and most importantly how it feels.

As a clinical (mental health) sports and exercise psychologist, and teacher in nutrition and exercise physiology, and a deeply experienced Brainspotting practice with over 5000 hours of interventions, it places me in an ideal position to recognise the symptomatic presentation of mental health issues, including anxiety depression disordered eating, dehydration, loss of balance, sleep disturbance, nausea, headache, sweating, and indeed a history of hiding symptoms which almost certainly would have prevented them from being selected to play. I have also witnessed appalling decisions made by medical doctors, and sport managers and coaches, to force players to continue playing in key games and competitions, sometimes with protective masks, without due regard for their safety, and future wellbeing. A history of American Football and the development of Chronic Traumatic Encephalopathy, leading to permanent brain damage, disturbingly illustrated by the 2015 film *Concussion*, shows what can happen.

Chapter 9 includes anonymised case notes from concussion interventions I have conducted with athletes, primarily over the internet via Skype or Zoom, using Brainspotting techniques. Brainspotting uses eye positions linked to subcortical memories of traumatic or impactful events. These eye positions are connected to physiological, emotional, and cognitive responses tied to those memories. By holding these targeted eye-positions, the trauma stored within the SNS can be released and processed through the parasympathetic nervous system (PSNS). Simultaneously, the previously blocked connections between the left and right hemispheres of the brain are automatically reprocessed, allowing for the formation of new neural pathways and a reorganisation of the brain's response to the event.

Osgood-Schlatter Syndrome is a condition commonly experienced by a significant number of young athletes, often referred to simply as 'growing pains' **(WW61)**. It manifests as a painful, bony bump on the shinbone, just below the kneel, and typically occurs in children and adolescents undergoing growth spurts during puberty. This condition is most prevalent in young athletes involved in sports requiring running, jumping, or quick changes in direction—such as football, basketball, figure skating, and ballet. Managing Osgood-Schlatter Syndrome involves periods of rest and recovery, and it usually resolves naturally. The condition commonly affects boys aged 12 to 14 and girls aged 10 to 14.

Drugs, Doping, Lifestyle, and the Law

During periods of injury, illness, intensive training, or performance loss, athletes may use medication or supplements that could unknowingly include substances banned by their sport. It is often the responsibility of the coach, along with any medical practitioner involved, to provide guidance on which medications are permitted within the rules of each individual sport. In such situations, it is strongly recommended that parents consult both the coach and the responsible medical practitioner to ensure that any substances being used do not jeopardise their child's participation in their chosen sport.

The use of illegal drugs, such as **cannabis**, generally becomes more likely around the age of 15 within society. However, among athletes, the use of such substances tends to be minimal, as most are focused on enhancing performance or finding healthier ways to relax. That said, cannabis use may arise in cases where families are experiencing distress, such as during a divorce or parental separation, and it is worth being mindful of this possibility with athletes or performers if they become depressed or long term injured, or some other life event, especially linked to relationships.

More recently, cannabis oil and other non-tetrahydrocannabinol (THC) derivatives have been legalised for the beneficial treatment of certain illnesses, highlighting a distinction between medicinal and recreational use. When it comes to illegal performance-enhancing drugs, this remains a challenging area for parents of promising athletes. International organisations responsible for testing are ultimately the most reliable source of information to help navigate these concerns and ensure compliance with their regulations.

Corner 3: Social

Skill Acquisition and Elite Player/Performer Development

Learning new skills of competence and capability in life, art, and sport performance is central to training and development. Such skills are learned and practised repeatedly. It is believed that it takes 7,500 to 10,000 hours of practice and competition to become an elite athlete before the age of 19. A key issue in sport is the use of psychological support to enable this process, as well as the prevention of overtraining and psychological burnout from pushing beyond one's limits. In this respect, I now turn to the impact of social relationships, which are essential to life, art, and sport performance achievement, or indeed to its detriment.

When you consider an athlete's training and competition career from the age of 7 to 17 or 18, just to become an accomplished athlete, imagine the commitment required from parents over all those years! The miles travelled by car, train, or aeroplane; the journeys to home and away matches, often in the most inhospitable weather—it's a phenomenal effort.

Not surprisingly, conflicts can arise along the way: between parents and their children, between children and their coaches, between coaches and parents, and even with teachers and friends. This triangular relationship between coach, parents, and athletes is a unique and complex dynamic, and referred to as the parent, coach, athlete Triad.

At the heart of this book lies this section, focusing on the critical key relationships within the contexts of sport and the performing arts. It examines how children and parents manage everyday life, education, and their emotional and intellectual development— ideally, one hopes, satisfactorily. However, this section focuses more on what happens when things go wrong, how these issues can be fixed, and, crucially, how they might be avoided in the future. Prevention is always better than cure.

Bullying and Trauma

In 2009, while delivering a show jumping workshop with Australian Olympic squad rider Warren Lamperd, one of the participants broke down in tears as she remembered being thrown from her horse. The horse had rolled on top of her, causing multiple injuries. Unaware until that moment, she had been living with undiagnosed post-traumatic stress disorder (PTSD) for five years. Over several sessions, her trauma was resolved, prompting me to write an article for the *Horse and Hound* magazine to raise awareness. Following its publication, I was inundated with telephone calls from female riders sharing similar experiences.

In discussion I asked the questions: "What was the variable elements in cases where precisely the same type of accident, known as a **'rotational fall**,' occurred, and why some riders fully recover both physically and mentally, while others failed to recover mentally and developed PTSD, given the life-threatening nature of these falls?"

My discovery revealed that 8 out of 10 riders who met the criteria for PTSD had all been **bullied at school**—not only by other children but also by teachers. Teachers, along with sport coaches, can be significant sources of bullying behaviour, often unknowingly **(WW63)**. I have witnessed this behaviour at every level of sport and in the performing arts. While it is evident across various sports I have worked in, it seems particularly prevalent in football. Rugby seems to be a notable exception, although not entirely free from such issues. When left unresolved, the effects of bullying are often carried into adulthood. See Chapter 9 for related interventions.

What seems to happen is that the trauma response, described in more detail in Chapter 8, suppresses the immune system. The term "psychological immune system" is used to encompass various biases and cognitive mechanisms that protect the person from experiencing extreme negative emotions, often through numbing and avoidance, both consciously and unconsciously.

Biologically, the immune system defends the body from foreign substances, cells, and tissues by producing an immune response. However, when subjected to pressure at future points in life, this robust ability to recover may either weaken or strengthen. In the case of rotational falls from horses, the difference lay in the brain and body's protective mechanisms, which were previously less robust for some individuals.

I have since recognised that earlier strong negative experiences—both physical and emotional—become encoded as brain-body memories. These memories can be subconsciously triggered, leading to disproportionate reactions that are not 'intended' but are instead driven by these past imprints.

Bullying, as defined by StopBullying.gov is "unwanted, aggressive behaviour among school-aged children that involves a real or perceived power imbalance. The behaviour is repeated or has the potential to be repeated (fear), over time. Both kids who are bullied and who bully others may have serious, lasting problems" (59).

Bullying in the form of physical or emotional abuse is often traumatic for young people and, sadly, often lingers into adulthood. It is a precursor to depression, chronic anxiety, lower self-esteem, and, not surprisingly, a loss of performance. So, what should you look for? It is important to note that not all children who are bullied will display warning signs. However, some indicators that may point to a bullying problem include the following **(WW64):**

- Unexplainable injuries
- Social media trolling or humiliation on platforms like Facebook

- Lost or destroyed clothing, books, electronics, or jewellery
- Frequent headaches, stomach aches, or complaints of feeling sick, sometimes faking illness
- Changes in eating habits, such as skipping meals or binge eating; children may come home from school hungry because they avoided eating lunch
- Difficulty sleeping and/or frequent nightmares
- Declining grades, loss of interest in schoolwork, or avoiding school altogether
- Sudden loss of friends or avoidance of social situations
- Feelings of helplessness or decreased self-esteem
- Self-destructive behaviours, such as running away from home, self-harm, or talking about suicide.
- Substance misuse, including drugs and alcohol

When considering the major characteristics of PTSD—or prolonged duress stress disorder (PDSD)—it is helpful to use the acronym ANIA to help recall: **Arousal, Numbing, Intrusion, and Avoidance (WW65)**. Numbing suppresses unwanted negative emotions; unwanted intrusive thoughts develop; and avoidance of people, places, or specific situations often occurs. Alongside these, hyperarousal—characterised by high levels of anxiety, panic, freezing, or phobias—is commonly present.

Parents, teachers, and coaches should take note that bullying is traumatic and often leaves a lasting impact.

The Art and Science of Communications with Others

In previous chapters, I have outlined how couples can significantly improve their communication with each other. That simple framework of feedback can also be used with your own children, coaches, teachers, and others—especially when addressing something difficult. I describe two golden rules for presenting information to others, focusing on the essence of what we **intend** to communicate to another person or group.

Golden rule 1: Speak from Personal Experience (WW66)

When we speak from our own experience, starting with "I" or "my," we cannot be criticised, as this perspective is unique to us. If criticism does arise, it is often more of a projection ("their stuff") from the speaker rather than an issue with us. Focus on speaking about your perspective: my view, my perception, my understanding, what I feel, what my instinct tells me, my reaction, my response. These phrases reflect personal experience and are not subject to criticism. Others may disagree, and that's perfectly fine.

Golden rule 2: Evidence-Based Statements (WW67)

Like writing an essay for a college course, any statement we make requires to be evidence-based to carry validity. In other words, our statements must be supported by reliable information, with the source clearly identified, ensuring the evidence can be independently verified. This approach not only validates what we say but also enhances credibility.

Over many years of observing the language people use, I have discovered that when individuals speak in generalisations, their statements often lack substance and knowledge. Under questioning, they frequently reveal that they do not actually know what they are talking about **(WW68)** When asked to clarify their comments, they tend to become avoidant or defensive, often repeating the generalisations with phrases like, "Well, of course, everyone knows that." They fail to provide specific evidence.

Of particular concern is when people persistently use non-validated statements and avoid taking ownership of their words.

In my experience, this is often linked to a history of a depressive phase in their lives This conclusion is not only based on my observations of over 2,000 clients during a long career in mental health but is also supported by numerous articles in the British Psychological Society's *The Psychologist* magazine. Furthermore, a recent journal article by Yahya and Rahim confirms this connection, stating that "sensitive markers of depression namely first-person singular pronouns, negative emotion words, and absolutist (exaggerated and global) words as they reflect increased self-focus, negativity, and absolutist thinking in depressed individuals" (60).

What seems to happen when people become depressed in mood is a consistent tendency towards social isolation. They withdraw from others and begin 'ruminating,' deeply reflecting on their feelings of sadness and sometimes their desperate situations, but without sharing these emotions. This isolation and lack of expression further deepens the depression. Over time, the combination of suppressing unwanted feelings and not expressing them leads to a loss of the language needed to communicate emotions. In essence, individuals become disconnected and dissociated.

So, parents, coaches, or teachers, take note: your children or pupils may exhibit this behaviour. Be **'Socratic'** in your approach—ask open ended questions to explore the depth and accuracy of their statements. This will help validate their thoughts or reveal a lack of substance. And ask yourself: why is this happening?

In Chapter 4, I describe **Transactional Analysis (TA)** as a straightforward method of understanding interpersonal dynamics—the transactions between people—enabling a clearer grasp of their intentions and actions. Are they engaging as an adult or a child? Are they exhibiting inappropriate parental or childish behaviours? In such cases, it is important to remain firm in the 'adult' self-state: listening, understanding, repeating, and responding appropriately.

This approach allows the other person the opportunity to mirror your appropriate behaviour. Otherwise, they may stay entrenched in a parental authority role or a victim-child mindset.

I see language as a window into the mind **(WW69)**. Phrases like I can't, I should, I must, I never, obviously, of course, it's impossible, I don't, are inherently limiting or make assumptions based on limited knowledge. These types of language create barriers to performance.

Obviously and Of Course = Assumptions (WW70)

Nothing is truly obvious—except to the person speaking! These words reflect assumptions and align with limiting self-beliefs, such as:

- Nobody loves me.
- I'm not good enough.
- I can't do it.
- Everybody hates me.
- We can't win.
- I will fail.
- I'll be too nervous.
- They will see my fear.

These types of statements demonstrate how the 'game' is often lost before it even begins, becoming self-fulfilling prophecies. Simply by neutralising and avoiding the use of such limiting words and phrases, you shift from negativity and a downward spiral into a place of possibility—and that feels different! Words like should, must, never, always, everyone, and can't, also be reconsidered for their impact.

It's not just Buddhists who benefit from mantras. **Affirmations** such as, "I am beautiful," "I can do this," "I am a winner," "I can live my life's desires," "I can be accepted as I am," and "I love myself" can be powerful tools for anyone.

When working with individuals, I often ask them what they feel. If they respond with statements like, "I probably feel sad," "I might feel," or "I guess I feel sick in my stomach," they are speaking from a detached, disconnected, or dissociated part of themselves **(WW71)**. They do not own or fully recognise these feelings, nor do they take responsibility for them. This lack of connection with their emotions and body is often a sign of trauma. **Dissociation** is a mechanism through which we separate ourselves from our own mind and body, perceiving experiences as if from a third-person perspective, and failing to remain fully 'present.'

In a podcast episode I shared with Dr Steve Peters for BBC Radio 4, we discussed the language of sport psychology as a preamble to the 2012 Olympics (61). I shared how I had worked with Bristol squash player Sam Ellis, who joined Dr Peters and me for the episode. In our first four hours of sessions, Sam could only respond with, "Don't know, don't know." This was a disconnected, resistant, and defensive reaction. Sam was very low in mood at the time, and the first breakthrough came when he said, "I'm not sure right now!" Why was this significant? Because it introduced the idea of possibility, rather than limitation. Over time, Sam, like both of his parents before him, became a world-ranked squash player. In the podcast episode, he demonstrates how much more articulate and happier he is now!

So, parents, pay attention to what people say and how they say it. In Chapter 8, I explore how even subtle factors like head and eye positions can influence voice volume, energy, and the production of negativity.

Coach, Player, and Parent Relationships

One of the most challenging aspects for parents in managing their children's sporting or performance career is navigating the relationship between their children and their coaches, instructors, teachers, choreographers—and knowing when or if they should intervene. At the same time, these professionals are expected to be sources of knowledge, information, and skill, ideally taking major responsibility for providing effective feedback.

However, many of the athletes and parents I work with report receiving very little professional feedback, particularly feedback that is individual and performance focused. Part of the problem is that some professionals lack the skills to deliver feedback effectively, fail to recognise their avoidance of it, or adopt styles and approaches that have limited positive impact. Yet, the ability to provide meaningful and constructive feedback is surely a fundamental skill for successful coaching.

Like parenting, our role models for coaching often tend to be our own coaches, and parents. Whether we aim to emulate them or strive to be different, the way we were parented, and coached, becomes ingrained in our own perception and actions, subconsciously driven by the subcortical brain—sometimes despite our best intentions to change it. In my view, coaching support continues to struggle to move away from the **command style** of "do as I say," where feedback often takes the form of comments that are either negative or positive but are usually personalised. This approach is typically adapted from how coaches themselves were coached or taught. Comments like, "You did this badly today," "You made that pass when I told you not to," "Where were you when that ball came across?" or "You could've done better" are frequently delivered in front of the entire team. These remarks can leave young athletes feeling embarrassed, disappointed, and even humiliated. Is that truly the way forward? What impact does this have on a young person already struggling with their sense of identity? It traumatises them.

In March 2018, Josè Mourinho, then manager of English Football Premier League team Manchester United, having spent over

£250 million on players, publicly sought to humiliate several players over the season. Personally disappointed with their performances, he emphasised his authority in the power dynamic. One notable target was young defender Luke Shaw, whom Mourinho criticised on multiple occasions in front of a global audience. Many considered this behaviour to be bullying, even from someone as famous, talented, and historically successful.

Mourinho's coaching style often directed players to perform exactly as he instructed. When they failed to meet his expectations or the standards he sets, he expresses his personal disappointment. During his final two seasons, first with Chelsea and then with Manchester United, he publicly criticised players, refused to cooperate reasonably with the press and media, and alienated a significant proportion of the fan base. Despite these players being worth hundreds of millions of pounds collectively, they were not performing to their potential according to Matthew Syed in *The Times* (62).

If such methods are prevalent at the highest levels of professional sport, they inevitably influence the generations that follow. These limiting and undermining approaches reinforce the status quo and make positive change less likely. A shift from a command style to **cooperative coaching** methods appears to be the best option, and happily the most successful.

There is a valuable lesson here for our schools and universities as well. As psychotherapist Carl Rogers demonstrated, adopting 'person-centred' methods fosters better outcomes. For examples of this, look to Jurgen Klopp, Pep Guardiola, and Gareth Southgate, David Moyes, Arne Slot, and Mikel Arteta.

The coach-athlete, manager-player, or teacher-student relationship is complex and deeply significant—not only within the context of their primary purpose, such as sport, but also in the broader human development of a young person. It is not surprising that young athletes often view their coaches in a 'parental' role or even idolise them. These young individuals are navigating how to act, how to respond, how to be themselves, and how to meet the expectations of their parents and coaches.

I firmly believe that within these connections and relationships there is an invaluable opportunity for someone outside the family to truly believe in a young person's talent and ability. Feeling special, acknowledged, and inspired through such relationships can be a priceless and life-changing experience for young people. However, these same relationships can also be devastating when coaches, managers, or teachers act from a position of power, projecting their own insecurities onto their athletes. Such behaviour undermines trust and can have a lasting negative impact on the young person's development, even without them realising it.

As Sophie Jowett has extensively researched (63), the coach-athlete relationship is, at its core, a power relationship. It often carries a maternal or paternal dynamic and involves significant role-modelling, much like the relationship between teachers and students in schools. However, when this relationship breaks down, it can disintegrate into something **abusive**, creating problems that affect not just the athlete but the entire group—teammates, parents, and even other family members. In such situations, parents often feel powerless to intervene. This sense of helplessness can immobilise them and even leave them traumatised. For me, there is still much work to be done in coach education to address and change these dynamics.

External Influences: Sport, Work, Culture, Media, and Role Models (Sources of Inspiration)

Humans are inherently social beings; we are not 'designed' to live in isolation. The concept of family—whether nuclear, close, or extended—provides us with essential connections that ideally help to define us positively. Families, and parents in particular, play a significant role in shaping who we are, for better or worse.

One particularly devastating aspect of bullying is the exclusion of a young person from the group, especially in sport, whether by teammates or even the coach. This form of social isolation directly impacts an individual's sense of self-worth and self-acceptance, often with profound emotional consequences for their daily lives. It can lead to depression, suicidal ideation, eating disorders, acute and chronic anxiety, self-harming behaviours, sleep deprivation, and demotivation. In essence, is a deeply traumatic experience.

If you find yourself as part of team or group engaging in such behaviour—regardless of the reasons you might think are justified—take a moment to consider the significant and lasting damage this can inflict on another human being.

Social Inclusion (WW71)

Social inclusion affirms that we are acceptable, valued, fun to be with, interesting, talented, and recognised as a friend, teammate, or partner. Being part of a team, particularly a successful one, fosters enhanced self-confidence, assertiveness, and opportunities for self-expression. It encourages cooperation, support and genuine care for teammates.

As a team member, you share a common goal, with each individual fulfilling their role to achieve success together. This idea is powerfully illustrated in **Al Pacino's motivational speech** from the film *Any Given Sunday* (64). In a pivotal scene, Pacino's character addresses his team during what he describes as the most critical moment of their careers, urging them to rise above their challenges.

"Either we heal as a team, or we are all going to crumble inch by inch, play-by-play, till we're finished… We can fight our way back into the light," he says, introducing the concept of "**game inches**." Pacino expands on this idea, highlighting how small, incremental changes, and efforts, can make the difference between success and failure: "You find out that life is just game inches. So is football. Because in either game, life or football, the margin for error is so small. I mean one half step too late or too early, and you don't quite make it. One half second too slow or too fast, and you don't quite catch it. The inches we need are everywhere around us. They are in every break of the game, every minute, every second."

The concept of "game inches" underscores the importance of small, incremental adjustments that collectively contribute to the team's capability and performance, even in the most challenging situations.

In my view, Pacino speaks about each individual player finding an aspect of their performance they can improve immediately. His goal is to motivate them not only from within themselves but also to inspire cooperation and support for each other as a team **(WW72)**.

"Cause we know when we add up all those inches that's going to make the f***ing difference between winning and losing, between living and dying. On this team, we fight for that inch; because that is what living is. The six inches in front of your face."

Here, the coach provides a framework where each member of the team improves themselves individually for the benefit of the whole team. In psychological terms, this approach initially activates **extrinsic motivation**, as the influence has come from 'outside'— the coach. However, the individual's response to this, when they realise the coach is asking them for self-responsibility, commitment to the team, and determination to achieve a common goal—to win the game—transitions into **intrinsic motivation**. This internal drive is fuelled by the emotional inspiration sparked by the coach's words.

Notably, in the film, Pacino's character deliberately seeks out individual players while speaking, making direct eye contact with them. This sense of personal connection resonates with those individual players, many of whom are natural leaders within the team. It demonstrates how a tailored, personal approach can inspire players to elevate both their individual efforts and their contributions to the team as a whole.

Leadership is both an internal and external process through which an individual seeks to positively influence other members of their group or team towards a mutual goal (65). In examining the common characteristics of leadership, Stuart Cotterell (66, p. 123) identifies the dominant presence of an individual's personality within a group. The essential characteristics of leadership appear to include:

1. Concern for task
2. Concern for people
3. Directive leadership
4. Participative leadership

The role of captaincy is explored by Sam Walker in his book *The Captain Class* (67), where he emphasises the importance of having a true leader within a team: the captain. Walker spent 20 years researching the world's most successful teams in the world and identified key characteristics that define effective captains. These include inspiration, dedication, commitment to the team's goals, the ability to unify the team, and a sense of responsibility in achieving these objectives. This collective effort and unity foster what is commonly referred to as group cohesion.

I have my own story related to this, from my time living in the countryside and becoming a beekeeping teacher. Observing these 'social insects' in their colony, I recognised that the queen bee demonstrates leadership, role clarity, and cooperation—all directed toward a common goal: survival. A bee colony, which can contain up to 60,000 honeybees at its peak, must be highly organised. The queen serves as the head of the colony and is solely responsible for laying eggs in each of the cells, which eventually develop into either worker bees or drones (males). The queen is significantly larger than any other bee in the colony. Male bees, known as drones, have only one primary function—to fertilize the queen, and, rather dramatically, when they fulfill this duty, they explode and die!

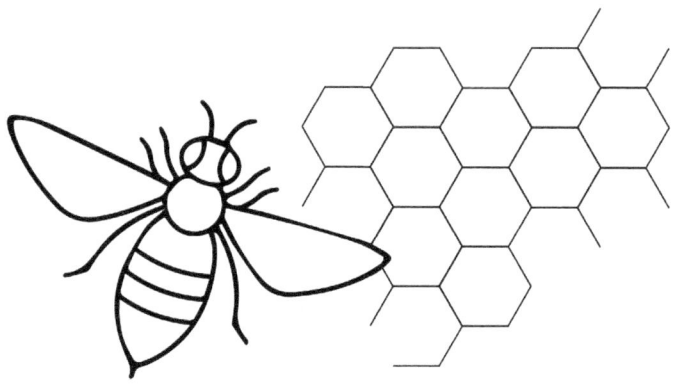

The queen cannot feed herself and relies entirely on worker bees to provide her with honey, and pollen. Despite this dependence, she exhibits total leadership within the colony. She achieves this in several ways. First, she releases pheromones—a scent that spreads throughout the colony each day. This chemical signal functions much like charisma, influencing the entire hive. It creates an almost tangible ambiance, generating a cohesive "vibe" that maintains order and unity. Additionally, as she moves through the hive, laying eggs and interacting with other bees, she physically touches them. This contact also spreads her pheromone, fosters a connection, much like an attachment to a mother. Her pheromones act as the glue that binds the colony together, much like how strong leaders create cohesion within a team.

Nature has its own way of ensuring the survival of the fittest, and the beehive is no exception. Queen bees typically last around two to three years in their role, maintaining the colony by consistently laying eggs. However, as the queen's egg supply dwindles, so too does the strength of her pheromones. At a certain tipping point, the worker bees sense this shift within the hive. In a seemingly subconscious collective decision, they determine that the queen must be replaced—much like an outgoing football manager who has lost influence in the dressing room. To replace her, the worker bees select an existing egg, enlarge its cell, and increase the supply of royal jelly (notice the queen reference here). This protein triggers a biological transformation, turning the developing bee into a new queen. The enlarged cell protrudes noticeably above the others, marking it as special. Once the new queen is born, she must establish dominance. She may force out the old queen herself, or the worker bees will remove or even kill the former leader. However, this transition only occurs once the new queen has completed her maiden flight, during which she is fertilised by male drones to activate her egg-laying capacity. If she fails, the worker bees eliminate her and start the process again ensuring the colony's survival. Voila! Nature's ruthless efficiency.

What this tells us about leadership is that sustaining influence over a long period while maintaining high levels of success is incredibly challenging. This has been wonderfully demonstrated by Sir Alex Ferguson and Arsene Wenger, two of the most successful Premier League football managers in history. We can also add Pep Guardiola, Jürgen Klopp, and Thomas Tuchel to that list now.

Parents, teachers, and coaches, have the ability to identify leadership characteristics in young people and encourage their development in this area **(WW73)**. However, it is also recognised that leadership responsibilities can sometimes be overwhelming, reducing an individual's capacity to sustain their own high-performance levels. In my view, particularly in team sports, it is essential to have both informally created and formally designated leaders—whether captains, leadership groups, or assistant leaders—who share responsibility and facilitate crucial communication. This structure helps implement tactical and strategic plans effectively within a team. The England football team adopted this approach at the 2018 World Cup and Euro 2020, integrating leadership support into their squad dynamics. Better late than never.

The way individuals are influenced in performance, from a psychological perspective, is described by Steven Covey's concept of the **"Circle of Influence"** (68). Whether you are a world-class tennis player supported by an elite team or a budding 12-year-old gymnast, this circle of influence naturally develops around you. At the centre of the circle is the individual athlete. Surrounding them in the inner circle of influence are key figures such as coaches, teachers, parents, siblings, teammates, friends, physical therapists, nutritionists, and psychologists. However, if anyone within this inner circle—whether an individual or a group—disrupts the balance through negativity, jealousy, egotism, or self-interest, they undermine the positive influence essential for success.

I witnessed this dynamic first hand in Monaco within Novak Djokovic's support team, and it was even more visible in Andy Murray's career. More recently, Emma Raducanu's post-2021 US Open struggles highlight the challenges of managing a stable and effective support system at the highest level of sport.

For young people, especially those under the age of 13, it is essential that parents serve as guardians of the circle of influence. They play a crucial role in observing, understanding, and sensing the influences surrounding their children to ensure safety, positive support, and balance. However, in some cases, parents themselves can become a source of pressure. By placing excessive expectations on their children to perform and win, they risk creating a negative influence within the very circle they are meant to protect.

The ability to perform under pressure falls within the realm of **Mental Toughness** and can be both demonstrated and self-measured. In this context, it becomes clear that parents, not just young athletes, also need support, as they play a crucial role in shaping their child's mindset and experience. Psychological interventions can be beneficial not only for young athletes but also for the parents who significantly influence their children, whether positively or negatively. Parents are not always neutral in their impact, and their own awareness and support can enhance their child's development. The importance of effective communication, both within oneself and with others, is explored further in Chapters 7 and 8.

Social Connections, Networks, Hobbies, and Personal Interests

In the journey toward becoming a well-rounded individual, rather than developing a sole (or soul) identity as a performer or athlete, it is crucial for young people to cultivate supportive social networks—in real-time, with real people—not just through social media. **Friendships** serve as a recreational source of human connection, fostering mutual satisfaction, empathy, and shared experiences. They teach young people to consider others, not just themselves. Similarly, **love** is not only a romantic experience but also a profound emotional connection with another person. We seek relationships that offer reliability, mutual support, understanding, and shared interests—another form of intimacy**.** This concept is explored in greater depth in Chapter 10.

One way young people attract others to themselves is by participating in shared activities **(WW74)**. While the pursuit of elite athletic success requires significant time and effort in skill acquisition and competition, it is equally important to develop interests beyond education, performing arts, and sport. Parents play a crucial role in encouraging these broader interests, particularly in families with multiple children. Not all siblings will share the same talent or passion as their high-performing brother or sister. By fostering diverse interests, parents help cultivate social inclusion, ensuring that young people are accepted for who they are not just for what they achieve.

Transitions in Sport and Performance: Career Changes and Financial Planning

We often notice athletes and players reaching a point where they can no longer sustain the level of performance required to maintain their professional status. Some officially retire, only to make a comeback—something rock stars seem to do regularly, as Sir Mick Jagger and the Rolling Stones keep on rocking! However, in sport, the physical demands on the human body, combined with the natural ageing process, play a significant role in determining an athlete's longevity. **Career transitions** are not always associated with young athletes and performers, but recognising and preparing for them early presents a valuable opportunity—one that is often overlooked.

Consider the different stages of an athlete's development— U10, U16, U21, reserve teams, high-performance groups, podium programmes, juniors, seniors, and beyond. At each stage, young athletes undergo significant physiological changes, including the challenges of puberty and brain development, as described in **Piaget's Four Stages** in Chapter 1. It is essential for parents to recognise and help manage these transitions. They need to be informed by coaches, physiotherapists, managers, and teachers about what to expect at each stage of development. Additionally, the risk of overtraining must be carefully monitored to ensure long-term performance and wellbeing.

Managing an education programme is also a crucial factor, particularly when teachers expect students to give their best effort academically while coaches in sport or performing arts demand peak performance. The dual pressures from both academic and athletic commitments can create conflicts that often lead to fatigue. For further discussion on navigating these challenges, see Chapter 7.

Corner 4: Psychological

You may wonder why, as a psychologist, I have placed this as the fourth rather than the first corner. This reflects a fundamental shift in understanding—many other factors influence and activate our responses before the mind consciously recognises them. "**Psychology** is defined as the scientific study of the mind and how it dictates and influences our behaviour, from communication and memory to thought and emotion" (69). Notably, physical aspects are absent from this definition.

Mental Toughness is a measure of individual resilience and confidence that may predict success in sport, education, and the workplace **(WW75)**. As a broad concept, it first emerged in the context of sports training, referring to a set of attributes that enable an athlete to perform at their best while effectively managing challenging training and competitive situations—all without losing confidence. Marc Jones and colleagues' Self-Determination Theory developed in 2007 has made significant contributions to the understanding of Mental Toughness, exploring its core characteristics and how they support high performance.

Self-Measure Scale for Mental Toughness

Mental Toughness can be assessed using a self-measure scale that evaluates four key aspects of resilience and confidence. To determine your Mental Toughness percentage, rate yourself on a scale of 1 to 10 for each of the following areas, where 1 represents limited ability and 10 represents peak ability:

1. **Ability to Recover from Setbacks** – How well do you bounce back from challenges and failures? 1–10=?
2. **Robust Self-Belief** – How strong is your confidence in your abilities, even under difficult circumstances? 1–10=?
3. **Determination** – How persistent are you in achieving your goals despite obstacles? 1–10=?
4. **Ability to Perform Under Pressure** – How effectively do you maintain performance in high-stress situations? 1–10=?

Once you have assigned a score to each category, add the four numbers together to get your total score. Then, multiply this total by 2.5 to calculate your Mental Toughness percentage. For example, if your total score is 28, you would calculate: 28×2.5 = 70% Mental Toughness. This self-measure provides insight into your current level of mental resilience and highlights areas for potential growth. My view is that scores from 70% demonstrates a high level of psychological strength. Therefore 8+ is excellent.

In assessing the Ability to Recover from Setback, consider a scenario where a football or rugby referee makes a decision which you strongly disagree with. How do you react once it becomes clear that their ruling is final, even with the use of VAR? Managing the emotions and thoughts that arise in such moments are crucial. If you allow frustration and negativity to linger, they will almost certainly interfere with your focus and ability to stay in the moment.

Distraction leads to a drop in performance. Developing the ability to let go of these thoughts quickly and refocus on the game is essential for maintaining Mental Toughness and peak performance under pressure.

In 2004, while working at Liverpool Football Club's Academy, I helped players manage their emotional responses to setbacks. One player, unable to accept a referee's decision, allowed frustration to affect his concentration. His opponents took advantage—he lost possession due to poor focus, became angry, and, feeling embarrassed in front of the Anfield crowd at just 17 years old, lunged into the player who had dispossessed him. As a result, he was sent off. He literally saw red.

If that sounds like you, your likely score is below five on the Mental Toughness scale for recovering from setbacks. However, if you can accept the referee's decision and move on without losing focus, you could score seven or higher.

That said, setbacks don't always happen in the moment—they can linger. Penalty misses, goalkeeping errors, or gymnastics falls that cost medals can stay with an athlete for days, weeks, or even years. If setbacks continue to impact performance long after they occur, your score would again be below five. It is likely this memory was traumatic.

Robust Self-Belief was explored in earlier chapters, emphasising the importance of trusting in your own abilities and consistently delivering strong performances **(WW76)**. This belief remains firm despite difficult environments and challenging opponents, allowing you to meet both your own expectations and those of others with confidence.

A higher score on the Mental Toughness scale—7 or above—indicates greater consistency, resilience, and predictability in performance. Ultimately, our beliefs operate on a subconscious level, driving both our behaviours and actions in high-pressure situations.

Determination reflects your motivation to train, perform well, and strive to win. It is a key indicator of how, over the years, you have set goals and worked to achieve them. Determination is also evident in your attitude toward recovery—how you approach rehabilitation after injury, your readiness to make a comeback if you have been deselected or benched, and your ability to learn from mistakes by adapting your training to improve.

While it is important to self-assess your determination as an athlete, it can also be valuable to seek external feedback from a coach, teammate, or mentor for additional perspective. If your score is below 7, it may indicate underlying issues that need to be addressed to strengthen your resilience and long-term performance.

Finally, the **Ability to Perform Under Pressure** challenges how well you manage different environments in which you compete or perform. This includes handling travel demands, large audiences, crowds, and criticism, as well as maintaining the ability to enjoy the performance itself. A key measure is whether, even after making mistakes or experiencing a narrow loss, you still feel that you gave your best effort. A strong ability to manage pressure is reflected in a score between 7 and 10.

Performing under pressure reveals any vulnerabilities an athlete may have. While 25% of performance-related influences come from the sport or performance environment (such as stadiums or arenas), the remaining 75% is shaped by life experiences—as explored in the other three corners of the framework. Performance is not just about competition; it is deeply influenced by personal resilience and everyday challenges.

Now that you've completed your **self-assessment**, perhaps with input from a coach or parent, it's time to evaluate your scores.

- Scores below 7 indicate areas that may need further development in each category. Identifying these areas can help target specific improvements.
- Scores of 7 and above suggest consistency in performance and mental resilience.

Using the concept of "game inches"—where small, incremental improvements lead to greater success—you can work with your coach to design specific training programmes aimed at enhancing your strengths and addressing any weaknesses. Focused development in these areas will ultimately elevate your performance.

When considering which of these four categories is the most crucial, you may be surprised to learn that it is **Determination**. This is because Determination is more of an innate characteristic, whereas the other three elements—Recovering from Setbacks, Self-Belief, and Performing Under Pressure—can be trained and developed over time.

If your Determination is low, especially if this is uncharacteristic of your usual performance or self-perception, it may indicate underlying issues such as increased anxiety, worry, or low mood. In such cases, the possibility of overtraining, burnout, or unresolved trauma—whether inside or outside of sport—ought to be considered and addressed.

When working with Mental Toughness, I have observed that athletes scoring below 7 often share a common experience—low self-esteem. Self-esteem is rooted in a strong sense of self-worth, built upon authentic self-belief and assertiveness—the ability to positively represent oneself in the world. Often, young athletes with low self-esteem have experienced past events that led to a loss of confidence. These are frequently tied to negative feedback from coaches, bullying, peer group issues, team dynamics, or family challenges such as sibling rivalry or parental relationship difficulties. Recognizing and addressing these underlying influences is essential for rebuilding confidence and fostering long-term mental resilience.

The benefit of the self-scoring approach is that it provides insight into **how young athletes perceive themselves**, revealing potential discrepancies between self-perception and actual performance **(WW77)**. Some athletes may overestimate their abilities, scoring themselves higher than their true level of performance, which can lead to overconfidence and missed opportunities for growth. Conversely, others may underestimate their strengths, undervaluing their own positive attributes and potential. This lack of self-recognition can hinder confidence and mental resilience. When considering these scenarios, it is essential to bridge the gap between perception and reality, using self-assessment as a tool for growth, self-awareness, and targeted development.

Anxiety, Trauma, and the Pressure to Perform

A report on British Gymnastics revealed allegations of a "culture of body-shaming," where teenage gymnasts were required to "starve themselves" to meet target weights, subjected to "punishment conditioning," or forced to wear a "fat suit" if they failed to reach the required weight. These experiences shape deep-seated beliefs that, in turn, direct behaviour and attitudes—often in ways that are inconsistent with healthy performance and undermine self-worth.

I have worked with several gymnasts who have endured similar experiences. The 306 pages of the Whyte Review, published in June 2022, investigated abuse in British Gymnastics (70) and found that young gymnasts had been weight-shamed, subjected to psychological trauma, and even suffered physical injuries. The report received over 400 submissions from across the UK, naming more than 90 clubs and 100 coaches. For many, these experiences have led to life-changing trauma.

At its core, **belief,** is defined as the mental acceptance of and conviction in the truth, actuality, or validity of something or someone (Oxford Dictionary). When those beliefs are shaped by shame, fear, or coercion, they can have lasting psychological consequences, deeply affecting an athlete's mental health and performance.

Anxiety is a natural phenomenon, essential for self-preservation—without it, we might not survive. It is triggered by the 'ancient' reptilian brain as part of the body's fight-or-flight response. However, anxiety exists on a spectrum, ranging from a normal response to threats to a clinical mental health disorder that significantly impacts wellbeing. The medical definition of anxiety is an abnormal and overwhelming sense of apprehension and fear often marked by physical signs such as tension, sweating, and an increased pulse rate. It is accompanied by doubts concerning the reality and nature of the threat, as well as self-doubt about one's ability to cope with it.

Anxiety is a multisystem response to a perceived threat or danger, influenced by a combination of biochemical changes in the body, personal history and memory, and social context. Unlike other animals, which clearly experience fear, human anxiety is unique because it involves the ability to use memory and imagination to move backward and forward in time. This capacity means that much of human anxiety is produced by the anticipation of future events—a phenomenon I refer to as "anticipatory anxiety."

The anxiety experienced in post-traumatic syndromes illustrates how human memory is far more complex than animal memory. Anxiety is often fueled by anticipated scenarios rather than immediate, present dangers. Without a sense of personal continuity over time, our memory, we would lack the cognitive, thinking, reflective, considered framework required for anxiety to develop from these historical memories that shape our perception or what is happening to us in the here and now. This is the brain's system for keeping us safe from danger.

It is crucial to distinguish between anxiety as an emotional state and an anxiety disorder as a psychiatric diagnosis. A person may feel anxious without having an anxiety disorder. Similarly, when an individual is confronted with a clear and present danger, their physiological arousal is not necessarily classified as anxiety but rather as an appropriate stress response. Additionally, anxiety frequently occurs as a symptom in various other psychiatric conditions.

With these definitions in mind, it becomes easier to understand how **performance anxiety develops.** While it is often assumed that performance anxiety arises just before a competition or event, many athletes and performers experience anticipatory anxiety weeks or even months in advance. Some begin worrying two to three weeks before a major competition, while others—especially those preparing for events like the World Championships or the Olympics—can feel the pressure years ahead.

There is a direct connection involving emotion and physiological responses, which manifest in a state of **arousal**. Initially, this arousal is purely physical, but as anxiety intensifies, it can interfere with our ability to focus, and affects confidence, and overall performance. Recognizing this relationship is key to managing and overcoming performance anxiety.

As an equestrian psychologist, I have worked across every discipline in horse riding, including carriage driving with Team GB. Among the riders I've worked with, a high proportion experience anticipatory anxiety—worrying excessively about potential issues before they even occur. They ruminate over travel logistics, arrival at the competition, and their performance, often creating scenarios in their minds that may never happen. Unlike other sports, equestrian competition involves an unpredictable partner—the horse. One of the most striking aspects of rider anxiety is its direct impact on the horse's behaviour. **Horses mirror (or reflect) the emotions of their riders**, meaning that projections of anxiety are felt by the horse or pony, often leading to a drop in performance. This can manifest as body tension, restricted movement, excessive reactions, tightness in the reins, and poor posture or balance **(WW78)**. This mirroring is also beneficial and used in equine therapy for addiction and helping with facets of autism, as examples. Interestingly, this phenomenon is not exclusive to horses—it also occurs with dogs, further highlighting the interconnectedness between human emotion and animal response.

When we examine the underlying causes of these worries and anxieties, they often stem from a wide range of concerns, including the fear of injury to either the rider or the horse. Riders may also fixate on potential opponents, competition environments, weather conditions, and any number of things that could go wrong, including their equipment. The impact of these anxieties during training is significant and often debilitating, not just for the rider but for the horse as well. The cycle of worry can create tension, hesitation, and reduced performance, further reinforcing the rider's concerns. When additional external pressures are introduced, such as parental expectations, academic demands from school or college, and the need to maintain high performance in multiple areas, the competition itself can become either a moment of relief or a complete disaster, depending on how these stressors have been managed.

Another psychological component of anticipatory anxiety is the tendency to dwell on negative thoughts about one's capabilities and recall past failures, leading to **self-fulfilling prophecies** of doubt and poor performance **(WW79)**. Riders may think, I won't win, I'm not good enough, I will let my horse down, my parents will be angry, my saddle is too uncomfortable, and so on. These recurring thoughts reinforce anxiety and increase the likelihood of an undesired outcome, further perpetuating the cycle of fear and self-doubt which become fulfilled.

The origin of anxiety is stored in the brain's unconscious memory of past events, but it is also **imprinted in the body's memory too (WW80)**. Both the brain and body retain experiences, even when they are not consciously recalled. These memories are held in the amygdala, a region of the brain responsible for emotional processing, physical memory, and decision-making. The amygdala operates subcortically, meaning it functions below the neocortex, the part of the brain responsible for thinking, reasoning, and problem-solving. The amygdala plays a central role in managing trauma.

The hippocampus, hypothalamus, and amygdala receive information from what is sometimes called the **"second brain"— the stomach (WW81)**. This gut reaction, along with signals from the skin and vagus nerve, drives the sympathetic and parasympathetic nervous systems, sending sensory information through the spinal cord into the brainstem. These signals reach the amygdala dominantly in the right hemisphere of the brain half a second faster than information transmitted through the eyes to the visual cortex before travelling to the amygdala. These are the gut reactions and feelings on which we act upon driven from our unconscious. For a deeper exploration of these mechanisms, see *The Body Keeps the Score* by Bessel van der Kolk (33), and chapter 8, 9, 10 of this book.

All of this activity occurs subconsciously. When the brain recognises a past experience that is similar to the current situation and associates it with a negative outcome, it automatically triggers a physical, and emotional response. This leads to the release of hormones, including cortisol and adrenaline, into the bloodstream, preparing the body for a fight (anger) or flight (fear) response in anticipation of a perceived threat. This reaction is self-protective, part of the autonomic nervous system, and not consciously chosen.

The intensity of the physical and emotional response—whether fear, anger, or distress—can be so powerful that it **overwhelms the brain's left hemisphere** and its ability to process information logically **(WW81)**. When this happens, individuals may experience panic attacks, phobias, "choking" under pressure, or immobilization, all formally known as hyper-arousal. Because this reaction is subconsciously driven, it can be difficult to control, even with deliberate effort to suppress or avoid it.

As an illustration, Client No.4 suffered a head injury after diving into a river in New Zealand. He immediately felt the blood rolling down his face, triggering fear and immobilization until help arrived, almost drowning in his helplessness. When asked if he was OK, he was informed that he needed to go to the hospital. With assistance, he was helped out of the river onto a rocky ledge, where he sat and recalled shaking uncontrollably—a classic sign of desensitization. At that moment, he became hyper-aware of pressure on his forehead and the top of his head.

He was then walked to a car, taken back to base camp, and eventually airlifted by helicopter to a hospital. During the flight, wearing a neck brace, he focused on keeping his head still, fearing that he might never play rugby again. This thought process led to a negative cognitive shift—from the euphoria of receiving a university offer to perceiving his injury as life-threatening. The belief, "I was so stupid" took hold, reinforcing a sense of self-blame and regret, making him feel as though he had sabotaged his future.

At the hospital, he had to wait three hours for his results, during which he imagined the worst-case scenarios. When the results finally came back, he was relieved to learn that he did not need the neck brace—only painkillers and physiotherapy. However, despite the reassurance, the pain lasted for two days, and since then, his neck has never felt the same. He frequently experiences a knot in his shoulder, which he believes may have contributed to a later shoulder injury. He also struggles with full rotation of his head, suggesting ongoing physical tension.

His Subjective Units of Distress (SUDS) score was 7. He described an image of sitting on an uncomfortable chair, feeling distracted, frustrated, and slightly angry with himself. Reflecting on his recovery process, he recalled rushing through rehabilitation and, with both of his shoulder injuries, returning too early to active play, only to get injured again.

We explored the role of **extrinsic motivation**—doing things to meet the expectations of others. He remembered an experience from ages 9 to 10, when he scored 60 goals in a football season. The following season, the expectation to repeat his success was immense, and he found it increasingly difficult to score. This led to what can be described as sport-related trauma, where he felt, "Nothing would go right. I was frustrated. I had lost my touch. Everyone expected me to repeat it." At that moment, he felt physically unwell, experiencing stomach reflux—an overwhelming sense of frustration that marked the beginning of his pre-game nausea. Now he understands where it all began.

In Chapters 8 and 9 it will be demonstrated how these negative experiences can be fully neutralized, and released, allowing individuals to focus on their performance without the inhibiting and limiting reactions that block high-level achievement. These unresolved experiences often contribute to poor performance in critical moments, such as heavy legs and arms in swimming trials, missteps in gymnastics routines, memory loss during school exams, and even the emotional toll of bullying and abuse.

In the working definitions of "sport trauma" (71), various factors contribute to the experience beyond triggered performance anxiety. Past injuries, low self-esteem, parental pressure, and internal pressure to meet one's own expectations all fall into the category of personal disappointment, embarrassment, and humiliation, which can become traumatic events. This perspective is key to an expanded definition of trauma.

Triggered Memory like the rings in the river fisherman's keep net, each section is a symbolic representation of different stages in our lives and our trauma history. As I sat editing this story on concussion and the way that the impacts historically in the here and now, I suddenly found my head tingling strongly, and then my whole body. At first, I had no idea what this was and became somewhat concerned, I started to feel dizzy, and the feelings in my head strengthened. As I moved away from the desk, I noticed that my eyes were taken to a particular point, and so I held the position and suddenly my legs involuntarily shook, and on the measurement, I use with others, SUDS it was the level of eight. As I closed my eyes I remembered around the age of 12, standing outside my friend's garage, where he'd brought out one of his father's golf clubs, known as a 'wood', as that was its construction, but with a metal edge to it. It's the biggest and strongest club for a golfer. He went to demonstrate the shot and the swing, and I stood behind him thinking I would be clear of the of him. Unknowingly in his preparation for the stroke he swung backwards and hit me on the head.

My wound started to bleed immediately, and within several minutes a large lump had developed, which was frightening. His mother placed a cold compress on my head and I pretended that it didn't hurt, I remember feeling dizzy and nauseous, and for a while unable to move. In previous work on myself with other concussions I thought that I had included this and desensitised it. It was therefore more than a shock when I realised what was happening to me, that I had been triggered by my client's story of diving into the shallow river and banging his head severely.

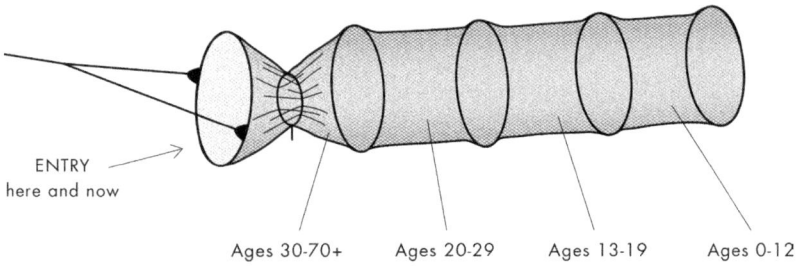

ENTRY
here and now

Ages 30-70+   Ages 20-29   Ages 13-19   Ages 0-12

The ringed sections of the net represent stages of our lives where memories are triggered subconsciously, by something current which is similar such as bullying.

I notice several eye positions and holding them in sequence each time releasing, my legs shook so involuntarily it seemed unreal. I used one of my pointers for Brainspotting, placing it on my head with the metal end on the strongest point of reaction at the back of my head. This is called body-spotting and connects the brain more directly to the point of injury. I started to experience sharp pain, and further reactions in my shoulders, my neck and my left knee. This continued for about 10 minutes, during which I would close my eyes at different times and feel a sense of unease around them. As I opened my eyes initially the vision was fuzzy, and then with several blinks would reveal complete clarity, and surprisingly enhanced sharp vision and focus. This happened several times over a period of 15 minutes.

I began to feel nauseous in my stomach, triggering a different eye position, and with each of these I would experience discomfort around my eyes, and building pressure behind them, the significant symptom of release from concussion. This process took approximately 45 minutes, and 2 1/2 hours later my head still feels lightheaded, tingling, and my arms trembling, all indications of trauma release. In some ways I feel utterly blessed that I can be healed by my own interventions, as indeed can you all if you know the indicators and the techniques. I am equally shocked by the strength of my reactions to this triggered response but recognise retrospectively the depth of the concussion, when my skull would have been softer, and the power of the swing from the golf club would have had maximum momentum. Whilst my friend was deeply apologetic, I had not been prepared for the extent of the swing, and so the shock was significant. I'm recovering, thank you brain!

One aspect of team sports is **deselection** from the starting lineup or being placed on the **substitutes' bench (WW83)**. This experience carries a range of psychological challenges, often difficult for athletes to articulate. Not being the first choice is a common reality in professional sports and performance, but how it is managed makes a crucial difference.

When combined with low self-esteem, a coach's avoidance behaviour, or a lack of reassurance, deselection can become a major emotional setback. I have observed many players with deflated body language warming up separately from the starting team, reinforcing feelings of exclusion. This separation, both physically and mentally, is not only felt by the athletes themselves but is also exposed to the crowd, making it an even more isolating experience. The psychological impact of being sidelined ties directly into Mental Toughness, influencing an athlete's ability to stay motivated, maintain confidence, and cope with setbacks. At Monaco the substitutes were kept separately from the selected starters during the warmup on the pitch in the stadium, whereas for most teams now they are included. Whilst this almost certainly has changed now, the body postures of the players were clear to see, not just to me but the spectators too, often their heads lower, and low energy, it may well have been humiliating for some, but I was not in a position to influence, as that would have been considered 'coaching' and I did not have that authority even though I am a professional qualified football coach.

These sport and life traumas can be resolved through Brainspotting, the focus of Chapters 8 and 9. Building self-esteem is a key element of personal development, essential for increasing and sustaining high performance. When the sporting life traumas described above are resolved, performance feels different, thought processes shift, and actions become more fluid and confident. Athletes often find themselves progressing beyond their previous best performances, free from the psychological barriers that once held them back.

The Art and Science of Communication: Understanding Belief Systems

Limiting self-beliefs are often the fundamental **barrier to high performance**. The challenge I've discovered through years of observation and experience is that these beliefs become difficult to recognize—and even more so to change—without the increasing support of a higher self-value. For this to develop, I consider it necessary to address what I conclude to be a trauma-based historical experience, whether this arises solely within sport or, more commonly, outside of sport and subsequently impacts it. Like a bang on the head from a golf club.

The first element of self-help is reflected in the language we use, which can either block or limit us or, conversely, open up capability and opportunity **(WW84)**. **Realizing the presence of limiting self-beliefs** relies on recognizing that these ingrained perceptions of ourselves and the world around us are no longer relevant. When this happens, people can become very angry upon realizing they have restricted their own potential for success due to an erroneous, untrue belief—untested and inaccurate—sometimes for years, often since childhood.

Changing these **beliefs** requires a different kind of language—one that no longer includes negative or **blocking words (WW85)**. These have been previously described as *don't, won't, should, must, can't, will not, never, always, obviously, of course, impossible, not for me, not a winner, we can't beat them,* and more. Neutralizing these negative words and replacing them with possibilities and opportunities transforms language into terms such as *could, possible, open, determined, accepting, visionary, positive, supportive, inclusive, loving, acknowledged,* and *humble*. Listen to the BBC Radio 4 podcast *The Language of Sport Psychology* recorded in 2012 for more on this topic (61) **(WW86)**.

The Four Agreements: A Practical Guide to Personal Freedom, written by Don Miguel Ruiz (17), seeks to reveal the source of self-limiting beliefs that rob us of joy and create needless suffering **(WW87)**. Based on ancient Toltec wisdom, *The Four Agreements* offer a code of conduct that can help transform our lives into a new experience of freedom, happiness, and **love**.

1. **Be impeccable with your words**. The negative and limiting words mentioned earlier are replaced, ensuring they no longer harm us.
2. **Don't take anything personally**. This can be a challenge, but by choosing our words openly and positively, we not only feel the difference ourselves but also influence

those around us. Recognizing the distinction between a personal attack and performance feedback is essential—something we have already considered in the coach-athlete relationship.

3. **Don't make assumptions**. This manifests in everyday life, particularly in how we consume newspapers, news broadcasts, and media interviews. "Obviously, we all know that, of course we do." No, we don't! Such statements assume that everyone shares the same understanding, yet to verify this, we would need to know what everyone else is thinking. This assumption can place people in situations of potential embarrassment, unconsciously undermine them, and reveal an arrogance that suggests we know best. You may be surprised to realize how often people use these phrases and how many reminders they need before they stop.

4. **Always do your best**. This is not about perfectionism but about maintaining a positive attitude—connecting with our values and embodying them through honesty, integrity, generosity, effort, listening, understanding, and respect. Imagine if our teachers, coaches, parents, and newsreaders adopted these simple guidelines—how different might the world be? See later: Striving for Excellence and not Perfection.

Mental Skills Training

Concentration, attentional focus, negative self-talk, anxiety and arousal management, imagery, goal setting, building positive self-beliefs, and relaxation techniques—these have long been the foundation of sport psychology and are rooted in cognitive behavioural principles. Throughout this text, reference has been made to these fundamental skills, which contribute to consistent, high performance in any sphere of life, art, or sport.

Comfort Zones in Sport Performance by Johnson and Cotterill (72), provides a framework for **supportive change** that allows us to begin the task of explanation **(WW88)**. It helps us conceptualize the various transitions that occur when moving from one state to another. In a sporting context, individuals often limit themselves within comfort zones, restricting both their ability to perform consistently at their optimal level and their capacity to raise the bar of their performance.

There is a paucity of research on the use of words and lexicon to define these transitions and express the concept of comfort zones. The terminology available was so limited that we had to start from the beginning and, indeed, create an entirely new framework of words to describe the process.

This framework provided a basis for researching and recognizing changes in state positions, allowing us to understand dynamically, in action, how these transitions are represented. Through interviews with Jack Russell (England cricketer and artist), Professor Stewart Cotterill, and myself, we reached a consensus that comfort zones are a *state of being*, quickly acknowledging a *plateau* element of performance in which participants experience both positive and negative thoughts.

The framework also highlighted transitions between *zones*, identifying the thinking and behaviours that facilitate movement from a *rigid position* into a **transitional phase**, and ultimately into a *changed and actualized position*, leading to improved performance. While this process can occur over a short period, it can also be seen in the progression from academy player to reserve team and then to the first-team squad. These stepped movements include a **plateau** phase, during which skill, knowledge, and experience are integrated and processed.

The importance of choosing specific supportive language in developing and understanding comfort zones was evident, as there were no established terms to describe the concept, particularly in 2008 **(WW89)**. Words that have helped frame and clarify the concept include *state, awareness, challenge, High Performance Zone, rigid position, transitional phase, changed position, plateau, static, momentum, below-par, feedback, physical, creating arousal, acceptance,* and *can do better.* The introduction of the term *High Performance Zone* was particularly significant, as it immediately broadened the understanding of the concept for others, contrasting with the notion of *comfort*, where everything stays the same *'ceteris paribus'* in Latin.

The essence of this research led us to identify the crucial elements of comfort zones in how we organise and understand ourselves within High Performance Zones. The key insight is that individuals need support during the transition state to sustain success throughout the process. This serves as an important marker for parents, coaches, and teachers and lies at the heart of effective coaching and teaching.

Mental Health and Wellbeing: Clinical Issues and Mental Disorder

While it is not possible to explore this topic in detail here, it is increasingly important for parents, coaches, and athletes to recognize the major presentations and symptoms of common **mental health disorders**. As a clinical psychologist, clinical social worker, and lecturer in Mental Health Law and Practice, I have 15 years of experience working in hospital-based psychiatric units and developing the first of four Community Mental Health Teams in England.

There is also a challenge for practising sport psychologists in the UK, who traditionally receive limited training in these areas of mental health—though this is evolving. High-profile figures have helped bring public awareness to mental health issues, including Princes William and Harry, Premier League footballer Aaron

Lennon, and many others, highlighting the depth of distress such experiences can cause.

Few cases have been as widely televised as Emma Raducanu's burnout and performance anxiety during Wimbledon 2021. After winning the US Open, she prioritized her wellbeing, taking time to rest and recover. Similarly, Simone Biles made headlines after withdrawing from the women's gymnastics team final at the Tokyo Olympics due to mental health concerns, following a vault routine that earned her lowest-ever Olympic score. She returned in 2024 and struck gold!

Depression is classified as a **mood disorder** and is defined by a loss of pleasure or interest in aspects of life that would typically bring joy, satisfaction, and even a sense of self-preservation. It affects a range of behaviours:

Do you recognise these features in athletes you know?

- **Appetite:** Loss of weight and nutrition
- **Sleep:** Initial insomnia and/or early morning waking
- **Energy:** Fatigue and low energy, often accompanied by poor concentration
- **Motivation:** Loss of interest in things and people around them
- **Emotion:** Negative feelings of guilt and worthlessness, leading to low self-esteem, as well as a sense of blame or shame for something they may or may not have done
- **Feelings of hopelessness:** These can lead to suicidal thoughts (ideation) and, in some cases, suicide itself.
- **Cognitive difficulties:** Challenges with thinking, concentration, and decision-making (73)

Depression is a chronic, relapsing condition, characterized predominantly by persistent feelings of sadness and/or a loss of enjoyment in previously pleasurable activities. These feelings differ from transitory mood changes related to everyday stresses, depending on the extent to which they interfere with daily functioning. What distinguishes a depressive mood from clinical depression is the duration—typically lasting weeks or months— and the impact of low mood on an individual's ability to carry out normal activities.

Suicide is often driven by despair or linked to underlying mental illness, including depression, bipolar disorder, schizophrenia, alcoholism, and drug abuse (74). Increasingly, public humiliation through social media has also been a factor in young teenagers taking their own lives. The Beck Depression Inventory, *Public Health Q9* (PHQ-9), and *Generalized Anxiety Disorder* (GAD-7) are available on the web for self-assessment.

Addiction, Dependency, and Substance Misuse: The Cycle of Dis-Ease and Self-Soothing Behaviours

Carl Gustav Jung wrote, "Every form of addiction is bad, no matter whether the narcotic be alcohol or morphine or idealism" (75). In the **sporting context**, the 'win-at-all-costs' attitude that pervades modern sport culture has, in many cases, overshadowed the values and benefits of sport. Athletes across various sports and competition levels use and abuse drugs. Anabolic steroids, amphetamines, and caffeine are commonly taken to enhance muscle development and recovery, while depressants and stimulants— including alcohol, cocaine, marijuana, and tobacco—are used to temporarily relieve stress and induce feelings of euphoria (76).

Addiction can be defined as "a process whereby a behaviour, that can function both to produce pleasure and to provide escape from internal discomfort, is employed in a pattern characterised by failure to control the behaviour, powerlessness, and continuation of the behaviour despite significant negative consequences" (77, p. 1404).

For young athletes and those in the performing arts, addiction is more commonly linked to exercise addiction, gaming, and excessive internet use, while exposure to cannabis remains a growing modern-day concern (**WW89**). I would advise parents that **social withdrawal** is one of the key indicators connecting various mental health issues. This is often accompanied by secrecy, avoidance, disturbed eating and sleeping patterns, poor communication, and uncharacteristic outbursts of anger.

As part of **the psychological revolution**, there is a **redefinition of 'addictive behaviours',** and a reconsideration of its classification as a 'disease' within the medical model framework **(WW90)**. In my experience, and in the shared experiences of many colleagues in the Brainspotting community, what we observe and encounter in addictive and repetitive behaviours is their **'self-soothing nature'**—what can be understood as **'Dis-Ease.'**

Through Brainspotting, I and others have repeatedly demonstrated in practice that these self-soothing behaviours often originate from depression and early dysfunctional attachment to primary caregivers. The avoidance of people, places, situations, and events—along with the numbing of unwanted emotional and physical feelings, hyper-arousal, and intrusive thoughts—are all rooted in trauma.

When self-soothing or addictive behaviours stop or are significantly reduced, there is, without exception in my experience, an underlying trauma behind the depression. When these traumas are identified and desensitised, the dis-ease—the lack of ease in life and the associated stress—can be alleviated. As a result, the need for self-soothing behaviours diminishes.

One crucial element, with few exceptions, is a history of limited affective attachment to parents. This is especially evident in cases where a parent struggles with substance abuse, gambling, or other addictions themselves. In such circumstances, individuals who develop addictive behaviours often do so as a means of self-soothing seeking the safety, security, and love that were missing in early attachment experiences.

Disordered Eating and Body Image: Understanding Eating Disorders and Body Dysmorphic Disorder

Eating disorders are described as illnesses characterized by irregular eating habits and severe distress or concern about body weight or shape. According to the *Diagnostic and Statistical Manual of Mental Disorders (DSM-5)* (78), eating disturbances may include inadequate or excessive food intake, ultimately damaging an individual's wellbeing. The most common forms of eating disorders include Anorexia Nervosa, Bulimia Nervosa, and Binge Eating Disorder, affecting both females and males. Sports such as gymnastics, swimming, dance, and equestrianism tend to have higher prevalence rates of eating disorders.

Body dysmorphia is often an element of eating disorders but can also be a distinct condition. According to the *DSM-5*, **Body Dysmorphic Disorder (BDD)** is a mental health condition characterized by an obsessive preoccupation with perceived flaws in body shape or appearance. England's National Health Services reports that BDD is most common among teenagers and young adults, affecting both men and women. No part of the body is exempt from concern, and BDD often coexists with other mental health conditions.

Abuse in Sport: Recognizing and Addressing Harmful Practices

I am indebted to Dr. Misia Gervis at the University of Brunel, with whom I worked alongside during her tenure as the sport psychologist for the England Women's Football Team and the GB Olympic Team in 2012, for her contributions to the following work on abuse in sport.

Physical abuse includes hitting, burning, and biting; giving children alcohol or drugs, including performance-enhancing substances; attempted suffocation or drowning; and enforcing excessive or inappropriate training regimes. Examples include denying a child water during training or imposing training regimens that exceed the child's developmental capacity. Additionally, the use of physical punishment to maintain power and control is a form of abuse (79).

Sexual abuse occurs when an adult exploits a child to fulfil their own sexual needs. This can include a range of acts, such as engaging in any sexual act, indecent exposure of an adult to a child, any physical contact with a child's genitals, making a child watch pornography, or using a child to create pornography (80).

Emotional abuse occurs when a child is threatened, humiliated, or taunted. This can also include persistent disregard for a child's effort or progress and a lack of concern for their emotional wellbeing. The adult's behaviour is repeated and frequent, defining the nature of the relationship. Key behaviours exhibited by adults that constitute emotional abuse include ignoring, isolating, shouting, belittling, threatening, humiliating, and rejecting (82).

Finally, within the sporting context, there is one more type of abuse that is not commonly reported in the general child maltreatment literature. This is a relatively new area of research in sport abuse and is important to consider here.

Forced physical exertion occurs when physical training no longer serves a legitimate purpose in enhancing sport performance. There is a fine line between intensive training that enables children to reach their potential and training that becomes abusive and exploitative. Grange and Kerr (79) identified key factors that help distinguish between the two. When assessing a coach's behaviour in relation to the physical demands placed on young athletes, **the following questions should be considered (WW91)**:

1. Is there potential harm?
2. Is there any actual or perceived athletic benefit?
3. Is there an absence of consent?
4. Is it being used as a form of punishment?

This framework serves as a valuable tool for evaluating training sessions. If any of the above behaviours are observed, they may indicate child abuse. For an example of this, see the first story included in Chapter 9.

Anxiety and Obsessive-Compulsive Disorder (OCD): Understanding and Managing Performance-Related Anxiety

Anxiety is defined as an emotion characterized by apprehension and somatic symptoms of tension in which an individual anticipates impending danger, catastrophe, or misfortune. The body often mobilizes itself to meet the perceived threat: Muscles become tense, breathing is faster, and the heart beats more rapidly. Anxiety may be distinguished from fear both conceptually and physiologically, although the two terms are often used interchangeably. Anxiety is considered a future-oriented, long-acting response broadly focused on a diffuse threat, whereas fear is an appropriate, present-oriented, and short-lived response to a clearly identifiable and specific threat.

OCD is an anxiety disorder characterized by obsessions—recurrent and persistent thoughts, images, or impulses—and compulsions, which are repetitive behaviours such as handwashing, checking, ordering, or other ritualistic actions (81). For individuals with Obsessive Compulsive Disorder OCD these obsessions are distressing, intrusive, and inappropriate, while the compulsions are intentional behaviours or mental acts applied rigidly as a response to the obsessions. The American Psychological Association defined this as a disorder characterized by recurrent intrusive thoughts, obsessions, that prompt the performance of neutralizing rituals, compulsions. Typical obsessions involve themes of contamination, dirt, or illness (fearing that one will contract or transmit a disease) and doubts about the performance of certain actions (for example, an excessive preoccupation that one has neglected to turn off a home appliance). Common compulsive behaviours include repetitive cleaning or washing, checking, ordering, repeating, and hoarding. The obsessions and compulsions—which are recognized by affected individuals (though not necessarily by children) as excessive or unreasonable—are time consuming (more than 1 hour per day), cause significant distress, and interfere with functioning. Although OCD has traditionally been considered an anxiety disorder, it is increasingly thought to be in a separate diagnostic category; *DSM–5* and *DSM-5-TR* classify it under the category **obsessive-compulsive and related disorders**, along with body dysmorphic disorder, hoarding, trichotillomania, and excoriation (skin-picking) disorder, among others (APA, 2023).

It is estimated that OCD affects approximately 2.5% of the population (81). Clark and Beck note that "an even larger number of non-clinical individuals experience milder and less frequent obsessional phenomena that would not meet diagnostic criteria" (83, p. 451).

I am grateful to Dave Alcock, Sport Psychologist at the University of the West of England (UWE), for his contributions in explaining OCD. Research has explored the connection between feelings of guilt and OCD, suggesting that an intense **fear** of experiencing guilt may be an underlying component of the disorder. Studies indicate that 'guilt sensitivity,' as measured by the guilt sensitivity test, is highly correlated with compulsive checking behaviours, such as repeatedly returning to verify that a door is locked.

When there is a historical loss of control associated with guilt—particularly when an individual feels unable to resolve something from the past—OCD appears to create a sense of consciously and subconsciously 'control.' In my experience, perfectionism also stems from a traumatic event linked to personal disappointment, embarrassment, or humiliation, where a deep sense of powerlessness is felt. Like OCD, perfectionism seeks to provide control, yet it has distinct disadvantages:

1. Perfection is transient in nature, if it can be achieved at all **(WW92)**.
2. We set ourselves up to fail.
3. We are highly self-critical when we fall short.
4. There is no lasting satisfaction, even when external validation is received.

By accepting and letting go of perfectionism, we allow errors and mistakes to become a crucial part of development and skill acquisition.

More recently, I have identified additional mechanisms that clients use to support both their perfectionism and their struggle with loss of control. One common concept is the 'light at the end of the tunnel'—often used as a metaphor for hope or motivation. However, this can also manifest as a form of 'tunnel vision,' shutting out unwanted thoughts or feelings while focusing on an end goal that is, in essence, unachievable. This is where the shift toward **'striving for excellence'** provides a realistic alternative. Unlike perfectionism, striving for excellence allows for both **quantitative and qualitative measurement**, making it a more sustainable and achievable mindset.

Imposter Syndrome

Imposter syndrome is the experience of feeling like a fraud—believing one is not truly competent or capable of meeting expectations. Individuals with imposter syndrome often compare themselves negatively to others, assuming that others are more skilled or deserving. This creates a psychological state in which they feel as though they are impersonating someone more capable or that they themselves are an imposter.

To reframe this perspective, I explore two key elements: 'fear of failure' and 'fear of success.' The imposter element stems from not feeling good enough or from occupying a position that exceeds one's own expectations—such as unexpectedly winning a race or a tennis match against a world champion despite being ranked significantly lower.

In my experience, when athletes approach the finish line, subconscious messages of past failures or near-misses are often triggered and brought into conscious awareness, reinforcing a limiting self-belief: *"I can't do this. I won't win."* (Note the subconscious *won't*). At its core, imposter syndrome is linked to low self-value, which fuels limiting beliefs about oneself and others.

CHAPTER 7: PSYCHOLOGICAL APPROACHES AND INTERVENTIONS

Winning Ways for Parents, Athletes, and Coaches

Career Transitions / Stages of Change / Self-Mastery

Coaching Styles / Communication Skills / Personal Boundary Development

The Hula Hoop / Brainspotting and Releasing Life Trauma

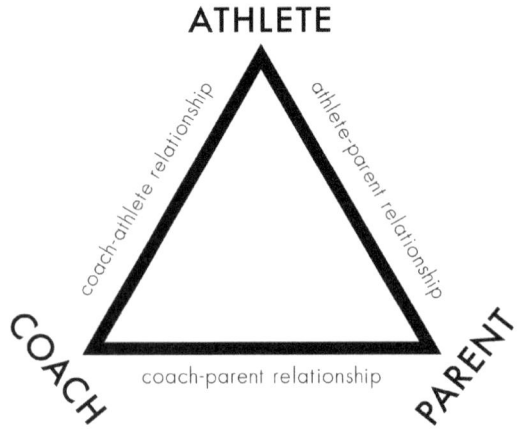

The 'Athlete-Parent'

The essence of this book is to provide knowledge, information, and resources to help parents support their talented children—regardless of age—while maximizing their performance in both life and their chosen performance 'arena,' both literally and metaphorically. In doing so, it is important to remember that the **family functions as a system,** where one action can influence the behaviours of other family members. At times, this influence may need to be more direct, involving control and the imposition of boundaries within the contexts of home, education, performance, and training.

In psychology, **'context is everything'**—the environment in which behaviours occur plays a crucial role in shaping them. This includes the setting, the people involved, and the specific event taking place. So, what can parents do to improve their own performance, positively influence athletic or performance outcomes, and integrate their responsibilities for education—all while occasionally taking time off to relax and have fun?

Supporting 'In-Career and 'End-Career' Transitions

Paul Wylleman is an expert in understanding the transitional challenges athletes face during the **initiation, developmental, and mastery stages** of their athletic careers. Providing support to athletes during these transitions is a key role for both parents and coaches—but recognizing when a transition is happening is the first step!

Consider how, in junior school, children move up a year together as a class, maintaining familiarity, friendships, competition, and progress, even though their teacher may change. In contrast, transitioning to secondary school is far more disruptive, involving changes in environment, rules, teachers, subjects, and classmates. While this transition is widely recognized, even the smaller shift from year 5 to year 6 can present challenges.

Teachers have both a responsibility and a moral duty to be empathetic to children's needs and to help manage these transitions. Similarly, recognizing the shift from 'tumble tots' to 'beam' or trampoline requires a supporting 'hand' and an understanding of the concept of moving from 'novice to expert.' So, what can be done?

Planning for Success: Failing to plan, is planning to fail (WW93)

More information is needed about what changes in the next phase— what the outcome goals are and what can realistically be achieved. Meeting new coaches and teachers, familiarizing oneself with the stadium, theatre, or gym, adapting to new routines, managing time effectively, and acclimatising to the environment are all part of the process. Simply getting used to something new is an important step.

Transitions involve moving from one level or state to another, pushing us out of our **comfort zones**—and this applies to parents as well. Connecting with others who have already navigated this stage can be a valuable resource, so don't hesitate to ask. Scheduling a one-to-one meeting with the coach to clarify key details— such as training schedules, kit requirements, travel logistics, role expectations, nutrition plans, progression pathways, and even introductions to other parents—can help ease the transition.

This is also a crucial time for observation—identifying what works and what doesn't. In unfamiliar settings, we notice things that feel 'out of place,' are difficult to understand, or require clarification. Based on my observations, it typically takes six to eight weeks to fully integrate into a new 'system,' after which our objective perspective on its limitations or opportunities for growth may diminish. This is the critical window for noting concerns and acting. It's the perfect time to ask, "Have you always done it like this? And if so, why?" Often, the response will reveal that no alternative has ever been considered!

The Stages of Change: Navigating Growth and Transition

Stambulova (84) identified these stages from an athlete's perspective.

1. Specialisation
2. Development of intensive training
3. Seeking high achievement
4. Transitioning from junior to senior/adult levels of performance
5. Mastery and becoming professional
6. Retirement or stopping

Challenges such as losing a coach, de-selection, moving from regional to national competition alone, or sustaining a season-ending injury introduce new and often unexpected difficulties. These stages are also influenced by age, biological changes (such as body development), as well as social and emotional factors.

From the earlier chapters, it is evident how the lost adolescence impacts young athletes. Many enter an almost obsessive phase of development in pursuit of achievement, requiring ongoing parental support and commitment. Additionally, there is often a **loss of 'self'** as their personal identity becomes closely tied to a social identity— whether as a footballer, gymnast, or violinist. This performance-based identity creates variable outcomes, further shaping their experience.

Effective Communication for Growth and Development

The role of clear, clean, understandable, age-appropriate communication is central to a young person's development and their ability to translate guidance into meaningful action. Unfortunately, across all sports, my own observations—and those of colleagues—highlight the widespread dominance of command-style coaching, often marked by a limited ability to explain what coaches seek to convey. This is not to say that coaches lack good intent or personal connection with their athletes, but rather that their feedback and guidance are often unclear—or, in some cases, absent altogether.

In command-style coaching, repeated failures among athletes and performers often stem not from a lack of ability or capability, but from a lack of understanding. Coaches may not always recognize how to guide an athlete toward a higher threshold of performance. Many coaches might strongly reject this critique, but the reality is that these communication gaps exist at every level of the coaching hierarchy. Some coaches, particularly when challenged by parents, react defensively seeing the feedback as personal criticism rather than an objective assessment of performance. Much like parenting, coaching is often shaped by personal experience; many coaches replicate the methods they were taught, for better or worse.

The most successful coaches are great communicators. They foster healthy human connections, listen attentively, empathize, and engage in cooperative, shared experiences with their athletes. When combined with parental pressure to perform, poor communication can lead to loss of motivation, burnout, disengagement, heightened performance anxiety, and ultimately, dysfunctional performance.

What can be done? During times of transition, both parents and talented children may lose perspective, feeling lost, confused, or uncertain about what to do and when to do it.

Intrinsic Motivation and the Key to Success: I'M SMART (WW94)

Setting goals using the I'M SMART model provides a structured approach to achieving success. This model allows the big picture to emerge, offering a foundation for training programmes, time management, and realistic expectations. Each element plays a crucial role in goal setting.

I'M SMART Model:
- **I** – Intrinsically **M** – Motivated
- **S** – Specific **M** – Measurable **A** – Achievable **R** – Realistic **T** – over Time

While the SMART goal-setting model has been widely used for years, in 2009, I introduced I'M to emphasize the importance of intrinsic motivation. Deci and Ryan, in their book on *Self-Determination Theory* (21), highlighted that goal achievement often falters when motivation is primarily 'extrinsic'—driven by external influences such as coaches or parents. Crucially, success is far more likely when goals are Intrinsically Motivated (I'M)—when individuals pursue them because they genuinely want to, rather than because others expect them to.

This is not considered 'selfish'—wanting something for yourself is, in fact, an essential ingredient for success. It is crucial for both parents and their children to understand this dynamic and to find a balance between parental expectations and the child's own aspirations.

Another key factor in failing to achieve goals is an unrealistic time frame. A simple adjustment can make a significant difference—add 25% to 50% more time than initially planned.

My research indicates that a critical period for change occurs between the ages of 14–16, coinciding with Piaget's fourth and final stage of brain development, where conceptual and abstract thinking emerge **(WW95)**. Around this time, young athletes begin making decisions about their future in sport and performance, particularly regarding the pursuit of a professional career. There is a natural shift in motivation—from a **50:50** balance of extrinsic and intrinsic motivation toward **75:25** in favor of intrinsic motivation. Like slices of a cake, this transition is a positive and natural development, though in some cases, it may be delayed.

Developing Media Skills

If you become a high performer, whether you actively seek attention, the press and media will take an interest—you become a story. Gaining experience and training in handling media interactions, including journalists, radio, and television, can help reduce stress, increase confidence, and provide a greater sense of control. A successful career will inevitably involve media connections, whether through interviews or, increasingly, social media. For valuable insights on this topic, see Chris Green's book *Every Boy's Dream* (5).

The Role of Sport Psychologists and Clinical Psychologists

Supporting athletes, performers, and parents with the guidance of professional sport and clinical psychologists allows for meaningful dialogue that ensures communication is clear, understandable, and supportive. This, in turn, helps individuals manage pressure more effectively, anticipate and resolve potential challenges, and approach their development with acceptance and confidence.

Over the past 15 years, UK Sport has incorporated Performance Lifestyle Coaches (PLC) to help elite athletes maintain a balance between personal and professional development, ensuring they stay on track both in and beyond their sporting careers.

Parental Powerlessness and Resolution (WW96)

My role in supporting parents developed from recognising their sense of powerlessness, particularly in navigating delicate communications with their children's coaches and teachers. When working with young athletes through their traumatic experiences, I often found that parents, too, became traumatised and required intervention. This inability to effectively intervene—especially when their talented sons or daughters are subjected to emotional abuse by coaches or others—becomes a primary source of parental powerlessness. **Immobilised by fear**, anger, frustration, or shame, parents witness their children experiencing performance anxiety, sleep disturbances, disordered eating, low self-value, limiting self-beliefs, and, in more severe cases, depression.

In such situations, a sport psychologist familiar with the context, language, and culture of sport or performance environments can help devise strategies for change and support parents in developing assertiveness. Essentially, the family unit itself can become immobilised by trauma. However, not all sport psychologists are trained in mental health assessment, family dynamics, or therapeutic interventions. In some cases, parents may need to seek additional support from specialist counsellors, therapists, general practitioners, or psychiatrists (medical doctors specialising in mental health).

There is a distinct role for clinical psychologists in these cases. While Clinical Sport Psychologists—like myself—are formally recognised in the USA, their integration into support systems elsewhere is still evolving so that clinical psychologists may well benefit from having knowledge of the sporting environment.

Self-Management: The Locus of Control

You may have heard the phrase **'controlling the controllables,'** a concept central to sport psychology. *Locus* refers to the 'point or location of something,' and as individuals, we can control our thoughts, ideas, and actions—making us the centre of our own world, our **Locus of Control**. Beyond that, our influence may be limited, and in some situations, we must accept that we have no impact at all.

Worrying about losing control of the ball hours before a match serves no meaningful purpose—it only distracts from healthy focus, undermines self-belief, and drains vital energy. Similarly, feeling demotivated by the size of an opponent's goalkeeper—something entirely beyond one's control—illustrates the importance of distinguishing what lies within our Locus of Control from what does not. The key is to recognise what we *can* control while acknowledging what we *cannot*, and in between, we find opportunities for *influence*.

In refereeing terms, once a referee has made a decision—at least before the introduction of VAR—it was highly unlikely to be overturned. However, appeals made before the decision was final could influence the outcome, demonstrating how behaviour and decision-making can sometimes be shaped within this space of influence.

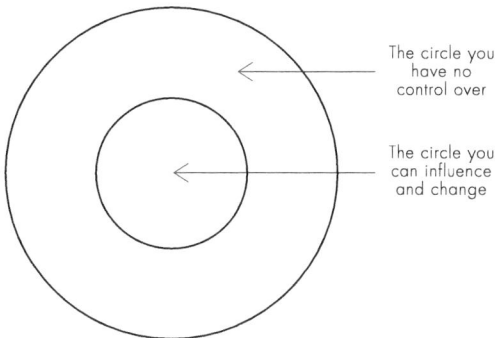

The circle you have no control over

The circle you can influence and change

The Circle of Influence

At the centre of two outer circles lies our *inner circle*—those closest to us. These are the people whose advice we listen to and may act upon. In sport and performance, this typically includes a coach, teacher, physical therapist, parents, and friends.

However, if any of these influential figures are negative or even abusive, it may become necessary to act—whether by reducing their influence, setting boundaries, or removing them altogether. Equally, we must recognise that influence is a two-way process; just as others affect us, we, in turn, impact those within our own circle.

culture and society

industry and government

community

school and peers

family and home

CHILD OR ADOLESCENT

As individuals and as parents, we must make conscious choices about *who* belongs in our circle of influence. Are those closest to us offering positive support or creating negativity? If the latter—STOP. Below are societal influences often framed by 'culture'.

Managing Different Environments

Personal Space

Most parents strive to provide the best they can for their children, and as young people grow, one crucial element is 'personal space'—a safe place where they can feel calm, relaxed, and in control. However, finding the right balance is essential, as too much solitude can lead to social isolation and withdrawal. Family mealtimes have traditionally served as a valuable opportunity to bring everyone together, check in on how things are going, and maintain connection—though they should never become a setting for conflict.

'Personal space' is also an integral part of our sense of **'personal boundary.'** I developed the concept of the 'Hula Hoop' as a symbolic representation of this boundary. Imagine the hoop encircling you—it defines your personal space and represents the idea that no one should enter it without invitation. The 'stop' hand signal, commonly used by police officers to halt traffic, can serve as a clear message to others when we need to maintain our space. Conversely, an open palm gesture toward the sky or ceiling symbolises an invitation to 'come in.' These signals play a fundamental role in safety and trust—'this is my space.'

The **'Hula Hoop'** concept has since evolved **(WW97)**. To introduce it practically, visit a local shop and choose an adult-sized Hula Hoop in any colour or style. Place it over your head and slowly lower it to just above your hips. At this point, the Hula Hoop becomes 'magical'—hovering invisibly to create a **permanent personal boundary**, one that exists as an abstract yet powerful idea. Since its inception in 2023, I've recently added another dimension, by introducing a 'shield' which is attachable to the hula hoop. The shield is traditionally concave, so that it can deflect oncoming aggression.

The use of the shield provides additional protection when others are aggressive towards us, projecting blame onto us, moving closer into our space. It also deflects energy, aggressions, strong negative emotions, but equally able to form the strength of barrier that causes it to bounce back to other person, so that they can take responsibility for their own experience and self-responsibility. You can simply hold the shield with your imagination, or have it attached to your hula hoop. The shield can also have 'microdots' which allow good energies or emotions to be filtered through.

This practice can also facilitate 'inner child healing.' A younger version of yourself, perhaps a child who experienced early trauma, can be represented by selecting a 'Hula Hoop' that resonates with them. Further, in a guided visualisation process, an even younger self—perhaps aged six or seven—can be ceremonially 'gifted' a smaller, age-specific hoop, placed around them as they are watched over by their older selves. Whether you are six or sixty, this simple yet profound ritual can be deeply healing and empowering.

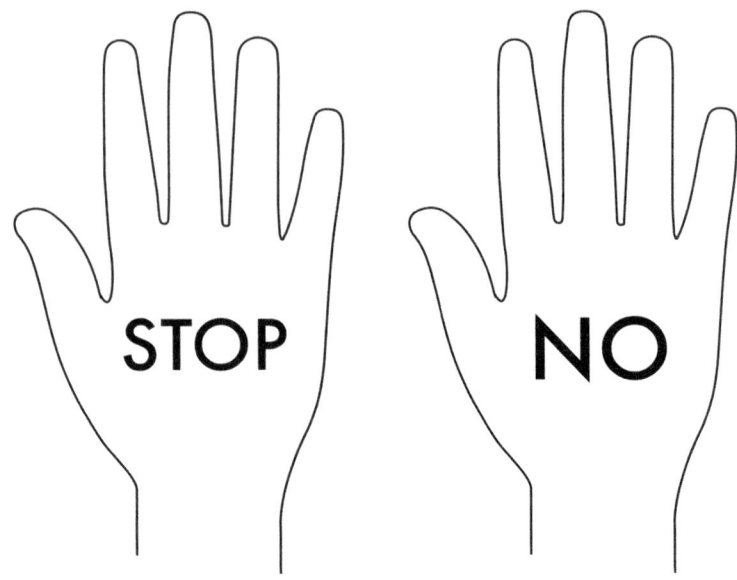

Professional and Competition Environments

Stadia, training centres, and camps can influence reactions and responses, so careful planning is essential. Arriving in good time, ensuring proper nutrition and hydration, and being prepared with the programme are all crucial—though plans can often change unexpectedly.

It is important to be aware of the 'atmosphere' and maintain 'attentional focus,' which, by definition, requires minimising distractions. Finding a quiet space, listening to music, or spending time with a trusted coach or teammate can help with preparation and create a sense of readiness.

At these moments, the way parents provide support and intervene can be key in maintaining an athlete's state of readiness. **Managing expectations** and effectively 'coping' with parents—particularly when they become intrusive or overly anxious—can make a significant difference in an athlete's ability to focus and perform.

The Pressure to Perform

One of the greatest challenges for athletes, performers, and coaches is the often-**unintended pressure from parents** for their children to perform well. Many well-documented cases highlight successful parent-coach relationships in sport. Tennis legends such as the Williams sisters and Andy Murray; motor racing stars like Lewis Hamilton, Damon Hill, and Max Verstappen, and footballers such as Peter Schmeichel and Jamie Redknapp all exemplify this dynamic. However, not all stories are positive—Andre Agassi's account of the cruelty he experienced from his father as a young tennis player was deeply troubling, contributing to his later struggles with depression. His autobiography, *Open*, is one of the most insightful and entertaining sports memoirs I have ever read (50).

The change for Agassi came when his brother introduced him to tennis coach Brad Gilbert who in a matter of hours transformed his mentality, challenging the limited self-beliefs that had been holding back his performance. Gilbert identified several critical issues: Andre believed his opponents could predict his serves, causing him to change direction at the last second and resulting in more faults. Secondly, Andre put himself under immense pressure by attempting to make every shot a winner. Thirdly, he prioritized making his strokes look aesthetically pleasing rather than focusing on effectiveness. Finally, Andre had a tendency to hit the ball directly toward his opponent, making returns easier for them.

Gilbert's coaching approach was transformative. He convinced Andre that opponents couldn't actually anticipate his serves and encouraged him to commit to his initial serving decisions, which dramatically improved his focus, accuracy, and success rate. Gilbert also persuaded Andre to stop forcing winner shots and instead extend rallies by playing the ball away from his opponent, putting pressure on them to make mistakes. Though Andre initially struggled with the concept of forcing opponent errors rather than executing perfect passing shots, this strategy proved highly effective. Gilbert also shifted Andre's focus from making shots look good to making them effective, emphasizing that winning mattered more than aesthetic beauty. These fundamental changes in approach—improving his serve, reducing perfectionism, strategically pressuring opponents, and embracing "ugly" winning points—led Andre to an unprecedented streak of victories including four Grand Slam titles. This positive coaching methodology directly countered the negativity that had been instilled in Andre by his father (2009, p188-9).

Within the pressure to perform, there are often multiple perspectives. Overzealous parents, heated arguments on the tennis court, emotional outbursts on the golf course, or tears in the gymnastics arena all illustrate the tension that can arise. Some parents, particularly those with real or perceived expertise, can be highly critical of their child's performance. At such times, young athletes may feel deflated, upset, or even humiliated. The public expression of disappointment and frustration by a parent at competitions can be traumatic, demoralising, and anxiety-provoking. In these moments, the 'coach' in the parent takes over, rather than the unconditional love of a parent.

It is often suggested that some parents attempt to relive their own unfulfilled ambitions through their child's success. In other cases, they may have been pressured by their own parents and, without realising it, pass this behaviour on to the next generation.

For young athletes and performers, the drive for high performance can sometimes stem from a belief that they must *repay* their parents for the time, effort, and financial support invested in their journey **(WW98)**. At nine or thirteen years old, a young person may not yet fully grasp the concept of **unconditional love**—that their parents ultimately want them to be happy and enjoy what they do. In many cases, sport psychology interventions help to bridge this communication gap, offering a much-needed opportunity to mediate and align these contrasting, often misunderstood, expectations.

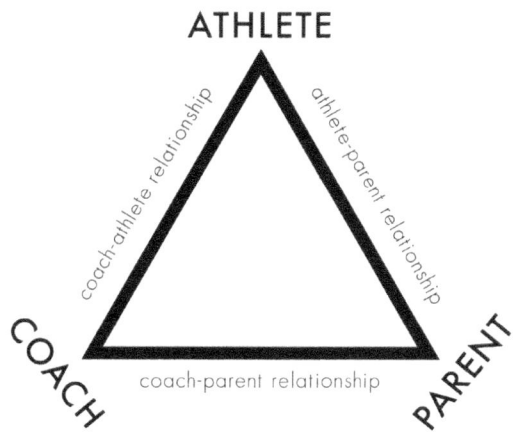

Balancing Education and Elite Sport: Managing Competing Demands

There can often be a struggle for time and effort between education and elite sport. Teachers expect full commitment to academic learning, while sport coaches or music teachers demand the same level of dedication to training and practice. Parents must remain observant to ensure their children have sufficient **rest, recovery, and relaxation** while balancing the demands of both academic and athletic pursuits.

I previously discussed burnout, which is 95% psychological, highlighting the importance of managing these competing pressures effectively.

Coping with Loneliness

Loneliness is the emotional and mental discomfort experienced when alone or feeling isolated. Various psychological disciplines interpret this differently: social psychology frames it as emotional distress from unmet intimacy needs; cognitive psychology views it as discomfort arising from the gap between desired and actual relationships. Meanwhile, existential and humanistic psychologists consider loneliness "an inevitable, painful aspect of the human condition" that may ultimately foster "increased self-awareness and renewal" (APA 2018). While I have alluded to this earlier in the book, the nature of traumatic events—whether stemming from disappointment, embarrassment, or humiliation—often leads to emotional disconnection and, in turn, a strong tendency toward social isolation and loneliness.

Parents need to remain vigilant, as their child may become secretive, fearing the perceived consequences of admitting to something they feel ashamed about. It is important to approach them gently, seeking to understand—without judgment—what may be troubling them and to reassure them that help is available, including professional support if needed.

However, being alone does not always equate to loneliness, which is inherently a negative state. Solitude, in contrast, provides an opportunity to be free from external influences, including noise, allowing us to process experiences, reflect on significant relationships, and gain clarity on the direction of our lives. When the mind is 'quietened' rather than overwhelmed, we can cultivate deeper self-awareness. Practices such as yoga and mindfulness facilitate this process, encouraging moments of meaningful solitude.

Alain de Botton and *The School of Life* (54, p. 74) suggest that many people feel ashamed of experiencing loneliness, yet "a high degree of loneliness is an inexorable (impossible to stop) part of being a sensitive, intelligent human—a built-in feature of a complex existence." In essence, part of **loneliness stems from feeling misunderstood**, which is why therapy can be so beneficial.

In Chapter 8, solutions to these challenges are explored through a combination of approaches, including Eye Movement Desensitisation and Reprocessing (EMDR), Somatic Experiencing, and Brainspotting: The Psychological Revolution!

CHAPTER 8:
A PSYCHOLOGICAL
REVOLUTION

Brainspotting in Action: Four Phases of Transformation

Phase 1: Desensitising Trauma History

Phase 2: Physical Emotional Reconnections and Resolutions

Phase 3: Resolving Intergenerational Trauma

Phase 4: Achieving Higher Performance and Winning Ways

A New Era in Psychology: The Rise of Brainspotting and Healing Trauma

It has been a long wait for a **psychological revolution**—albeit an evolutionary one! In my view, the development of Brainspotting quite literally turns psychology on its head, particularly in the realm of trauma. Unlike traditional approaches that focus on the neocortex, where cognition, thinking, and most psychological problem-solving processes occur, Brainspotting is directed at the lower and midbrain regions. These subcortical areas play a crucial role in processing trauma, making this approach fundamentally different from conventional methods.

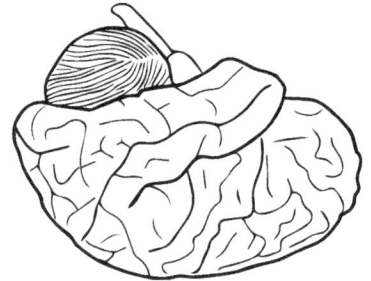 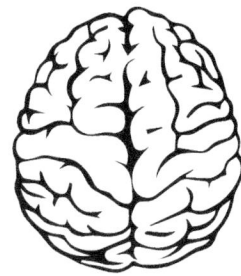

In 2011, while writing a chapter on trauma in sport, I discovered that there were limited examples within the field of sport psychology in the UK. It was then that I came across Dr Alan Goldberg, a sport psychologist based in Amherst, Massachusetts, USA, who was engaged in similar work to me. He generously introduced me to three key trauma-focused approaches he was using—Eye Movement Desensitisation and Reprocessing (EMDR), Brainspotting, and Somatic Experiencing—specifically within the context of sport and performance.

He first described **EMDR**—a technique designed to release trauma by using rapid eye movements, similar to those that occur during Rapid Eye Movement (REM) sleep. This process enables the body's sympathetic nervous system (SNS) to physiologically discharge stored trauma to the Parasympathetic Nervous System to be deactivated, while the individual recalls a past negative event, with attending eye position.

The originator of this approach, American psychologist Francine Shapiro (91) conducted extensive scientific research into how trauma is encoded in the brain, its impact on individuals, and, crucially, how it can be resolved. She demonstrated that guiding the eyes from one side to the other repetitively—REM—can facilitate trauma processing and integration.

When a person experiences a sudden shock or fright, such as a car accident, the impact is stored within the sympathetic nervous system (SNS), which is responsible for mobilising energy and responding to stress. Under normal circumstances, this activation is counterbalanced by the parasympathetic nervous system (PSNS), which deactivates, releases stress responses and promotes relaxation. However, in a traumatic event, the shock remains trapped in a **'freeze'** state within the SNS, unable to be discharged through the PSNS. This 'freeze' response disrupts the brain's normal processing, preventing the right and left hemispheres from effectively communicating about the specific memory, leaving it unresolved.

In a state of stress, the brain releases cortisol, adrenaline, and other hormones, triggering a *fight* (anger) or *flight* (fear) response to perceived 'danger,' worry, or distress. The intensity of these physical and emotional reactions—primarily governed by the right hemisphere of the brain—can overwhelm the left hemisphere, which is primarily responsible for logical processing and making sense of experiences. When this overload occurs, it can result in a sense of being **overwhelmed**, leading to states such as **'choking,' panic, phobias,** breathlessness, sweating, and ultimately immobilisation, known as the 'freeze' state.

Live MRI scans of individuals recalling intense negative experiences, such as a fear of snakes or spiders, reveal that the amygdala—the subconscious part of the brain responsible for emotional memory—becomes highly activated. This confirms that traumatic memories are stored both physically and emotionally within a specific region of the brain, forming what is referred to as a Brain Spot, predominantly located in the subcortical, lower part of the brain. The amygdala crosses both the right and left hemispheres.

Shapiro and others demonstrated that EMDR—through REM—can desensitise and release trauma from the SNS, allowing it to naturally shift into the PSNS. Furthermore, the two hemispheres of the brain, previously disconnected for that specific memory, are automatically reintegrated, enabling the brain to **reprocess** the experience and form **new neural pathways**.

Over the past 20 years, EMDR has been widely used as a first-line treatment for PTSD. However, it has certain limitations, as it relies on Rapid Eye Movements and follows a structured protocol, which can lack flexibility and creativity in its delivery. Many clients find this approach difficult to manage, and research indicates a success rate of approximately 50% (86). There appears to be less emotional connectivity given the following of strict protocols and more technical. Although qualified in EMDR, I have used it twice, but the science is excellent.

Brainspotting was introduced and developed by Dr David Grand in 2003 (86) after working with a female ice skater who had experienced an anterior cruciate ligament (ACL) injury while attempting a triple loop manoeuvre. The trauma of her fall had left her unable to complete the jump for five years, as she feared reinjuring herself, leading to high levels of anxiety.

During an EMDR intervention, instead of following REM guidance, the skater maintained a fixed eye position. Recognising this, Dr Grand intuitively allowed her gaze to remain in that position. As a result, she began to feel less anxious. Using a **static eye position** rather than REM, she was able to **discharge the physiological, emotional, and cognitive aspects of her trauma**. The following day, she successfully completed her first triple loop jump in five years, landing it correctly.

This moment marked the beginning of Brainspotting, which, using eye positioning, has demonstrated a success rate of over 85%.

The Science and Definition of Trauma

To understand the application of Brainspotting in sport and performance, it is essential to define key terms and explore the different dimensions of trauma.

Post-Traumatic Stress Disorder (PTSD)

A medical diagnosis of PTSD requires specific symptoms to be present for at least three months following a traumatic event in which there was a perceived threat to life—either to oneself or others. This can include serious illness, the death of a close friend or relative, the aftermath of a car accident, or a life-threatening injury. Psychiatric diagnoses are categorised in the DSM-5 (78), the diagnostic manual published by the American Psychiatric Association, which outlines all recognised mental health disorders for both children and adults.

PTSD is a psychiatric disorder that may develop in individuals who have experienced or witnessed a traumatic event such as a natural disaster, serious accident, terrorist attack, war/combat, or rape, or have been threatened with death, sexual violence, or serious injury.

PTSD has four main characteristics: Arousal, Numbing, Intrusion, and Avoidance (ANIA). For a medical diagnosis, these symptoms must be present in relation to a past event where there was a perceived threat of death to oneself or others.

- **Arousal**: A heightened state of constant wakefulness and alertness, often leading to hyper-vigilance, sleep disturbances, and difficulty concentrating.

- **Numbing**: Emotional detachment from people and events, often presenting as depression, loss of interest in activities, reduced ability to feel emotions (particularly intimacy, tenderness, or sexuality), irritability, and hopelessness. A lack of physical connection to oneself is a key element of trauma.
- **Intrusion**: Recurrent and unwanted recollections of the traumatic event, including dreams, intrusive memories, flashbacks, and exaggerated emotional and physical reactions to trauma-related reminders, triggering a present-moment response.
- **Avoidance**: A persistent fear and avoidance of people, places, thoughts, or activities associated with the trauma, often leading to anxiety disorders such as generalised anxiety disorder, panic disorder, and specific or social phobias.

Prolonged Duress Stress Disorder (PDSD): Understanding Trauma Beyond Life-Threatening Events (WW100)

Prior to the 2013 edition of the DSM-5, it was acknowledged that many individuals exhibit some or all the primary symptoms of PTSD without experiencing a life-threatening event. In addition to these reactions, PDSD encompasses responses to **non-life-threatening events** such as personal disappointment, embarrassment, and humiliation.

This expanded understanding of trauma provides valuable insight into how life events impact individuals, particularly children. Research suggests that the brain does not distinguish between life-threatening and non-life-threatening trauma in terms of felt experience, meaning the psychological and physiological responses may be similar (86).

Personal disappointment arises from the dissatisfaction that follows when expectations or hopes fail to materialise. While it is like regret, the two emotions differ in focus. Regret centres on personal choices that led to an undesirable outcome, whereas disappointment is directed at the outcome itself. This distinction is crucial, as disappointment can become a significant source of psychological stress.

The study of disappointment—its causes, impact, and the extent to which individuals make decisions to avoid it, is a key area in decision analysis. Research highlights disappointment as one of two primary emotions that influence decision-making, shaping how individuals assess risks and weigh potential outcomes.

Embarrassment is often grouped with shame and guilt as a self-conscious emotion and can have a profound impact on a person's thoughts and behaviour. It arises when an individual perceives that they have failed to meet social norms—whether real or imagined—and fears a loss of social standing as a result. Embarrassment often triggers a strong physiological reaction, even when someone tries to hide it, and may be accompanied by awkwardness, exposure, shame, regret, or a loss of control.

Social embarrassment occurs when a person becomes aware of an unintentional violation of social expectations, such as making a mistake in public, being caught in a lie, or committing a social faux pas, a slip or blunder in etiquette, manners, or conduct. The individual may fear judgement or ridicule, leading to discomfort or distress.

Personal embarrassment arises from unwanted attention on private matters, personal flaws, or mishaps. Examples include being seen in a vulnerable state (e.g., in underwear or naked), being the victim of gossip, being rejected by another person, or having a parent reveal childhood photo in a social setting. Additionally, personal embarrassment can stem from the actions of others who place someone in an awkward position, such as a public comment about their appearance or behaviour.

Embarrassment often manifests through physiological responses, such as blushing, sweating, or changes in posture. While some individuals may perceive an embarrassing act as inconsequential, others may experience intense apprehension or fear, particularly if they are shy or highly self-conscious.

Humiliation is considered deeply traumatic within the framework of trauma psychology. It involves the act of making someone feel less important or less deserving of respect and is often associated with a sudden loss of social status, whether by force or circumstance.

Humiliation can result from intimidation, physical or mental mistreatment, deception, or public embarrassment—particularly if an individual is exposed for committing a socially or legally unacceptable act. Unlike humility, which can be self-imposed as a way to diminish the ego, humiliation is imposed by others, whether intentionally or unintentionally.

A person who experiences severe humiliation may suffer from major depression, suicidal thoughts, and severe anxiety states, including PTSD (WW99). The loss of status—whether through losing a job, being unfairly discredited, or labelled a liar—can lead to an inability to function normally within a community. Humiliated individuals may become vengeful, craving justice or retribution, while others may feel worthless, hopeless, and helpless, increasing the risk of suicidal ideation if they perceive no resolution. However, humiliation can also lead to new insights, activism, and solidarity with marginalised groups.

Feelings of humiliation can trigger **'humiliated fury,'** according to Donald Klein's Theory of Humiliation (88), which, when turned inward, can result in apathy, depression, and self-hate. When directed outward, it can manifest as paranoia, sadistic behaviour, and fantasies of revenge. Klein explains: "When it is outwardly directed, humiliated fury unfortunately creates additional victims, often including innocent bystanders. When it is inwardly directed, the resulting self-hate, renders victims incapable of meeting their own needs, let alone having energy available to love and care for others. In either case, those who are consumed by humiliated fury are absorbed in themselves or their cause, wrapped in wounded pride." Understanding these psychological mechanisms highlights the importance of recognising, defining, and processing our emotions when we experience humiliation.

One of the clearest examples of humiliation occurred to an 11-year-old boy in a classroom. While reading aloud from a book, he made a mistake, prompting laughter from his classmates, who found it amusing. Initially, he felt personal disappointment and embarrassment at their reaction. However, when his teacher pointed at him and called him "stupid," the situation escalated into humiliation. This a real experience for an academic.

Years later, despite becoming an internationally regarded physicist, he still experienced intense anxiety when speaking at conferences. As he stood at the lectern, his shirt would be drenched with sweat, a physiological remnant of that early experience. However, after 45 minutes of Brainspotting, he was able to desensitise and reprocess the early humiliation. Since then, he has spoken publicly without fear or physiological reaction, demonstrating the transformative power of Brainspotting in addressing trauma.

Key Characteristics and Elements of the Brainspotting Framework

Brainspotting is an evolution and expansion of Eye Movement Desensitisation and Reprocessing EMDR, originally developed by Shapiro in 2001 (91). While it utilises elements of EMDR, including its scientific foundation and understanding of trauma origins, its Rapid Eye Movement protocols can lack precision. Brainspotting, however, employs **eye positioning** to desensitise and release trauma more deeply and accurately, addressing the physiological component of trauma with greater specificity. This method enables automatic reprocessing between the left and right hemispheres of the brain, ultimately reducing future triggered responses from their history.

Brainspotting is a **brain-based relational therapy** that acknowledges the role of relationships in shaping daily experiences. It helps individuals identify recurring thought and emotional patterns, fostering a deeper understanding of how they relate to themselves (3).

One of Brainspotting's defining strengths is its flexibility, allowing it to be adapted to suit the state and age of the client. It is structured around the principle of **'dual-attunement,'** in which the therapist or practitioner's presence and sustained rapport form one element, while the technical guidance of eye positioning forms the other. By targeting the physiological and emotional activations associated with trauma, this process allows for desensitisation and release. Today, there are in excess 50,000 practitioners and over 100 trainers worldwide. I have been a Brainspotting trainer since 2016.

Dual Attunement

Mario C. Salvador, a leading Brainspotting trainer, describes dual-attunement as follows: "Attunement to the patient/client at the relationship and psychological level is a concept that, as far as I know, does not exist anywhere else in psychotherapy. Only in this 'double (shared) relationship' is it then possible for the brain to activate in that 'healing bubble'" (95).

Brainspotting makes **no assumptions** about the client, maintaining a non-judgemental approach that follows the client's lead.

The therapeutic connection mirrors early-life attachment processes, fostering a safe space for vulnerability, emotional expression, and physical release. This presence manifests in reflective listening, validation of experiences, and deep understanding, allowing the client to look within, with clarity and courage.

Salvador further speaks of **"the loving observer, a compassionate therapist"**, who facilitates an awakening process on **cognitive, emotional, developmental, and spiritual levels**. He describes this experience as phenomenological—where healing occurs not only through words and expression but also through deep, embodied experience. The presence of the therapist, as part of dual-attunement, has a profound impact. By neutralising personal projections, the therapist creates more space for the client's healing. "From here, we create a space for the **divine and spiritual nature to surface.**" (p10 95)

Through this perspective, Salvador and other Brainspotting trainers **introduce love, compassion, observation, and spirituality as fundamental components of dual-attunement**. Without realising it at first, I had drawn the same conclusion through my own years of Brainspotting practice—that loving observation naturally expands into a non-religious spirituality. As I completed this manuscript, I recognised that what had been missing was precisely this conversation—What is love? How does love deepen in relationships, and how does deeper intimacy move us beyond the self into spirituality, strengthening our sense of purpose in life? To explore answers to these questions and delve deeper into the spiritual aspects of Brainspotting, see Chapter 10.

In Brainspotting, a key focus is managing dysregulation—the inability to regulate and process emotions—by helping clients become more grounded and connected to themselves. As Schwartzberg asserts, "grounding brings homeostasis, balance, and uniform coherence in the here and now" (95b). By supporting the strengthening of personal boundaries and creating space for growth, this transformation leads to a paradigm shift, nurtured by the presence of the loving observer. How good is that?

Another essential aspect of Brainspotting is the recognition and management of **loss and grief**, including pet loss. Debora Antinori, a specialist Brainspotting trainer in loss and grief, highlights the importance of limbic countertransference—the emotional responses a therapist experiences at a subconscious level while working with a client. The therapist's limbic system may be involuntarily activated in response to the client's emotions, reinforcing the need for therapists to develop awareness, self-regulation and control, in their practice (95c).

The Importance of Silence

David Grand, the founder and developer of Brainspotting, with whom I did all my training, has emphasised from the beginning the critical role of silence in the therapeutic relationship—particularly in Brainspotting. Unlike cognitive behavioural therapy, where activation occurs in the thinking neocortex, Brainspotting operates within the midbrain and subcortical regions, where physiological and emotional memory and dysregulation is stored. Intervening too much in the client's process can disrupt this regulation and slow or even halt the healing process.

As Salvador explains, "This structured silence is the condition (context) through which experience reveals itself in an intimate and compassionate relationship. These experiences may be divine, sacred, and deeply human. A transformational arc takes place when the process has been completed" (95).

One of the greatest challenges for therapists is learning to stay silent and resist the urge to intervene. Brainspotting is particularly effective when working with adolescents, who may struggle with verbal expression. Instead of forcing conversation, this approach allows them to simply look, feel, and heal at their own pace. As they do so, they become more regulated in processing emotions, gaining the confidence to express their feelings verbally. Once these emotions are acknowledged, heard, understood, and validated, deeper healing can take place.

A helpful reminder in this process is the acronym WAIT—Why Am I Talking—which encourages therapists to pause and assess whether an intervention is necessary or if silence should continue.

Additionally, bilateral sounds—which alternate between the left and right ear during desensitisation interventions—are believed to accelerate processing by approximately 25%. This technique is also known to reduce or even eliminate pain when its origins are psychological, partially by disrupting the brain's perception of pain (3). In addition, Grand's concept of **the 'uncertainty principle'**, incorporates not making assumptions about the client or their history, and that it is unpredictable in nature, and unique in experience.

The **success** of Brainspotting in clinical mental health practice, sport and performance environments, and other therapeutic contexts is unprecedented. This approach enables practitioners to work three-dimensionally with clients by integrating eye positioning, focal techniques, and proximity, all while remaining attuned and connected with the client. This deep attunement provides a safe and supportive environment in which individuals can release their trauma history physically, emotionally, and cognitively. This foundational principle is a key element of Brainspotting's success.

There are several technical methods for identifying and maintaining eye positions. The most natural is simply **'gazing'**— much like unconsciously staring out of a classroom window, which, despite being an automatic behaviour, serves as a powerful eye position. Additionally, body reactions can indicate specific eye positions associated with trauma and scanning horizontally or vertically helps locate the strongest activation point, on the X horizontal and Y vertical movements. Holding this position allows internal physical and emotional connections to the trauma to be accessed and released.

A **resource** eye position, by contrast, induces a sense of calm, physically represented in the body, and mentally conscious. Eye positions can be switched from an activation position to a calming resourceful position as needed. This process of moving from one eye position to another is called 'pendulation' much like a classic clock movement for side to side. Further, when a pointer, finger, or pen is used to help more accurately connect with highest physiological activation in the body, its movement toward or away from the eye is known as **'proximity,'** which helps refine focus, creates a focal-point. This is a most powerful movement, changes the intensity of the experience, and forms a 3-dimensional response with the X & Y axis movements.

Additionally, **Body Spotting** is used when pain or a strong physical reaction is present. A finger or pointer is held on the area of pain, allowing the brain to focus more intensely on the sensation, often leading to a stronger release. Another body position of calm from the resource eye position mention earlier, can help ground this brain directed pain, and release it. Finally, Brainspotting can also be conducted with eyes closed, incorporating imagery as a tool for processing and integration. This I developed from my early training and development of imagework, and visualisation, and integrates with the eye movements, which are subconscious in nature. This is doubly powerful, as the picture image paints 1000 words, and allows continued process in the subcortical brain, further releasing trauma. Ultimately, we are healing ourselves, as we more than anyone, knows our own body.

The Four Phases of Brainspotting

The way Brainspotting works in both process and practice has evolved over my 14 years of experience in practice and training. To better explain the transformational process that clients undergo, I developed a structured four-phase model based on years of observation, feedback, and written reports, and presented it in Amsterdam in 2016 at a Brainspotting Training. This system highlights an often-predictable sequence of change, providing practitioners with a framework to guide their interventions and process effectively.

Phase 1. Interventions Target the Trauma History and Remove Barriers to Performance

In this initial phase, the defined and remembered trauma history forms a key part of the assessment. In Brainspotting, trauma is defined broadly to include personal disappointment, embarrassment, humiliation and injury, significantly expanding the scope of what is considered impactful not just life-threatening events. This history may emerge in a fragmented way, often referred to as 'parts' of the self—experiences from school, sport, peer groups, relationships, and other life events – are part of the jigsaw.

The approach is all encompassing, systemic and comprehensive, incorporating the Four Corners Framework from Chapter 6 – performance, physical, social relationships, and psychology. This framework allows practitioners to observe connections between themes in the client's history, like assembling the pieces of a jigsaw puzzle. The process is intuitive, absorbing and integrating historical, observational, physical, and emotional information to identify patterns, and connections. Another representation is that of inter-weaving like in a fabric, or embroidery. Once these linked experiences are recognised, interventions begin by targeting the most relevant or recent events, gradually tracing back to earlier experiences. The focus is to reconnect people to their feelings. This approach ensures that all connected experiences are comprehensively addressed, as they emerge.

A key focus in this phase is reducing debilitating anxiety. A useful metaphor for this process is a fishing keep-net—where the open section represents the client's current state, and the linked rings symbolise historical memories from different stages of life experience, that continue to trigger activated distress. By systematically desensitising and resolving past events, the client begins to experience a release from persistent anxiety and other emotional burdens.

Towards the end of this phase, emotional reconnection with the self becomes more evident. This is a critical shift, as at the point of trauma, the two sides of the brain are blocked from connecting messages for these specific events. This is experienced by dissociation, as though this event was someone else's, and unwanted depressive memories continue to be suppressed. Traditional talk-based therapies often fall short in addressing trauma because intellectualising an experience, speaking from a rational rather than a felt experience (processed in the neocortex) does not necessarily lead to emotional or physiological healing (which occurs in the subcortical brain where it is felt).

This limitation is evident in cognitive behavioural therapy, which primarily targets cognitive thinking appraisals in the upper brain but may not fully resolve deeper emotional wounds. Similarly, traditional counselling approaches that repeatedly ask clients to recount their trauma may re-traumatise them, especially when multiple professionals revisit the same painful experiences. Many of my clients have reported such experiences with other professionals.

In Brainspotting, we focus on the 'memory' of the event rather than insisting the client relive the experience itself, ensuring a safer, more effective healing process.

Phase 2: Emotional and Physical Reconnection and the Development of Self-Esteem Attachment

PTSD, whether from 'big T' or 'small t' traumas, is inherently dissociative and disconnecting. These experiences often stem from early disruptions in attachment with parents or other significant figures such as teachers or coaches. As a result, the child experiences a deep sense of rejection and abandonment, leading to heightened insecurity and anxiety, also known as separation anxiety. When triggered memories and flashbacks occur, these can induce a hyper-aroused state, a reaction that is subconscious and unintentional.

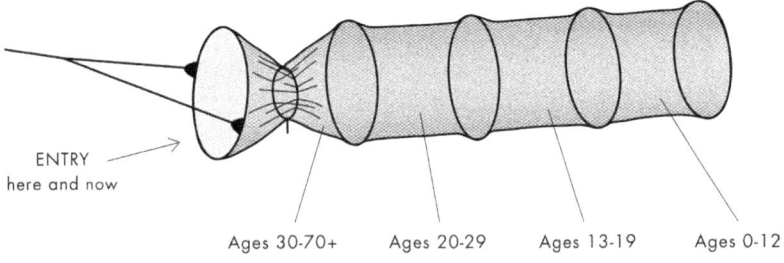

ENTRY
here and now

Ages 30-70+   Ages 20-29   Ages 13-19   Ages 0-12

The fishing keepnet symbolises the different stages of our lives which are triggered.

Since historical trauma blocks our ability to connect with ourselves, its desensitisation and release create the opportunity for reconnection with the 'younger self,' commonly referred to as **'inner child'** work **(WW101)**. This process also supports an increase in self-value, which is directly linked to self-belief. As the effects of past trauma are processed and released, triggered memories are reduced, allowing for a reshaping, and strengthening of self-perception, and naturally lift self-value. During this phase, clients develop a greater ability to access and reconnect with emotions, including feelings that were previously distant or suppressed. Emotions such as satisfaction, contentment, and happiness become more available as depressive states lift.

My extensive observations over the past 25 years, along with recent research from the British Psychological Society (BPS), suggest that many individuals who have experienced trauma or depression often lack, or lose the vocabulary to fully express their emotions. Furthermore, trauma can disrupt the ability to connect feelings with the meaning of words, making emotional processing more challenging. Through Brainspotting, these emotional connections can be restored, facilitating deeper self-awareness, confidence, and personal growth.

The **recovery from addiction**, whereby the nature of their self-soothing behaviours, regardless of drugs, alcohol, sexual obsession, gambling, shows a higher dissociation, and disconnection from felt sensations, suppress and avoid anger, sadness. In my view, there is an underlying depressive feeling within the trauma experience, which is particularly noticeable. By developing an expanding vocabulary with appropriate meanings, enables greater confidence in understanding these felt sensations, which we recognise as emotional feelings, and can then be better expressed. However, it is also important to acknowledge that the physical sensations that accompany them, such as 'butterflies in the stomach', are not always noticed. These changes improve communication skills within relationships and social situations in the form of self-expression, and formed part of my work at *The Sporting Chance Clinic*, a treatment centre for footballers with addiction.

Breakdowns in relationships are a major source of trauma and are often accompanied by limitations in expression for both parties. Through my observations of many clients, particularly those with addictive and self-soothing behaviours, along with underlying depressive feelings, I have seen an inability to express emotions outwardly, as detailed above. As a result, through a mixture of social withdrawal and imposed self-isolation, two key factors emerge.

Given emotional and physical disconnection, the numbing of feelings causes us to lose the vocabulary that would otherwise help us identify and articulate those experiences. In some cases, individuals may simply be unable to recognise what they are feeling. Introducing and encouraging the use of a wider **emotional vocabulary** is therefore welcomed, especially in communicating with a partner or family **(WW111)**. The six basic emotions are sadness, happiness, fear, anger, surprise, and disgust.

As trauma is discharged and a sense of connectedness is restored, clients experience a shift in how they perceive themselves and the world around them. This not only brings new insights but also strengthens **personal boundaries**, much like the concept of the **Hula Hoop** ring. This transformation is reflected in greater assertiveness—the ability to present oneself confidently in the world. During this phase, clients often become more aware of improved posture, a willingness to make healthier dietary choices, better hydration, and respective improvements in sleep, energy, mood, and motivation. These changes enhance performance in all areas of life.

Finally, as this phase progresses, clients can recognise **limiting self-beliefs** they may have held for years and begin to modify them.

However, this is only possible after a significant portion of their historical trauma has been processed and removed.

Confidence is a belief in oneself—the conviction that one has the ability to meet life's challenges, succeed, and act accordingly. Being confident requires a realistic sense of our capabilities and feeling secure in that knowledge (93). Confidence is a major area of development, particularly within social and performance environments. Without the previous limitations in self-belief, a wide range of actions and behaviours become possible, from winning Olympic medals to establishing and maintaining meaningful intimate relationships.

Intimacy, our sense of closeness, is often disrupted by trauma— not only in relationships with others but also in our relationship with ourselves. With the support of these newly developed feelings, intimacy can be restored or, for some, created for the first time.

A defining feature of Phase 2 development is the welcomed challenge of functioning within a new framework with guidance and support. Research on comfort zones highlights the need for ongoing support during periods of significant change from one level to another, and to achieve positive and lasting behavioural outcomes. In other words, effectively managing and supporting change.

Phase 3: Intergenerational and Transgenerational Trauma

In 2017, I had the opportunity to study with Dr Ruby Gibson from Colorado, USA, the developer of Somatic Archaeology© and Generational Brainspotting. While I had worked with these patterns before, I came to recognise that even after a client's presented trauma history had been desensitised, an additional, often unknown, blocking mechanism could remain. This emerged as intergenerational trauma.

Dr Gibson acknowledges through her work with Native American communities that individuals often inherit familial and cultural patterns of abuse, addiction, disease, and despair. Additionally, transgenerational conditions may stem from experiences such as war trauma, genocide, ethnocide, forced migration, and the removal from ancestral homelands.

Once intergenerational trauma has been acknowledged and processed, where it exists, it clears the path for Phase 4, allowing for further transformation and enhanced performance.

Phase 4: Achieving Higher and Sustained Performance

Whilst this phase of work has primarily focused on sport performance and other high-performance environments, achieving new and previously considered impossible goals becomes realistic when applying the I'M SMART model (see Chapter 7). In sport, athletes, teams, and players are often subject to external influences, as described in **Povey's Circle of Influence**. Recognising that one's inner circle consists of direct influences—whether positive, negative, or neutral—is crucial in supporting change. For more on this, see **WW27, WW28, and WW94.**

Although external influences play a key role in social relationships, developing a strong **Locus of Control** is both individually empowering and essential for managing arousal, achieving goals, and maintaining personal boundaries **(WW97)**. These three interconnected elements of the Locus of Control, the Circles of Influence, and the Hula Hoop's Personal Space, are interlinked into a matrix of developing stronger personal boundaries.

In this fourth phase of development, new insights and beliefs about performance become more accessible, desirable, and attainable. This is largely due to the extent to which trauma history previously blocked and restricted performance improvements. The use of visualisation techniques, along with **resource eye positions**, proves valuable in this phase. These approaches, combined with enhanced communication skills and heightened awareness and sensitivity, contribute to sustained performance growth **(WW102)**.

While Phase 1 focuses on removing trauma history and other barriers to performance, unconscious unresolved trauma can still create resistance, preventing full progress. Two key factors often require further attention and resolution.

The first is **early attachment failures**, and disruption, which may not have been fully reconnected, particularly in cases where there is a history of addiction and self-soothing behaviours. These patterns are often linked to parental substance abuse, such as alcoholism or drug addiction, which can disrupt a child's sense of safety and connection.

The second factor, which can be more difficult to identify, is **intergenerational trauma** (Phase 3). This refers to the transmission of trauma effects down to younger generations, where the oppressive or traumatic impact of past events experienced by parents or grandparents is carried forward. This can result in coping mechanisms such as emotional detachment or avoidance, often seen in individuals who have endured experiences like childhood hospitalisation or sexual abuse. A deep-rooted sense of rejection or abandonment is commonly associated with this inherited trauma, further reinforcing patterns of emotional disconnection.

Exploring relationships with parents, and grandparents can help uncover these underlying issues and their impact on an individual's daily life. Since the transference of these experiences is often subconscious and not intentionally conveyed, understanding these dynamics is crucial **(WW103)**. Freud referred to this phenomenon as 'projection.' Once identified, these patterns can be desensitised and removed, preventing them from being triggered in the present and, importantly, from being passed on to future generations.

Brainspotting interventions offer a powerful approach to resolving trauma history physiologically, emotionally, and cognitively, leading to significant and lasting change. **The Four-Phase Model of Brainspotting** provides a structured framework for practitioners and clients to recognise the stages of development, transitions, and the timing of supportive interventions. The creation of positive eye positions as resources is an integral part of this process, fostering a sustained sense of calm, confidence, and security.

Once the four phases have been completed to the best possible extent, performance often exceeds previous levels. The impact of these changes will be explored further in practice in Chapter 9. However, when resistance or blocks persist, clients may become re-traumatised during sessions, or deeper layers of trauma may emerge as the healing process unfolds—much like peeling back the layers of an onion. The root cause of the stressor, such as emotional abuse from a partner or manager, may be linked to much earlier experiences that remain unconscious and unrecognised. In such cases, further investigation, recognition, desensitisation, and continued support are necessary for full resolution.

While the four distinct phases of the process have been observed, they are interdependent and often coexist during transformational change. This becomes particularly noticeable during desensitisation, when new feelings and experiences emerge, reopening past emotional connections that were previously closed. The process can be likened to peeling back the layers of an emotional 'onion,' gradually reaching the core of our often hidden and suppressed vulnerabilities.

Psychology and psychologists have traditionally focused on thoughts, emotions, and the interplay between them. However, while emotions such as love, fear, anger, shame, joy, disappointment, and sadness shape our psychological experiences, they also have a physiological origin. This is what makes the integration of brain-body approaches revolutionary **(WW104)**.

Trauma, first and foremost, is a physical experience. Conventional psychological interventions typically focus on thinking patterns, problem-solving, beliefs about self and others, and the emerging behaviours, are dominantly within the neocortex, and actions—all influenced by mood and emotional states. Yet trauma, which can block or prevent desired actions, operates largely at the subconscious level and is deeply physical. This is the distinct change that Brainspotting enables, beyond talking therapies.

There is another paradigm shift. Neurobiological attunement harnesses the body activation experienced in relation to a traumatic event, through a resonating spot in the visual field (an eye position), that releases experiences and symptoms that are typically out of reach of the conscious mind, and its cognitive and linguistic focus (Grand, 3).

Kaufman says "My assertion is that contemporary sports psychology does not typically utilise clinical knowledge readily at the disposal of trained clinicians, and most certainly does not incorporate conversion disorder or similar ideas into its assessment of sport performance problems. (Kaufman p210 95). Conversion disorder relates to an inability to explain a physical symptom neurologically or medically. The success rate of Brainspotting interventions in resolving trauma is over 85%, demonstrating that it is fundamentally successful as a brain-body intervention rather than a conventional talking therapy that does not reach the core of the issue, literally. The process is naturalistic, allowing the brain to heal itself through its inherent neuroplasticity—empowering individuals to take charge of their own healing and transformation. So here we go.

CHAPTER 9: BRAINSPOTTING IN PRACTICE

Ten Case Studies: Illustrating Interventions and Outcomes

These detailed interventions highlight the presenting issues, assessment processes, interventions, and outcomes. The ten case studies span a wide range of contexts, including sport, performing arts, and life challenges. Each story follows multiple sessions, illustrating key moments of desensitisation and reprocessing, including the release of trauma related to concussion and injury.

In addition to Brainspotting, other interventions and techniques are incorporated and described. Notably, I was among the first Brainspotting practitioners to observe that the brain continues to move the eyes even when the eyelids are closed, activating responses through imagery. Prior to my work with Brainspotting, I trained as a teacher of Imagework and Visualisation, which further informs my approach.

Case Studies

1. Gymnastics (Female) – Sharon
2. Gymnastics (Male) – J
3. Guitar / Music – Nick
4. Equestrian Show Jumping (Female) – D

5. Football (Male) – RT
6. Performing Arts (Music, Acting, Dance) – Natalie
7. Rugby Union (Mother and Son) – DB & S
8. Aerial Freestyle Skiing (Female) – RL
9. Classical Guitar – Michael
10. Motorcycling – Dean

Case Study 1: Gymnastics (Female) – Sharon

At the point of referral, Sharon's mother described her as a talented 12-year-old gymnast who had been involved in the sport since she was six. "She has performed at high levels of competition well beyond her normal age band and is an international hopeful," her mother explained. "She is normally a happy, confident child with a good sense of humour. We have had to let her opportunity for national representation go, and she is currently out of training, as suggested by a musculoskeletal physician, as her body was overreacting to each little twinge. She really needs someone with your expertise in sports psychology to try and get her back on track."

Her mother went on to describe how difficult the situation had been for Sharon, as well as for the family. "Poor Sharon thinks she is going mad as everyone keeps telling her it's in her head. She suffered two-foot fractures within eight weeks of each other. She has missed two national competitions and one international competition. She has now sunk into what appears to be PTSD—her body is hyper-alert, and her fight/flight reflex is working overtime. She is having nightly flashbacks of her accidents and recurring nightmares about monsters."

Sharon's parents were particularly distressed by the severity of her sleep disturbances. "The high levels of disturbance in Sharon's sleep have resulted in constant nightmares, leading her to bang and punch the wall," her mother said. "I have had to sleep in the same room for over two weeks to protect her from harming herself during her dreams, in which she becomes very frightened, with themes of monsters and death. Over the last few months, she has lost confidence, become more withdrawn socially, and is self-isolating."

In my observations there is a direct relationship between energy, mood, motivation and performance. As demonstrated in the self-rated questionnaire, 'S' is significantly affected by her loss of energy and has a very low mood.

Sharon's Four Corners Framework Assessment:

Physical/Psychological

From my observations, there is a direct relationship between energy, mood, motivation, and performance. As demonstrated below by Sharon's Overtraining and Burnount Self-Assessment results, she is significantly affected by her loss of energy and has a very low mood. These factors, combined with her disrupted sleep and increasing withdrawal, indicated the depth of her distress and the need for targeted intervention.

Sharon's Overtraining and Burnout Self-Assessment Results

Overtraining 57%	Burnout 95%
Poor performance	Low motivation or low energy ✔
Apathy	Concentration problems ✔
Lethargy	Loss of desire to play ✔
Sleep disturbance ✔	Lack of caring ✔
Weight loss	Sleep disturbance ✔
Elevated resting heart rate	Physical and mental exhaustion ✔

Muscle pain or soreness ✔

Mood changes ✔

Elevated resting blood pressure ✔

Retarded recovery from exertion ✔

Appetite loss

Overuse injuries ✔

Immune system deficiency ✔

Concentration loss ✔

Lowered self-esteem ✔

Negative affect ✔

Mood changes ✔

Substance abuse

Changes in values and beliefs ✔

Emotional isolation ✔

Increased anxiety ✔

Highs and lows variable mood

Sharon sustained an impact injury to her left elbow, which remained non-weight bearing for nine weeks, causing her to miss two competitions. Following this, she developed a mental block on performing a front somersault. Around the same time, she began experiencing severe migraines, which would leave her temporarily blind the following day, rendering her unable to see. After consulting a specialist, she was prescribed Sumatriptan 50 mg to take at the onset of an attack. The blindness typically resolved itself by mid-morning after the previous night's migraine.

Sharon's mother reported that her daughter had always exceeded the normal pain threshold for her age, consistently participating in gymnastics despite carrying pain and injury. While pain is meant to restrict movement and protect the body from further harm, Sharon had progressively overridden this mechanism. This level of pain tolerance is common in elite competitive sport but is rare in someone so young. Over the past three years, she had experienced a series of both minor and more significant injuries. It is likely that her migraines resulted from the cumulative stress on her body, emotional strain, dietary changes, disrupted sleep, and reduced immune system resilience. Migraine and headaches, particularly those occurring around sleep, can also be linked to dehydration, highlighting the importance of the Four Corners Framework approach in addressing the broader context of her condition.

Social

Sharon is well-liked both at school and within her gymnastics group. However, her competitive nature and intense focus sometimes lead her to 'disconnect' from her friendship groups. This is partly due to the demands of her gymnastics training, but it also contributes to a phenomenon often seen in high-level young athletes— 'lost adolescence'—where social development is unintentionally restricted.

Social and Psychological

Sharon is very close to her family, particularly her mother. However, her mother recognises that throughout this challenging period, she may have been 'over-indulgent,' leading Sharon to become 'clingy' and seek constant reassurance. These behaviours indicate attachment issues, particularly separation anxiety, which was exacerbated by her mother's hospitalisation. As Sharon progressed through the desensitisation process, she began regaining confidence and was able to separate more easily from her mother. This improvement allowed her to return to full-time schooling, which had previously been disrupted by her physical injuries, illness, and emotional difficulties.

Psychological

Sharon has felt intimidated by her coach, A, and sidelined by her new acrobatic partner for Team X, which has contributed to performance anxiety. Gymnastics is central to her identity—she sees it as her 'life'—and her sense of self-worth is heavily influenced by winning and losing. Philosophically, this aligns with the idea that individuals define themselves through their achievements and external validation. One of Sharon's key breakthroughs was learning to see herself as a 'whole' person first and a talented athlete second. While this is a complex concept, both she and her mother now understand it within the cognitive framework of a 12-year-old.

In summary, these challenges resulted in performance anxiety, loss of performance, reduced motivation, missed opportunities, social and emotional isolation, and low mood. Brainspotting interventions helped her process her injury history (including concussions), fears around separation from her mother, catastrophic themes in her dreams, and sleep disturbances. Most of the sessions were conducted with her mother sitting behind her, occasionally holding the 'pointer' (a pen or finger) used to establish focal points for eye positioning and adjusting intensity during desensitisation and reprocessing. Sharon found bilateral sounds particularly soothing, which facilitated the process and increased the speed of trauma release by approximately 25%. The intervention was conducted over Skype.

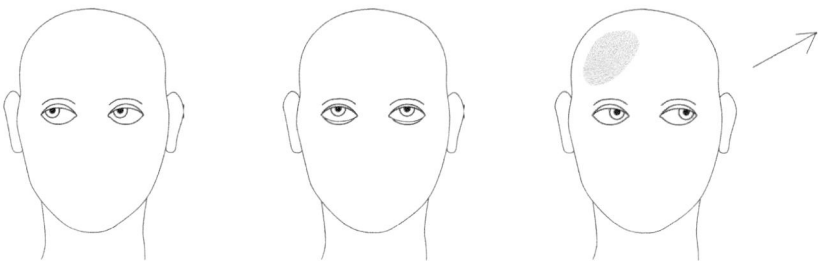

When we look to the left, the right hemisphere is dominantly activated, which holds our physical and emotional memory. When we look to the right, it's the left hemisphere, which is responsible essentially for problem-solving. When we look straight ahead, we are balanced and at our most positive.

During the period of burnout, it was agreed that Sharon would take a complete break from gymnastics, take up swimming, spend more time with school friends, and focus on recovering the joy in her life while reducing social isolation. After three months, she returned to gymnastics. However, her parents had also been deeply traumatised by witnessing their daughter's suffering and felt powerless to intervene in the emotional abuse she endured from her coach without jeopardising her chances of joining Team GB. It was essential to provide support and reflection for her mother, who needed to process the distress of watching her daughter bang her head against the wall in the middle of the night, attempting to shake off the demons in her dreams—subconsciously connected to her coach. Gymnastics, as is widely acknowledged, can be a highly demanding and pressurised environment for young athletes.

This reality was underscored in 2020 when British Gymnastics faced an unprecedented group-claim lawsuit from 17 former gymnasts. The lawsuit alleged widespread physical and psychological abuse by coaches, inflicted on children as young as six, under a "win at all costs" mentality. It also highlighted a "culture of body-shaming," with teenage gymnasts reportedly pressured to "starve themselves" to meet target weights and subjected to "punishment conditioning" or forced to wear a "fat suit" if they failed to do so. The *Whyte Review* (70), commissioned by UK Sport and Sport England, formally documented these allegations.

In July 2021, Sharon's mother wrote me a seven-page report detailing her daughter's return to gymnastics. By age 14, Sharon could no longer cope with the environment and, in essence, was retraumatized. She became clinically depressed and was diagnosed by a psychiatrist with generalised anxiety disorder. She was prescribed Sertraline at 100 mg per day to manage her symptoms, but her mental health continued to decline. She became suicidal and engaged in daily self-harming behaviours. Further assessments by educational psychologists resulted in additional diagnoses of PTSD, OCD, and ADHD, for which she was also medicated. Eventually, her mother decided to stop the Sertraline.

By the time I re-engaged with Sharon and her family, she was 16 years old, had stopped attending school, and had become severely dysregulated. She slept only during the day, exhibited extreme perfectionism, lacked personal boundaries, was chronically dehydrated, highly agitated, and catastrophized nearly every situation. Over the course of 14 Brainspotting sessions, combined with some talking therapy, we worked on rehydration, restoring normal sleep patterns, desensitising the four elements of PTSD, and addressing her agoraphobia, OCD, perfectionism, and disordered eating patterns, including episodes of overeating. Eventually, Sharon enrolled in a supported educational college, where she thrived. She was selected as a college ambassador and successfully passed her driving test. While she continues to experience occasional nightmares about her gymnastics coach, she has made significant progress in rebuilding her life.

The eye positions indicate that looking to the left activates the right hemisphere of the brain holding physical and emotional memory. Looking right activates the left hemisphere.

Case Study 2: Gymnastics (Male) – J

Imagine a 16-year-old gymnast—dyslexic, unacademic, yet brave, coordinated, extroverted, and charismatic—suddenly struggling with failure, developing performance anxiety, and sustaining minor injuries. This is J. He has a good relationship with his coach, but communication was not always as effective as it could be. The fear of failure, compounded by the fear of injury, creates a physical and mental imbalance, adding to his stress. Distractions at competition venues interfere with his training preparation, further weakening his ability to focus. Eventually, these anxieties led to panic in the middle of performances, particularly when set routines, once ingrained, are suddenly forgotten.

During the assessment and history-taking stage, we began to uncover past embarrassments with coaches, teachers, and peers. Early educational experiences were made difficult by the noticeable traits of dyslexia—struggles with reading, numbers, and feeling left behind. The frustration of these challenges left him feeling inadequate and unintelligent. However, when he entered the world of gymnastics and demonstrated high performance, he found a strong sense of capability and achievement. Gymnastics became a source of pride, self-value, and belief in himself. So, when his performance began to decline, these core aspects of his identity were noticeably shaken.

At one international competition, J's panic became so overwhelming that he felt hypnotised, trapped in a state of immobility and freeze for approximately 45 minutes. So-called friends cruelly referred to him as "stupid", a "retard", and "lazy", further traumatising him and deepening his feelings of sadness, anger, self-doubt, and demoralisation. Between the ages of 12 and 13, his sleep was severely disturbed for months, filled with anxiety about the next day at school and the next competition. The loss of quality sleep led to fatigue, impaired concentration, and more frequent errors. In an effort to maintain control and prove himself, he developed perfectionistic tendencies—an exhausting cycle in which every mistake became a personal failure, reinforcing his fears. Yet mistakes are crucial to learning and development. By setting unrealistic standards, he unintentionally set himself up to fail, punishing himself for the very errors that were an essential part of his growth.

Interventions focused on addressing J's overthinking, improving concentration and attentional-focus, overcoming his phobia of water, and desensitising injury memories related to his ankles. Additional areas of work included attachment issues to mother, the loss of close relatives, career transitions, and reducing performance-related anxiety while enhancing his self-value and belief. The goal in Phase 1 was to desensitise his trauma history, while Phase 2 aimed to build self-worth, modify limiting self-beliefs (barriers to performance), and create a sense of safety in the air and whilst landing, and managing parental and coach expectations.

Brainspotting sessions targeting past humiliations uncovered a range of memories from school years 7 to 10 and ages 13 to 14. This process released suppressed feelings of anger, sadness, and a deep-seated lack of trust in friends and adults. Despite his growing popularity, J had always been considered 'different,' which contributed to his emotional struggles. More recently his situation would fall into the realms of neurodiversity. Eye movement patterns revealed notable insights: when looking to the left, information was predominantly processed through the right hemisphere of the brain, whereas looking to the right primarily engaged the left hemisphere, though not exclusively. Looking down often brings negative thoughts and feelings, including shame.

When working on desensitising his ankle and elbow injuries, J's Subjective Units of Distress Scale (SUDS) rating would spike between 7 and 9 (indicating very strong distress). This was accompanied by physical symptoms such as shaking in the legs and arms, increased upper body temperature, and resurfacing pain-memory in the shoulders. His eye positions were predominantly located on the x-axis (horizontal), with significant activation in the lower right at a 45-degree angle and in the upper Y-axis (vertical). Some eye positions tracked upwards along the Y-axis, mirroring the body's experience of being mid-somersault, unbalanced, and landing poorly on his ankle. The SUDS scores were monitored throughout, with a target of reaching zero, indicating a full resolution of negative feelings associated with these traumatic memories.

Over eight sessions across three months, J significantly improved his performance, and for one six-week period, he secured two gold, one silver, and one bronze medal. This progress led to his selection for the national U-18 team, and he remains an Olympic hopeful. Many of his early traumas related to humiliation at school—largely stemming from his dyslexia—were successfully resolved. One key early memory involved an incident at age five when he and his brother briefly lost their mother in a supermarket, which was identified as an attachment issue. This event unconsciously triggered various anxieties, later compounded by the loss of two close grandparents within a year, both of whom he had a deep emotional connection with. While the supermarket incident contributed to separation anxiety from his mother, the unresolved grief following his grandparents' deaths left an emotional void.

These experiences were desensitised using Brainspotting, opened up with talking therapy to help J process the loss and separation. Given the family-wide impact of these events, both his mother and brother later engaged in sessions to address their own emotional responses. His mother, in particular, was deeply traumatised by the supermarket incident once she realised its long-term effects on her sons. Another significant breakthrough came from resolving J's body memory of two ankle injuries. Once desensitised, his body experienced greater flexibility—an essential factor in gymnastics.

It became evident that J's performance struggles were linked not only to sport-specific pressures—such as injuries, embarrassment with coaches, and performance anxiety—but also to personal challenges outside of sport, including attachment issues, grief, hyper-arousal, and humiliation at school. Parental expectations, both conscious and unconscious, further contributed to his stress. By supporting his parents in managing their own anxieties and reactions, the overall household atmosphere became calmer, leading to better competition preparation and higher achievement.

On a practical level, I attended a national competition to help J's parents regulate their nerves and avoid outward displays of anxiety. His mother had previously never been able to watch his performances due to her overwhelming fear of him getting injured. J was aware of this, which only intensified the pressure he felt to perform safely. Through breathing techniques and positive eye positioning, she was finally able to watch him compete for the first time in nearly four years.

Case Study 3: Bass Guitar Music – Nick

Nick's case highlights the profound impact that unresolved personal emotions can have on performance. As a professional bass player, he had never struggled with his solos before, but after one mistake during a concert in the Middle East, he found himself increasingly anxious whenever his solo approached. Over the following eight months, his concern about making another mistake grew, leading to heightened anxiety and loss of concentration.

During our session in Monaco, I asked him to reflect on what significant life events had occurred around the time this issue first appeared. Almost immediately, he recalled that his partner had announced she was pregnant. While he initially felt excitement, deeper emotions surfaced—his head lowered, his gaze shifted down to the left, and he became tearful. "I had a bad relationship with my dad," he admitted. "He was a drinker, violent to my mum. He had to leave, and my mum did everything. I don't want to be a father like him."

The connection between his personal history and his performance struggles became evident. His fear of fatherhood—rooted in childhood trauma—was manifesting as performance anxiety. When playing the bass, he described his technique as shifting between two forms: one like a heavyweight boxer, with power and aggression, and the other like a ballerina, light and fluid. While he was technically capable of both, he no longer felt them. In essence, he had become emotionally detached from his music.

Many musicians experience moments of performance anxiety, but what set Nick apart was his inability to shake it off. Like a footballer who misses an open goal and carries that disappointment throughout the match, Nick found himself stuck in a cycle of self-doubt. His challenge was not just about regaining his technical ability but reconnecting emotionally with his music and overcoming the subconscious fears that were interfering with his performance.

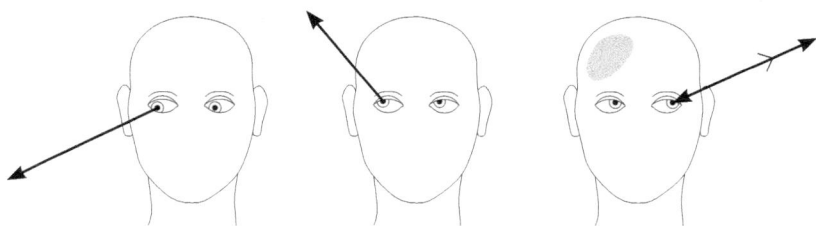

As we delved deeper, it became clear that Nick had suppressed a great deal of anger towards his father. This unresolved emotion, combined with uncertainty about his own ability to be a good father, was feeding into his performance struggles. When we shifted focus back to his bass solos, his body reacted immediately—his temperature rose, his palms became sweaty, and his shoulders, arms, and hands tensed. These physical responses indicated a fight reaction, a deep-seated anger manifesting as physical distress. At the same time, he felt disconnected from himself, his self-worth plummeting, and the embarrassment of freezing on stage weighing heavily on him. He described it as feeling like a football striker breaking towards the goal line but suddenly unable to kick the ball.

A major turning point came when Nick informed his father that he was about to become a parent. For the first time in 30 years, they agreed to meet. However, the stress of this long-avoided reunion overwhelmed him, leading him to emotionally shut down and attempt to block his feelings with drugs. During our session, his reactions were intense—his SUDS score rose to 9, and he was on the verge of tears. Yet, as he began to desensitise, the tension in his shoulders slowly started to release, marking the first step toward reclaiming his confidence both on and off the stage.

Nick's trauma history did not meet the criteria for PTSD, as none of the events he experienced were life-threatening. However, by all indications, he exhibited clear signs of Prolonged Duress Stress Disorder (PDSD).

Applying the Four Corners Framework, each corner revealed an area of dysfunction—whether in sleep, energy levels, social relationships, or communication. Psychologically, Nick struggled with low self-esteem and limiting self-beliefs, despite his sustained high performance and the recognition he received from audiences and fellow musicians. Once the initial trauma history was desensitised, the second phase of development focused on strengthening his self-esteem, self-value, self-belief, and assertiveness. Finally, in the fourth and final phase, the emphasis shifted to high performance.

After three Brainspotting interventions, Nick was once again playing his bass solos with excitement rather than anxiety. He sent a text from the Middle East, letting me know that all was well. His renewed enthusiasm extended beyond performing—he began channelling his confidence into his teaching, creating a positive ripple effect in both his professional and personal life.

Case Study 4: Equestrian Show Jumping (Female) – D

At the time of referral, D was a 20-year-old competitive show jumper struggling with anxiety and performance issues. Her mother, who attended all her competitions and managed her horses and equipment, expressed deep concern: "I'm looking for a sports psychologist for my daughter who is a show jumper. She has always suffered from 'nerves,' and this can affect her performance. We have discussed getting some help for this for a while, but after a very serious fall, I think it's imperative. She is really struggling. My concern is that she is very shut off, disconnected, and doesn't like discussing issues. I think it would be better for her to sit down with someone rather than avoid it. However, I'm sure you've dealt with this personality before. Although she is a reluctant patient, she has specifically asked me to sort something out for her."

Her history was marked by various traumatic events, both within and beyond the sport. These included experiencing a tsunami at age six, the sudden death of a trainer at 14, the loss of a grandfather, and several deeply disappointing performances in competition. Among these were a fall during the *Horse of the Year Show* qualifier at age 12, a poor round at *Olympia* leading to the immediate sale of her pony, and subsequently, several years later, a fall at the first fence in the *Under-26 Final* in Spain, despite winning against the same competitors the previous day.

D also endured low-level bullying when changing schools at age 11 and carried lingering embarrassment which impacted on her abilities to perform well with her ponies and horses. These bullying experiences caused perfectionism, negative self-talk, trust issues, and repressed anger, and were compounded by a history of poor sleep, frequent overthinking, and at least four concussions between the ages of 13 and 20.

Assessment & Mental Toughness Evaluation

D was assessed for key mental resilience factors using a self-rated scale (1–10). Her initial scores reflected moderate confidence but a significant struggle with setbacks and self-belief:

- Ability to recover from setbacks: 5.5.
- Robust self-belief: 5.0
- Determination: 4.0
- Ability to perform under pressure: 7.5
- Total 22×2.5 = **55%**

These scores, along with her trauma history, guided the interventions that followed.

Interventions

Concussion: The Rotational Fall

D's fall occurred when her horse, Jack, swerved abruptly at an 'oxer' fence and stopped dead. This fence is guarded by X positioned poles. She was thrown forward, when her horse stopped abruptly before the poles, and D landed between the poles. Upon recalling this memory, she immediately exhibited physical symptoms: sweating, shallow breathing, increased heart rate, and a tight chest—all indicators of a fight-flight-freeze response. She described feeling winded, shocked, and embarrassed, especially with the crowd watching.

Her body's reaction was intense. She experienced eye pressure, dizziness, and a headache behind her right eye—hallmarks of lingering concussion effects. Her SUDS score reached 8, with additional tension in her shoulders and stomach. Through Brainspotting, we identified five distinct eye positions (EPs) that corresponded to different moments of impact. The most activated eye position was looking right at 45 degrees, which intensified her symptoms, while a shift to looking left and slightly downward created an immediate sense of relaxation.

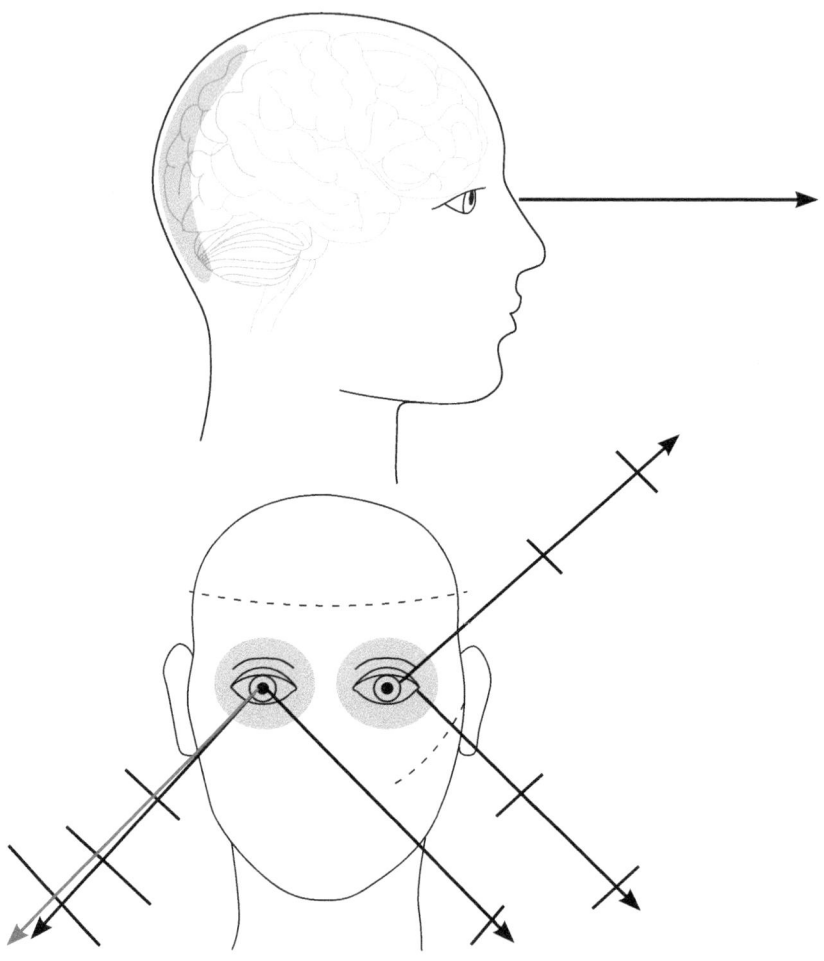

The short cross lines for the eye positions represent 'proximity', when the handheld pointer points are brought closer or further away from the eye, which alters the intensity of the physical and emotional feelings, for release. In concussion work the eye positions can be held in one position for several minutes whilst the brain activates changes. Release of concussion is dominantly through the visual cortex, experienced as dominantly internal pressure from behind the eyes, measured for the intensity of the pressure (SUDS) and indicates further release. The forehead, back of the head, brow and temporal lobes are most activated. Removal of concussion for people who are neuro diverse, ADHD / Autistic spectrum, can result in a significant increase in clarity of thinking, better information processing, and relief.

Concussion: The Jump-Off Disaster

In a high-pressure jump-off, D attempted a sharp turn to save time but miscalculated, leading her horse to stop suddenly. She was thrown head-first into a triple oxer and had to be lifted from the arena. Upon recall, her hands fidgeted in anger, her heart rate increased, and her breathing became shallow. She also experienced jaw tension and facial pressure, typical symptoms of concussive trauma.

Using Brainspotting, we located vertical eye positions that linked to the moment of impact. As she processed the memory, her physical reactions shifted—first to nausea, then to relief. She later recalled another fall while skiing at age 12, in which she fell backward after losing balance, hitting her head. This memory had been subconsciously linked to her later equestrian falls.

Concussion: The Rotational Fall with Pony

At 15, D fell from her pony during warm-up, aggravated by the absence of her mother at the event, triggering separation anxiety. The rotational fall resulted in the pony landing on top of her, causing facial abrasions and a concussion. While recalling the event,

D's body froze, her energy drained, and she became dizzy. Her hands twitched, and she felt intense pressure behind her eyes. She later remembered waking up in the first aid room, shaking uncontrollably for 15 minutes—her body's attempt to release the shock.

Through Brainspotting, she was guided through the sequence of events leading to the fall, including her hospital admission. The session triggered a further memory: another concussion, sustained only nine weeks earlier.

Concussion: The Career-Threatening Fall

D was competing in an equestrian event in the Six-Year-Old Class when she miscalculated an approach, panicked, and took off incorrectly to navigate the jump, resulting in another rotational fall. She fractured her collarbone, sustained a severe concussion, and was kept on the ground for an hour before being moved to the hospital. This event triggered powerful emotions, including deep-seated sadness and anxiety.

Processing this memory required using body-spotting, where D held a metal pen against her forehead to enhance somatic awareness. She also worked through limiting beliefs, such as "I'm not confident enough", replacing them with a new sense of self-belief.

Addressing Deep-Seated Trauma

As D continued to process her falls, another memory emerged—an experience at age 12 when a boy in her class humiliated her by calling her ugly. Soon after, she began wearing oversized glasses, symbolically 'hiding' behind them for the next eight years. Through Brainspotting and inner-child work, D revisited and reassured her younger self. At the end of the session, she was persuaded to take off her glasses, smiling through tears of relief.

At this stage, it became evident that her mother had also been deeply traumatised—not only by witnessing her daughter's many falls but also by experiencing a life-threatening tsunami in Thailand in 2004. In a separate session, we worked on desensitising the trauma her mother had endured, as parental anxiety can unconsciously transfer to children.

Progress & Outcomes

Over nine months and 12 sessions, D worked through 18 different horse-related events on nine different horses. By the end of the intervention, she reported:

- Improved sleep quality, feeling more rested upon waking.
- Increased confidence and energy levels
- Better competition performance, with major wins on horses she had previously struggled with.

Her mental toughness scores improved as follows:

- Recovery from setbacks: 5.5 → 7.5
- Self-belief: 5.0 → 7.0
- Determination: 4.0 → 6.5
- Performance under pressure: 7.5 → 8.0 Total 29×2.5 = **72.5 %**

At one competition, after winning on a horse she had previously given up on, she reflected: "I feel happy for the first time in my life. I held my own at a high-level competition despite famous riders around me. I just did my own stuff. I felt powerful."

Further breakthroughs occurred when she addressed unresolved grief from the loss of her grandfather and a beloved riding instructor. Additionally, she processed the devastating loss of a pony she had to put down due to injury.

Final Breakthrough

The last major session focused on a pivotal event: her experience during the tsunami at age six. D had long carried subconscious trauma from the hours spent separated from her family, worried for her mother and sister. In a symbolic moment, she described visualising a closed door. As she processed her trauma, she imagined opening the door to a new life, stating: "I deserve this."

Conclusion

By the final session, D had overcome most of her trauma-related blocks, improved her performance, and regained confidence. She even recognised how her own behaviours had affected her horses—an essential insight for an equestrian athlete.

Her journey demonstrated a fundamental principle in performance psychology: "Do the basics well, and you will always perform" **(WW46)**. Another lesson that emerged was "It's not about effort; it's how you use it" **(WW41)**.

D had finally stepped into her power, not just as an athlete but as a whole person.

Case Study 5: Football (Male) – RT

At the time of referral, RT was 17 years old, on the verge of quitting football altogether. His dream of becoming a professional footballer had soured, and he had lost all motivation. He felt overlooked by his manager, placed on the substitutes bench during games, and constantly scrutinised when he played. The situation had become so disheartening that he secretly hoped for matches to be called off or for the coach to leave him out of the squad.

Breaking Point and Burnout

Two months earlier, RT had reached his lowest point. His self-doubt had become overwhelming: "I'm not good enough. I'm not getting enough game time. I feel like I'm constantly being knocked down, and when it comes to playing, I'm overlooked because the second-year players get priority in my position. First-year players like me aren't accommodated the same way."

His confidence had plummeted. A burnout assessment in January revealed a score of 60%—a stark reflection of his complete emotional and mental exhaustion. Socially, he had lost his once lively personality, becoming unusually quiet in the dressing room.

His mental toughness scores reflected his struggle:

- Ability to recover from setbacks: 2/10 (Confidence dips, doesn't want to go)
- Ability to perform under pressure: 4/10 (Fear of losing the ball or being criticised)
- Robust self-belief: 4/10 (Inclined to pass the ball immediately out of fear)
- Determination to succeed: 7/10 (Despite everything, still holds onto some resilience – **42%**)

In addition to football-related struggles, RT was battling low self-esteem due to severe facial acne. He had been prescribed Accutane, a medication known for its side effects, including depressive mood, aching muscles, dry skin, and lowered serotonin levels. He recalled a particularly dark period after a hospital visit, where he felt completely closed off from the world, overwhelmed by fear, anxiety, and a sense of isolation.

His SUDS score during this recall reached 9/10. Physically, he felt tension in his back, heaviness in his chest and neck, and was close to tears. His EP during this recollection—looking 45 degrees left and down—revealed how deeply trapped he felt in his emotions.

Unpacking the Trauma Triggers

A series of events had contributed to RT's downward spiral, triggering emotional distress, and reinforcing his belief that he was failing:

1. Substituted after only 8 minutes – a humiliating experience that shattered his confidence.
2. Tour of Spain ended in tears – The manager, after drinking alcohol, spoke negatively about RT to other players. Later, he exploded in a rage in the dressing room, further humiliating RT in front of his teammates.
3. Fractured ankle – A career setback that left him feeling vulnerable and isolated.
4. Father's conflict with the coach – RT's dad once witnessed the coach jokingly tell his own son that he "wasn't good enough" in front of the entire team. The moment escalated into a major argument, leaving RT humiliated. As team captain, he refused to play.
5. Post-dermatologist appointment – The weight of his acne struggles, and medication side effects led to a moment of deep self-loathing, and suicidal ideation.

Interventions and Emotional Releases

During Brainspotting interventions, RT's head heated up, his stomach tensed, and he experienced a tightness in his throat, as if he were choking on his emotions. As the session progressed, he visualised a body scan, where he experienced a feeling of spaciousness in his head, an orange glow in his lower stomach, and tingling in his legs—all signs of physiological release.

Through targeted EPs, RT gradually desensitised his trauma responses:

- Central EP, looking right 20 degrees down: He felt his right shoulder relax, his body hydrated, and the hospital memory less oppressive. His mood lifted.
- Recalling the post-injury period: He acknowledged feeling sorry for himself and realised how injury had not just taken away his movement, but also his ability to engage socially, connect with teammates, and maintain a sense of purpose.
- Processing the humiliation from the coach: He initially felt heat and discomfort, but as he worked through the memories, his emotions shifted. He visualised washing under a waterfall, his skin feeling airbrushed clean, full, and thick—symbolising renewal and self-acceptance.

One of the most profound changes was in his mindset before games. He no longer spiralled into fear but instead built himself up with positive self-talk. He still got nervous, but it was a focused, confident nervousness, rather than the debilitating dread he once experienced.

This transformation aligned with the Inverted-U Hypothesis, which explains how optimal performance is achieved when anxiety is managed at the right level—neither too low nor too high. RT was finally regaining control.

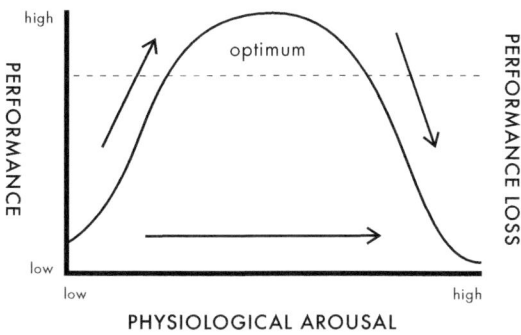

Social and Emotional Shifts

Outside of football, RT became more engaged in life. He found himself joking with classmates, laughing more with teammates, and generally feeling happier. His once-problematic housemate, J, seemed to bother him less—either because J had changed or, more likely, because RT was now emotionally stronger and more resilient.

Despite these improvements, his relationship with his coach remained difficult. RT did not respond well to negative reinforcement, and the coach's constant rants and public humiliations drained his motivation. Eventually, after a string of poor performances and worsening treatment from the coach, RT wanted to quit altogether.

Breakthrough and Final Transformation

RT's determination and motivation had always been his strongest qualities, and as he continued Brainspotting interventions, his performances skyrocketed. His best match of the season came in a game where he felt relaxed, focused, and powerful.

"I've got my mojo back again. I feel great. My legs feel good, I have more energy, and I want to stay and improve. I am good enough."

Even the coach, who had been a major source of stress, acknowledged his improvement, telling him: "You're playing really well."

His mental toughness scores improved significantly:

- Ability to recover from setbacks: 2 → 7
- Robust self-belief: 4 → 7
- Determination to succeed: 4 → 8
- Ability to perform under pressure: 7 → 7 (maintained high level of performance) = 72.5%

This represented a 30% increase in mental toughness, a clear indicator of how deeply his self-value, confidence, and belief had transformed.

Remarkably, his acne cleared without any medication, reinforcing the strong mind-body connection.

Career Decision and the Role of Parents

Despite receiving a professional contract offer, RT declined the opportunity because of the coach. The toxic relationship was too damaging, and he chose his wellbeing over a career under poor leadership. Two seasons later, the coach was dismissed, validating RT's decision.

For parents of young athletes, this case highlights the power dynamic between the player, coach, and family. RT's case was not unique—several players considered quitting football due to the coach's verbal abuse. However, it was the collective action of parents who challenged the coach's behaviour that ultimately led to change.

This is a textbook example of the Coach-Athlete-Parent Triad in action—a critical concept in understanding the complex relationships within competitive sports.

Final Reflection

RT's journey from nearly quitting football to rediscovering his confidence, joy, and self-worth is a testament to the power of emotional resilience and interventions. His ability to challenge limiting self-beliefs, process trauma, and rebuild his mental toughness did not just change his game—it changed his life.

Case Study 6: Performing Arts (Music, Acting, Dance) – Natalie

At 24 years old, Natalie was a multi-talented performer—a gifted singer, pianist, guitarist, songwriter, and actress. However, despite her abilities, she felt she had yet to reach her potential. During her first session, she admitted, "I was expecting to be further along my path by now."

She struggled with creative blocks, particularly in songwriting and performing her own music. "I have so much inside me that wants to come out, but I lack the courage," she confessed. Perfectionism had been a defining trait throughout her life, something she saw as both a strength and a curse. "I've been obsessed with perfection for as long as I can remember, at least with anything that's measurable. I know what's lacking, but I don't want this same approach for my music—it's not possible to achieve perfection there."

Performance Anxiety and Emotional Blocks

After an intense period of touring with her band, followed by three weeks of auditions at *The Conservatory*, Natalie found herself feeling exhausted, scared, and blocked again in her music. The pressure she placed on herself was immense, and it weighed heavily on both her mind and body.

A history of influenza, viruses, and colds had indicated her immune system was under pressure, which had already impacted on her academic performance, but rather than allowing herself to rest, she pushed harder, frustrated by the setbacks. This pattern of overworking and self-pressure had begun to take a toll on both her mental and physical wellbeing, a typical mindset of those who burn out, as they go beyond their limits.

A Need for Recognition and Early Influences

One of Natalie's most influential role models was a teacher she had between 11 and 12 years old, who encouraged her singing and acting. "He saw me. He gave me good parts in school plays, lead roles, and made me feel acknowledged," she said. This was a rare and deeply meaningful experience for her, as she had never felt truly seen or validated by her parents.

Her mental toughness self-evaluation revealed key insights:

- Ability to Perform Under Pressure: 6.5/10
- Ability to Recover from Setbacks: 4/10
- Robust Self-Belief: 1/10
- Determination: 9/10

While her determination was remarkably strong with a **51%** overall mental toughness score, her self-belief was almost non-existent.

Cultural Identity, Social Isolation, and Family Dynamics

Despite being well-liked by her peers, Natalie often felt like an outsider. She resented her mixed ethnicity, resulting in an internal conflict over her identity that added to her sense of alienation and self-doubt.

Natalie also carried guilt—not just for her own success, but for something deeper. She felt guilty for having mobility, something her father, who was wheelchair-bound from a childhood injury, did not have. His disability had created a ripple effect of intergenerational trauma, shaping how Natalie saw herself and her limitations.

Before she was born, her mother had developed pneumonia during pregnancy, leading to a Caesarean birth and four months of postnatal bedrest. Even before she was old enough to understand it, Natalie had absorbed a sense of being a burden—a subconscious belief that she had somehow caused distress in her family simply by existing.

Unlocking Early Traumas and Reconnection

In one session, Natalie described an overwhelming darkness in her classroom at six years old—a memory tied to her sense of alienation from other children. Through Brainspotting interventions, she reconnected with her younger self, imagining sitting her six-year-old self on her lap and watching colours brighten in the classroom. Her legs and arms felt lighter, and her breathing flowed like running water.

However, at 16, she had made a painful decision: "I forsook happiness for music." During the session, she felt her throat tightening, like she was being covered by a suffocating shower curtain. She felt isolated, sick, and trapped. Her Eye Position revealed activation looking down at a 45-degree angle—the posture of someone weighed down by emotional burdens. Shock...

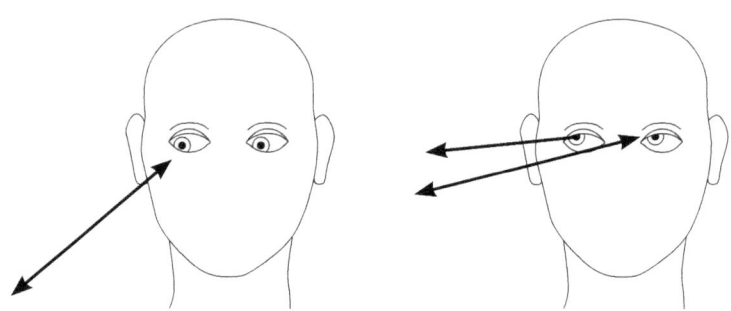

She then recalled an incident where she had written a song at 16, only for her mother to dismiss it as "no good." At that moment, she saw an image of a box with a lid on it. Encouraged to open the box, she found the same song she had written years ago. This time, she saw it differently. "It is good. I can play. I can dance. I feel light."

The Burden of Family Expectations

A year later, despite significant improvements in her performance and overall wellbeing, Natalie found herself drained again after visiting her parents. Following an intuitive question about a pain in her lower back, she revealed that she felt pain all over her back—a pain she had lived with for 10 years. When asked why she had never mentioned it before, she simply said, "I got used to it." The pain had begun a decade earlier, coinciding with her father's disability progressing. "He always looked forward to my concerts. He was so proud of me, and I felt I had to perform well for him."

Through desensitisation, she realised she had been carrying her father's pain, sorrow, and loss as her own. The guilt of being mobile when he wasn't had become a physical burden on her back. The pain never returned after processing this realisation.

Intergenerational Trauma and Self-Sabotage

Natalie's intergenerational trauma ran deep. She had always felt behind her peers, impatient with herself, and struggled with control. This manifested in perfectionism, determination, and addictive tendencies—including recreational drug use.

She described experimenting with the drug crystal meth (methamphetamine) with a boyfriend, which initially made her feel euphoric. However, the effects soon turned terrifying. "My jaw locked. I was in a busy public place, and I felt trapped, scared, unable to move." The experience deepened her fear of losing control and further reinforced her perfectionistic and self-punishing tendencies. This traumatic memory was desensitised during sessions.

Final Insights and Transformation

Natalie's formulation and summary revealed clear patterns:

- She was deeply talented but lacked self-belief.
- She had inherited a subconscious burden of guilt.
- She struggled with attachment issues and social isolation, despite being well-liked.
- She had a complex relationship with her family, including resentment toward her more successful sister.
- She self-sabotaged in both her music and personal life.

One of her earliest memories resurfaced—playing in a kindergarten sandbox. Another child claimed it was "her sandpit," making Natalie feel small and powerless (though not able to understand such concepts at the time). When she told her mother, her feelings were dismissed. It wasn't until her mother spoke to the teacher that she was reassured that she had just as much right to be there. Even at five years old, Natalie had learned to doubt her own experiences, setting the stage for a lifetime of self-questioning and seeking validation from others. However, through her journey, she gradually shed the burdens she had carried—both physical and emotional. With a renewed sense of self and freedom from past limitations, she was now ready to fully embrace her music, her artistry, and her life with confidence and authenticity.

She took her place at one of her nation's top music academies.

Case Study 7: Rugby Union (Mother and Son) – DB & S

This case study highlights a shared trauma between mother and son, demonstrating the effectiveness of dual Brainspotting, where both were treated simultaneously.

Reason for Referral

S's mother, DB, reached out for help, writing: "My son studies at university. He is an able rugby union player (number 10 fly half). He has always suffered from anxiety but recently mentioned that this is now severely affecting his performance, and indeed other aspects of his life. He even mentioned giving up! His coach mentioned that he had put his name forward for a professional rugby academy. S has long dreamed of being a professional player, but I feel he is overshadowed by his anxiety."

Physical Trauma History

S had experienced several sports-related injuries, including:

1. A fractured nose from a head-butt while playing football at age 9.
2. A second nose fracture from another head-butt in rugby at age 17.
3. A rotator cuff injury to his right shoulder at 17, which reoccurred after an unsuccessful return to training.
4. A sprained ankle at 18 that required six weeks of rehabilitation.
5. A kick to the face during a rugby match that caused dizziness and nausea, indicative of a concussion.
6. An impact injury to his right shoulder that left a lump and forced him to withdraw from a major varsity match.

Personal Trauma History

Alongside his physical injuries, S had accumulated emotional traumas:

- Bullying in school: In Year 7, a classmate repeatedly called him 'gay' to provoke him. This continued until S finally pushed the boy against a wall and put an end to it.
- Academic teasing: In Year 11, less academically inclined peers mocked him for his efforts, leading to a similar confrontation where he physically asserted himself.
- Shyness with girls: At 12, he avoided standing at a bus stop near girls from a neighbouring school, even waiting for a later bus to avoid them. Though his social confidence improved by 16–17, he still struggled with self-assurance around women.
- Anxiety at university: Upon returning to university, S experienced overwhelming anxiety about both his train journey back and a planned house party, feeling "weird, nervous, and like my thinking was speeding up."

Summary and Formulation

During desensitisation, S recalled a moment during a rugby match when he felt his head collide with another player's shoulder. While he hadn't previously considered it a concussion, he now recognised the symptoms. As he processed the memory, he felt drained and drowsy, with tingling in his head—a sign of reprocessing. I also pointed out that he had likely experienced depressive episodes after two major academic setbacks: failing the 11+ examination to go to a Grammar School and later missing out on his first-choice university. He admitted that both had left him in a deep low, and recently, he had again been feeling "not quite right."

While Brainspotting had significantly improved his confidence, anxiety crept back in. "I feel like I have to be anxious," he reflected. However, discussing rugby lifted his mood: "I feel more relaxed and different."

A new memory surfaced: during his gap year in New Zealand, he had been leading a group of teenagers on an outdoor programme when he decided to dive into a river. Moments before, he had received an email confirming his university offer. Feeling elated, he dived in—only to hit his head on the rocky bottom. His lower body never even reached the water. He recalled seeing a white flash before blacking out. At the time, his first thought was that he had broken his neck. "Everything felt hot," he remembered. "I kept all these thoughts and feelings to myself."

As we explored his emotional responses, more memories emerged. He recalled being substituted in a rugby game, and coming off the field unexpectedly, suppressing anger and his sense of humiliation. "I felt like crying, but I tried to forget about it," he admitted. But the brain doesn't forget. As we continued, he experienced symptoms of trauma release—tightness in his throat, aching limbs, a sore nose, and internalised frustration.

A positive resource memory helped to counterbalance these emotions. "Every year we go to a woodland, make dens. I feel happy and relaxed there, like I have no cares in the world," he recalled. This became a grounding point for his process, and a resource eye position.

Uncovering the Root Trauma

Eight months later, his mother contacted me again. S had once again become socially withdrawn and anxious, particularly around meeting new people—especially women. It was clear he had been re-traumatised, and we needed to find out why.

As we examined his history, DB remembered an incident when S was three years old. While playing outside with his cousins, he tripped over the edge of a partially buried barrel top, part of an ornamental garden. He fell head-first onto the barrel's metal corner, and his face into the water it had collected after rain, and then briefly losing consciousness due to the head impact. His cousins saw what happened, and while one ran for help, the other pulled him out. Bleeding and gasping for air, S was rushed to the hospital. "I wasn't a good mother," DB sobbed, overwhelmed with guilt.

Dual Brainspotting Intervention

I decided to conduct a dual Brainspotting session, a technique I had learned from David Grand. DB and S sat side by side, each focusing on a different eye position. I instructed DB to recount the incident while S listened.

As DB spoke, she wept, releasing nearly 20 years of guilt and shock. Meanwhile, S entered a trance-like state, staring ahead. His body twitched involuntarily as if reliving the experience. When he recalled the moment he fell into the water, he felt dizzy and sick to his stomach (SUDS 0–10=8). I moved the Brainspotting pointer closer to his left eye, triggering a response—pressure built in his forehead, exactly where his injury had occurred.

S then made an unexpected connection: after being rescued, he had felt ashamed that a girl had saved him. This subconscious embarrassment had carried through to his later struggles with confidence around women. His mother confirmed his feelings, adding that she had unconsciously become more anxious whenever he played outside, and later, whenever he played rugby. Her fear unknowingly projected onto him, exacerbating his anxieties.

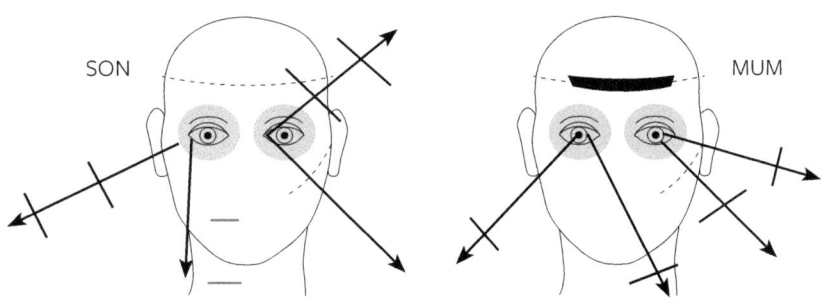

The Outcome

After the intervention, both DB and S experienced a profound shift. DB felt an immense sense of relief, no longer weighed down by two decades of guilt. S's confidence rebounded—his fear of social situations dissipated, his anxiety around women lifted, and he was able to reframe his past experiences in a more empowering way.

From then on, S's performance in rugby and academics improved, and, in a final breakthrough, he began dating confidently for the first time.

This case exemplifies the power of dual Brainspotting—healing not just an individual but an entire family dynamic. By addressing both DB's and S's unresolved trauma together, the cycle of fear, anxiety, and self-doubt was finally broken for both, and dad too.

Case Study 8: Aerial Freestyle Skiing (Female) – RL

RL was referred to me through a ski coach in freestyle aerial skiing. Her parents provided a detailed history of her injuries and wellbeing, revealing a pattern of physical trauma, repeated concussions, and chronic fatigue.

Injury and Health History

RL's history was marked by frequent concussions and physical injuries, many related to high-impact falls:

- Multiple head injuries from falls (ages 14–16), including a backward fall onto a stone floor, crashes while sledging, cycling, and scootering, and a trampoline accident.
- A series of concussions from sports-related falls (ages 17–21), including crashes in races, failed backflip attempts, and a severe skiing accident during a Europa Cup event where she hit her head and vomited afterward.
- Frequent illnesses, viral infections, and fatigue, often leading to missed training sessions and school absences.
- Burnout symptoms, with disrupted sleep, chronic headaches, and severe exhaustion, reaching a burnout scale of 60%.
- Struggles with perfectionism and self-judgment, particularly around her ability to perform complex aerial ski manoeuvres, leading to self-doubt and frustration.

These recurring injuries and illnesses created a cycle of physical and emotional depletion, leaving RL trapped between pushing too hard and feeling incapable of reaching her goals.

Uncovering the Core Issue: Perfectionism and External Pressure

Through our sessions, it became clear that RL was driven by external validation rather than intrinsic motivation. She was not skiing for the love of it but to meet expectations—her own and those of others. This loss of control and self-imposed pressure led to harsh self-criticism, disrupted sleep, and heightened anxiety. She would overthink her training, worrying about what her coaches, peers, and even younger teammates thought of her.

RL was also highly intelligent and trilingual, yet she struggled with processing information quickly, much like how she hesitated before executing complex aerial manoeuvres. This mirrored her academic challenges, where she needed extra time to absorb new concepts but felt pressure to keep up.

Interventions and Progress

The first interventions focused on her concussions, starting with a severe scooter crash that required hospital treatment. As she processed the trauma, she recalled earlier childhood injuries and experiences of humiliation in school—such as struggling with French pronunciation and feeling exposed in front of her classmates. These memories carried a SUDS level of 8, triggering physical symptoms like pressure in her right eye and feelings of frustration.

By session four, we desensitised multiple concussions, reducing the cognitive "fog" she frequently experienced. Her visualisation skills improved, allowing her to mentally rehearse complex ski rotations with greater confidence.

In June 2020, she attempted a backflip somersault on a water ramp but failed to complete the turn, crashing onto her stomach. This became a defining moment—she felt completely immobilised at the top of the ramp, unable to move forward due to fear. After processing the trauma through Brainspotting and open-eye visualisation techniques, she regained her confidence. In the next session, she successfully performed all the trampoline manoeuvres she had previously struggled with, reinforcing the connection between mental and physical performance.

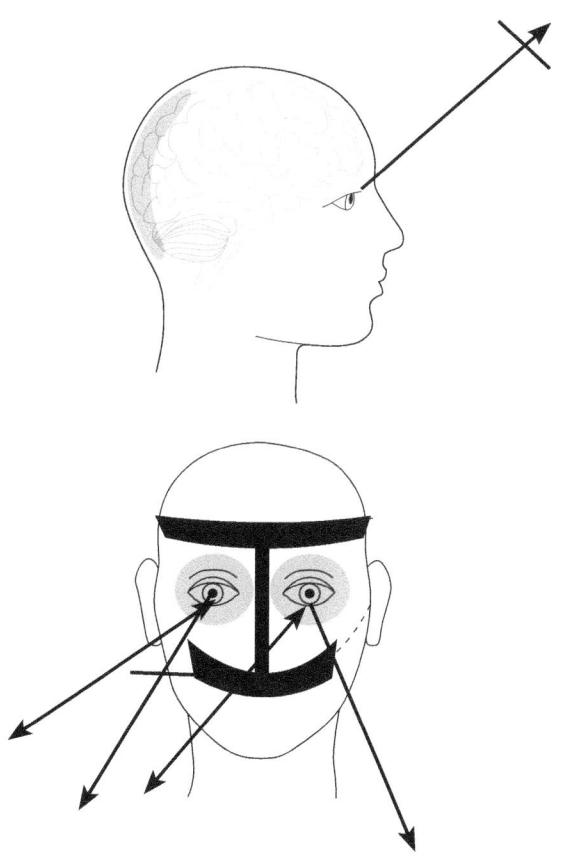

This was a complicated and deep concussion as the freestyle skier fell hitting the hardpack snow during an aerial backflip, landing on her back and head at an angle, hitting her face and impact from the protective helmet. 2020 – The pressure on release in the BSP interventions is entangled with the pain memory from the upper back which took most of the shock on landing.

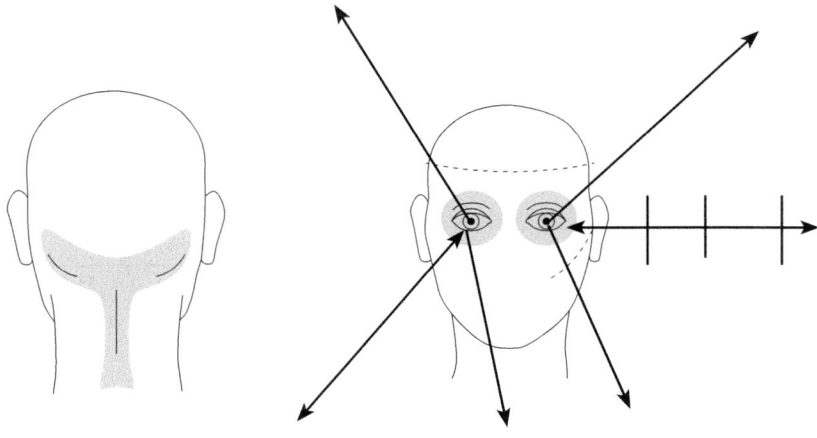

Ski fall 2025 Concussion

Case study 8 the release of concussion from the impact on the back of the head, was also releasing from the high proximity eye positions looking to the left, in the figure above. The spinal cord is connected both to the brainstem and the stomach. The stomach connection is the '2nd Brain", gut feeling, linked through the vagal nerve system, which operates the parallel Sympathetic and Parasympathetic Nervous System (PSNS), which drives both the 'fight flight freeze' response and the calm deactivated experience.

By session 12, I formally assessed her burnout scale, where she scored 60%. It was clear that anxiety, limiting beliefs, and social isolation were major contributors to her exhaustion. We began challenging her perfectionism, shifting her mindset from "pushing to the limit" to "striving for excellence"—an approach grounded in pacing and recovery.

Rebuilding Balance: Managing Burnout and Family Trauma

At this stage, we agreed that RL would stop skiing temporarily, focus on recovery, and allow herself time to rest. She struggled with this concept, initially feeling restless and frustrated. However, while on holiday at an Italian lake, she finally allowed herself to relax, spending a week floating in the water instead of competing with others. This was a pivotal turning point **(WW39)**.

As RL's performance improved, I identified an underlying family trauma. When RL was three years old, her mother was diagnosed with a brain tumour during a prenatal scan before giving birth to RL's brother. Though the surgery was successful, her mother was critically ill for three months, leaving RL unable to see her until she was out of intensive care. This early attachment disruption had left a deep subconscious imprint, shaping RL's need for control, perfectionism, and fear of failure.

To address this, I conducted a dual Brainspotting session with RL and her mother. As her mother recounted the experience, RL's SUDS level rose to 9, her heart rate accelerated, and she felt a rush of emotions she hadn't previously connected to the event. As we processed the trauma together, both mother and daughter experienced profound relief—allowing RL to let go of some of the pressure she had unknowingly carried since childhood.

Cognitive Training: Enhancing Learning and Processing

In the final two sessions, we addressed RL's academic struggles using chunking techniques **(WW53)** to improve information retention.

She had difficulty processing numbers and languages quickly, so we broke down learning into manageable segments:

- For numbers, instead of recalling 201210668765, we practiced recognizing patterns: 2012 – 1066 – 8765.
- For language learning, we created mental associations:
    - Burgundy → Burger → Red wine
    - Brittany → Britain → Brittany Spears
    - Haute France → High France → Calais ferry

This approach significantly improved her recall speed, and in her next test, she scored 80%.

Summary and Conclusion

From a young age, RL had relentlessly pushed herself in both sports and academics, often trying to prove her capability to others. Her parents, both athletic and high-achieving, had encouraged her drive, but this well-intentioned support had unknowingly contributed to her perfectionism. Over time, her internal pressure to succeed drained her energy, leading to injuries, burnout, and declining self-confidence.

In our final session, I encouraged RL to prioritise her wellbeing and rediscover the joy in skiing rather than treating it as a test of her worth. The fundamental truth is that athletes perform at their best when they are having fun—something RL had lost. By shifting her focus to rest, recovery, and self-care, she created space for her body and mind to heal.

The next time she puts on her skis, it will not be out of obligation—but for the sheer love of the sport. RL became a Junior Olympian and National Champion.

Case Study 9: Classical Guitar – Michael

Michael was first referred to me at the age of 22, with a medical diagnosis of Musician's Focal Dystonia (MFD)—a neurological condition that causes involuntary muscle contractions, loss of motor control, and tension, typically triggered when playing an instrument. MFD is often painless at first but becomes progressively disabling, impacting a musician's ability to perform.

In addition to MFD, Michael had **Chronic Fatigue Syndrome** (CFS), digestive issues linked to Irritable Bowel Syndrome (IBS), and a history of trauma, including a concussion and whiplash from a car accident in 2015. His asthma, diagnosed at age 3, had affected his breathing, and he frequently experienced hyperarousal, anxiety, and social withdrawal. His struggles were compounded by perfectionism and the pressure to over-practice, leading to severe muscle tension in his trapezius muscle—a common issue in musicians.

At music academy, Michael's teachers dismissed his need for a smaller guitar, despite the physical strain the large fretboard placed on his body. He described his teachers as bullying and controlling, further contributing to his declining mental health and sense of self-worth. When he was ultimately forced to stop playing, his self-identity collapsed, leading to shame and the deeply ingrained belief that he was not good enough.

Michael's personal history included parental separation at age 7, the death of his father, and the loss of his grandmother, who had been a central figure in his life. These experiences left him emotionally vulnerable and isolated, particularly as he had tied his entire sense of identity and self-value to his success as a guitarist.

In Session 4, we began Brainspotting to target his dystonia. His hands, arms, and legs reacted intensely, and his facial twitching intensified—a clear sign of deeply stored trauma being activated. Although his initial therapy funding was limited, the impact of Brainspotting was so profound that he later pursued training in the method himself.

A Return to Therapy:

Two years later, Michael self-referred after a personal crisis. His five-year relationship ended, sending him into a state of collapse, marked by chronic depression, financial struggles, and intensified symptoms of MFD. He also expressed suspicions of undiagnosed autism, OCD, anxiety, and Complex PTSD, stemming from his family upbringing and relational trauma.

A reassessment revealed:

- Generalized Anxiety: 7/10
- Depression: Moderate to Severe
- Burnout Scale: 58%

Interventions and Progress

Session 1: Processing Loss and Trauma

Michael struggled with flashbacks, grief, and poor personal boundaries. His facial twitching became highly activated, with 85%

intensity of stomach disturbance (SUDS 1–10 scale 8.5). Through Brainspotting, his eye positions shifted—first straight ahead, then lower right—indicating concussion release from a previous fall.

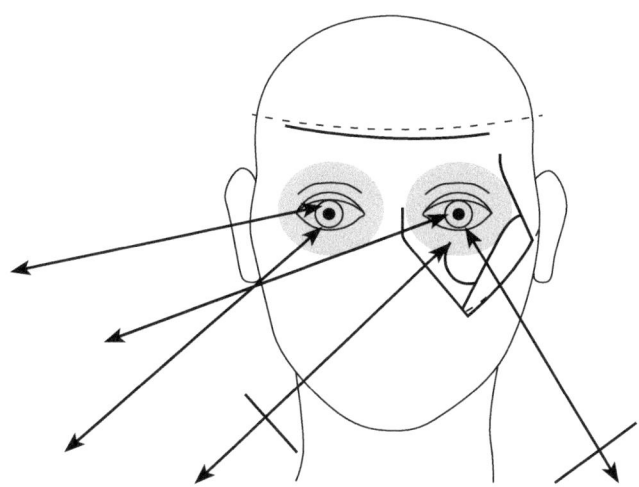

Michael Concussion and left eye twitching.

He also processed childhood memories of feeling unsafe when his single mother was working, which had left him emotionally hypervigilant from a young age.

Session 2: Reducing Isolation and Unlocking Suppressed Emotions

To counter his social withdrawal, Michael joined a sports club. He also began using bilateral sounds for calming his nervous system, especially before sleep.

He recalled that his facial twitching first appeared at age 9, along with jaw clenching and recurring dreams of being trapped. Remembering frequent fights with his brothers at the age of 10 or 11 triggered a 95% activation in his arms and hands. Through Brainspotting, he released long-held anger and sadness using two eye positions—one to the left horizontal and the other right 30 degrees upwards.

Session 3: Inner Child Healing and Regaining Creative Flow

Michael expressed **deep loneliness** after feeling rejected by friends. These emotions were linked to early life experiences of abandonment by his father and an underlying distrust of relationships. To reconnect with his younger self, we used visualisation techniques—he imagined taking his 9-year-old self into the woods, where they built a treehouse together and invited others in. This restored his sense of play and belonging, helping him realise that he wanted connection without feeling trapped or overwhelmed.

We also used an imagery technique where Michael visualised inserting a microscopic fibre optic cable inside his arm, allowing him to "conduct microsurgery" to release tension and restore movement. As he held his eye position, he felt lighter, calmer, and more connected to his body.

Session 4: Releasing the Burden of the Past

Michael's emotions intensified, particularly around his mother's depression and his role as a caregiver. Through imagery, he visualised carrying a heavy school rucksack filled with stones—representing his childhood responsibility for his mother's wellbeing. Once he threw the stones away, he felt physically and emotionally lighter.

Brainspotting also triggered his dystonia-related tension, linked to memories of being pushed beyond his limits at music academy. As he released anger and hurt, he remembered playing his grandmother's favourite songs—a reminder of the joy music once brought him before perfectionism took over.

Session 5: Establishing Boundaries and Letting Go of Ego

Michael forgave his mother, which helped them develop a more open and reciprocal relationship. He realised that his guitar had become his entire identity, and its loss had felt like an ego death. However, he now saw that his self-worth was not dependent on external validation.

To strengthen personal boundaries, we used the Hula Hoop Boundary System—a physical and psychological exercise in which he ceremonially placed a hula hoop around himself to create a protected space. This taught him to assertively say **"Stop" and "No",** preventing others from draining his energy. He then guided his younger self through the same exercise, reinforcing these boundaries at different stages of his life. We later introduced the shield to reinforce the protections.

Session 6: Releasing Armour and Embracing Vulnerability

Moving back home triggered childhood memories and overwhelm. Through Brainspotting, he identified an eye position (45 degrees left) that activated facial tension and left-side pain, indicating stored emotional defences. We used a visualisation exercise where his grandmother and uncle helped remove a full suit of armour he had worn for years. Piece by piece, they took off his gloves, breastplate, and helmet, allowing his heart to open. This symbolic act of shedding protection helped him accept love, support, and connection.

Michael also recognised that his relationships had often been codependent, with partners draining his energy. Using Brainspotting, we released wounds from past relationships, which activated strongly in his gut.

Session 7: Transformation and Self-Love

Michael noticed a radical shift in energy—he felt vibrant, more assertive, and no longer drained by others. As he cleared out old possessions, he was unexpectedly triggered by a piece of clothing linked to his time at music academy. His stomach clenched (SUDS 80%), revealing deep-seated anger and disgust at how he had been treated.

We reframed his perfectionism—instead of chasing an unattainable ideal, he embraced excellence, allowing a 30% margin for growth and learning. This removed the pressure to "always be the best" and helped him appreciate his journey.

Summary and Conclusion

Michael's case demonstrates the complex interplay of trauma, perfectionism, identity, loss, grief, boundaries, and physical symptoms. While MFD initially appeared to be a purely neurological disorder, it became clear that his struggles stemmed from deep-rooted emotional wounds. His physical symptoms (dystonia, chronic fatigue) were manifestations of trauma, exacerbated by perfectionism, bullying, and self-worth linked to external validation.

Through Brainspotting, imagery work, and boundary-setting, Michael transformed his self-identity, personal boundaries, and emotional wellbeing. His healing journey reinforced that music is not just about performance but about joy, connection, and self-expression—a profound realisation that set him free from his past constraints. He is now a Brainspotting practitioner, himself.

Case Study 10: Motorcycle Racing – Dean

Dean, aged 42, has a history of trauma that extends far beyond his years in motorcycling. His experiences of disappointment, embarrassment, humiliation, and injury have compounded over time, leading to Complex PTSD.

He presented with severe anxiety, chest pains, 'dark' thoughts of suicidal ideation. His sleep was significantly disturbed, and he suffered from chronic back pain. He exhibited classic symptoms of PTSD: hyperarousal, numbing, avoidance, and intrusive thoughts. Seventeen years earlier, he had been thrown from his motorcycle after losing control on a wet road. The accident resulted in a compression fracture of his T7 and T8 vertebrae, a herniated L4 disc, and multiple injuries, including a concussion, knee and ankle trauma, and persistent digestive issues requiring medication. His GP prescribed anxiety medication, and a later diagnosis of fibromyalgia, incorporating Myalgic Encopholomyilitis / (CFS) led to further prescriptions, including Pregabalin, Amitriptyline, and Codeine. These medications caused significant side effects, including uncontrollable muscle twitching, obesity (an 8-stone weight gain), and increased pain.

Dean's trauma extended beyond his personal injuries. In 2010, he witnessed a car crash with five occupants. Though they survived, the event unsettled him. Months later, he witnessed a fatal motorcycle accident, holding the rider in his arms as he passed. The rider was later found to be intoxicated, but for Dean, the trauma was profound. Other significant emotional wounds included his wife's near-death experience during childbirth and the loss of his beloved grandfather, leaving him with unresolved grief.

Upon assessment, his burnout scale revealed 60%. Symptoms included low energy, reluctance to participate in activities, low self-esteem, flashbacks, intrusive thoughts, and mood instability.

Intervention 1: Addressing Physical Symptoms

Electrolyte drinks were introduced to relieve muscle cramps, which ceased after two weeks. Bilateral sounds helped regulate arousal levels and improve sleep. On 19.2.24, his left hand and wrist pain rated 80%, while his right T7/T8 pain was excruciating at 100%. Using a guided imagery technique, he visualised microsurgery on his damaged vertebrae. He experienced tingling sensations and a 60% reduction in pain.

Intervention 2: Processing Trauma and Early Memories

On 21.2.24, Dean awoke feeling calm for the first time in years but later became tearful and dizzy. He recalled vivid memories of past accidents: falling from a mini motorcycle at age nine, burning his leg on an exhaust pipe, and suffering a head injury at ten. The recall of these childhood concussions, combined with his motorcycle accident and later head trauma, highlighted how the brain layers traumatic experiences together, intensifying their emotional and physical impact, with disproportionate reactions.

Guided imagery helped him reconnect with positive childhood moments, such as blowing on flowers and playing football with his father. By visualising a peaceful ride to his favourite beach, he momentarily became pain-free.

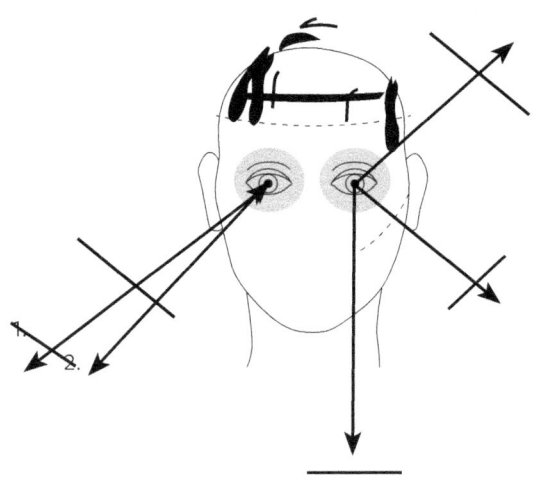

1. Dean fell in a restricted space. 2. Frontal collision with another car.

Intervention 3: Releasing PTSD Flashbacks

On 26.2.24, flashbacks of his motorcycle accident resurfaced, as well as the trauma of witnessing the car crash and the loss of his grandfather. Through Brainspotting techniques, he processed these memories, reducing dizziness from 80% to 30%. He found comfort in recalling the scent of lavender from his grandfather's garden, which brought unexpected relief.

For the first time, Dean recognised that his experiences were not a sign of madness but a logical consequence of accumulated trauma. Understanding this was profoundly liberating and further incentivised him to withdraw from all prescribed medication.

Intervention 4: A Turning Point

On 29.2.24, Dean described his transformation as "phenomenal." His hyperarousal decreased, and he expressed a willingness to taper off his six medications. His burnout scale dropped from 60% to 38%. He admitted an addiction to Tramadol, which had worsened his stomach issues, and resolved to withdraw from it. A visualisation exercise using traffic light imagery supported his decision to reduce Pregabalin. By 4.3.24, he had completely stopped taking it. It can take some people years to do this.

Intervention 5: Navigating Withdrawal

On 13.3.24, Dean experienced heightened anxiety, disrupted sleep, and intense emotions due to detoxification. Recognising the connection between magnesium depletion and sleep disturbances, supplementation improved his energy and sleep within three days. Processing unresolved grief for his father led him to re-engage with his neglected garden, a symbolic act of renewal.

Intervention 6: Reconnecting with Life

By 18.3.24, Dean had visited a garden centre with his wife and started planting shrubs. He noticed substantial improvements in sleep, energy, and emotional resilience. However, reflecting on his past use of

Pregabalin triggered regret and a deeper appreciation for his family's support. He described the experience as "setting himself free."

Intervention 7: Deep Trauma Processing

On 28.3.24, Dean realised that withdrawing from Pregabalin had unmasked suppressed emotions. A complex Brainspotting intervention addressed multiple trauma layers. Through proximity techniques, which adjust focal length to modify emotional intensity, he released further concussion-related distress. This allowed him to recall positive memories of motor racing events and regain confidence in walking alone, which he had not done for many years.

Intervention 8: Rediscovering Freedom

By 10.4.24, Dean was walking more, attending motocross events, and even riding a motorcycle again. His mobility increased, weight decreased, and overall wellbeing improved. Brainspotting supported his transition into an unfamiliar but liberating state, prompting him to stop taking Amitriptyline. His burnout scale dropped further to 25%.

Intervention 9: Addressing Residual Trauma

On 9.5.24, persistent lower back tightness and ankle discomfort were addressed through imagery-based body scanning, revealing, and releasing old scar tissue. A complex intervention targeted unresolved trauma from a 2009 car crash, unlocking suppressed anger and frustration. Dean acknowledged how much he had withdrawn from life and began reclaiming his sense of self.

Intervention 10: Releasing Self-Limiting Beliefs

By 30.5.24, Dean recognised and released deep-seated beliefs that had kept him stuck. Using Body-Spotting techniques, he identified and processed the physical remnants of trauma, reducing pain and increasing emotional resilience. His growing self-awareness allowed him to challenge past assumptions and embrace new possibilities.

Intervention 11: Breaking Free from Medication

By 19.6.24, Dean had been off Codeine for ten days, marking a major milestone. He experienced occasional anger and irritability but managed these through mindful breathing techniques. For the first time in years, his family noticed genuine happiness in him.

Intervention 12: A Complete Transformation

On 15.8.24, Dean completed his final session in person. He had ceased Esomeprazole after 16 years, lost another stone in weight, and returned to work with renewed focus. A holiday to Cornwall confirmed his progress—for the first time in years, he experienced no back or neck pain. His deepened self-awareness led to reconciliation with his mother, healing a lifetime of emotional disconnection.

Conclusion: A Seismic Shift

Dean's journey reflects a profound transformation. From a man immobilised by trauma, chronic pain, and medication dependency, he emerged with stability, optimism, and renewed family connections. His weight loss, expanded mobility, and increased social engagement marked a complete reversal of his previous existence.

His case highlights the limitations of conventional medicine in addressing deeply rooted trauma. Brainspotting, through compassion, humility, and love, facilitated his healing by integrating fragmented aspects of his life into a cohesive whole. This process extended beyond psychology, tapping into a broader spiritual framework that transcends traditional therapeutic boundaries.

Dean's story exemplifies the power of facing trauma head-on, transforming suffering into resilience, and reclaiming a life once thought lost.

1. Dean fell over in a restricted hallway area and banged his head, shoulder and leg. High pressure levels behind the eyes. SUDS = 6.5 shows after 7 minutes. EP Right 45 degrees. Lower back pain feels wobbly and sustain vibrations. Shaking is one way the body releases trauma. Yawning is also a positive sign of release and healing. Remembers being hit in the right eye, evidence of concussion through added anterior (behind) eye pressure. After 45 minutes using 4 eye positions EP, he feels a state of calm, clarity in the head. Bangs on the head have been a frequent experience.

2. When looking down and up, this indicates the position of the eyes in the sequence of the fall. Firstly, on the way to the floor, and then looking upwards having landed and twisted. When remembering the event, the brain -body connection is such that when the eyes follow a pointer, there is an activation at certain points indicating body memory. The neck and shoulders are often impacted and restrict movement even years after the accident. The brain also remembers previous similar events, and this case his fall from his motor bike, landing on his back, concussed, and showing also at the back of the head. It can take between 8–13 minutes before a concussion can show symptomology. This is a typical scenario in Brainspotting, when we WAIT, and allow the brain-body release without language, so that the client remains in connection with the subcortical brain, whereas talk causes the conscious neocortex to interpret the words, and thus away from the subcortical brain where the physical and emotional trauma are held in memory.

CHAPTER 10: DEVELOPING EXCELLENCE IN / LOVE / RELATIONSHIPS / INTIMACY / SPIRITUALITY / SELF-HEALING

What is Love?

What We Think Love Is, How We Use Love,
and How We Experience Love

Why Love Is Important in Developing Excellence

How Love Connects People in Relationships

The Spiritual Dimensions of Love and Relationships

Self-Healing, Love, and Intimacy

"Love is All You Need"—The Beatles

Having completed all the previous chapters I set out in 2018, and after reviewing them five times, I was left with the sense that something important was missing. Almost like the concept of the 'elephant in the room'—something so big I didn't notice it—**love** was my elephant. You could say love is all around!

Some elements of what we refer to as love affect us almost every day, shaping how we relate to ourselves and others. In the context of sport, performing arts, and life, we might ask: *"What's love got to do with it?"* Let's turn to the late Tina Turner, who suggests it might just be "a second-hand emotion."

The music and film industries, literature, poetry, storytelling, religion, spirituality, family, and sex—all place love at the heart of human experience. But what is love, really? That essential ingredient in life's recipe—the force behind our search for happiness, contentment, purpose, desire, and procreation?

How do we express love? Are we clear in its meaning, its intention, and its purpose in our communication? Ultimately, how does love effect our performance in daily life, the arts, and sport?

Is love an 'elephant in the room' for you? Let's reflect on what we truly feel.

In this concluding chapter, I am addressing the use of 'love' in the same way I have explored 'trauma,' 'depression,' and 'anxiety'—highlighting the need for greater clarity and a shared understanding of its meaning. To communicate effectively and meaningfully, we must establish some fundamental agreement on what 'love' intends to represent. Like 'self-esteem,' 'love' is a deeply significant topic, yet often misunderstood, especially in relationship. My observation is that people make assumptions about it, leading to miscommunication and, at times, deep misunderstandings.

To bring depth and perspective, I have 'invited' prominent voices to contribute their insights, offering a broader understanding of 'love' beyond a 'second-hand emotion.' These perspectives help us explore how we use, feel, and communicate love in modern life. Unsurprisingly—and thankfully—love is multidimensional.

During the Covid-19 lockdowns from March 2020 to March 2022, many young people reported feeling 'depressed.' Upon reflection, however, they were not necessarily 'clinically depressed' but instead experiencing a lower mood. Their emotional state may have been 'depressed'—pushed down—without meeting the criteria for clinical depression, though for some, the inability to function normally did make life unmanageable.

Similarly, 'anxiety' is a natural and essential response to life's challenges. It only becomes dysfunctional when it spirals into 'hyperarousal,' persistent worry, or catastrophizing—where the mind constantly anticipates the worst.

Despite the hardships brought by the Covid-19 pandemic, it was a defining, generational, and global experience. It reshaped the way we lived, worked, and connected. For many, it also forced families to spend more time together—for better or worse, in richness or in hardship—deepening relationships or, in some cases, straining them.

When we say, "I love you" or when we do something 'loving,' what does that really mean? Love is a major component of early attachment—in relationships, friendships, partnerships, teams, between coaches and athletes, musicians, and their mentors. It is all-pervasive. As the Troggs shared in 1967, *"Love is all around us."* So, in just a few pages, let's aim to understand it more clearly and refine our communication to enhance our experiences—not just in sport and the performing arts, but in life itself. Which came first: the love or the performance?

The APA defines **'love'** as "a complex emotion involving strong feelings of affection and tenderness for the love 'object', pleasurable sensations in their presence, devotion to their well-being, and sensitivity to their reactions to oneself. Although love takes many forms, including concern for one's fellow humans (brotherly love), parental love, erotic love, self-love, and identification with the totality of being (love of God), the triangular theory of love proposes three essential components: passion, intimacy, and commitment. Social psychological research in this area has focused largely on passionate love, in which sexual desire and excitement predominate, and companionate love, in which passion is relatively weak and commitment is strong." (15.11.2023 dictionary.apa.org)

To explore this further, I turn to Alain de Botton—honorary architect, writer, philosopher, and speaker—whose work offers a psychological perspective on love. His focus has been on helping us understand and respond to the complexities of love, including in *The School of Life* (54). Early in his career, he distinguished between 'romantic love'—often idealized and fleeting—and a more mature love, which requires life skills, knowledge, and understanding, particularly in communication.

In de Botton's *The Course of Love* (97), he illustrates this through the story of a couple married for 15 years who, during couples therapy, discovered they both held the same belief: that they were "not good enough for each other." For over a decade, this unspoken assumption shaped their interactions and, perhaps, even influenced their children—despite being entirely unfounded when tested against reality. How woeful is that? And what does it reveal about their communication, their belief systems, and the way we, too, construct our own narratives about love?

So often, in my experience, athletes, musicians, and parents tell me they have never felt 'good enough.' Yet, in any relationship, all we truly need to be is *good enough*—and no more.

Alain de Botton introduces a range of topics for us to consider in understanding love, drawing from various publications, but most notably from *The School of Life: An Emotional Education* (54). Rather than beginning with loving others, he argues that "self-love is the quality that determines how much we can be friends with ourselves, and day-to-day remain on our own side" (54, p. 43). Others support this view, as do I, through my concept of 'The Love Bank Account' **(WW25)**.

Similarly, de Botton highlights how the 'kindness' of another provides "the security needed to probe our inner selves constructively." He further emphasizes the importance of having someone truly 'listen' to us as we attempt to know our own minds—echoing Socrates' call to "know thyself." This role can be filled by a partner, friend, or therapist.

I often tell my clients that they cannot do this work alone. Left to their own perceptions and experiences, they will only ever see the world through their own eyes **(WW105)**. These are what we call 'blind spots'—unrecognised and subconscious elements of life. When brought to light, they become 'realisations,' from which we can begin to act differently and make new choices **(WW106)**.

I hold the view that we attract what we put out—whether this is through our energy, what others refer to as 'personality,' or our overall sense of 'being' **(WW107).** Until I discovered the *16 Personalities* framework through Exeter-based relationship 'guru' Nicky Dunn **(WW107)** (98), I was somewhat sceptical of personality theory—even as a psychologist—when it came to personality traits. I have always believed that personality is shaped more by nurture than nature (genetics). However, the depth of research conducted by the Cambridge-based company behind *16 Personalities* is impressive, offering analyses that provide a surprisingly accurate, detailed and insightful understanding of the self.

Romantic Love

What is love? Fantasy, fiction, felt, formidable, forgiving, f**king, fortuitous, friendship. The word 'love' has been used synonymously with enjoyment, enthusiasm, attachment, affection, sexual attraction, care, concern, loyalty, and devotion, etc. It is important to distinguish 'romantic love,' which has a more specific meaning. It refers to "intense attraction that involves the idealisation of the other, within an erotic context, with the expectation of enduring for some time into the future" (99).

Alain de Botton argues that "we need to learn that love is a skill rather than an enthusiasm. To correct our weaknesses and imbalances, love is a search for completion." (p6 97) This perspective is central to his work, particularly in *Essays in Love* (100) and *The Course of Love* (97). I highly recommend the latter when working with couples—each partner should have their own copy!

Romanticism is often associated with hopefulness, optimism, deep emotional connection, and the fusion of love and sex. It offers the promise of companionship and an end to loneliness, yet it often lacks practicality in truly serving both partners. De Botton suggests that, in essence, this idealistic approach does not work. Instead, he advocates for a more "psychologically mature vision"—what he terms a 'classical' approach—one that encourages us to adopt unfamiliar yet ultimately more effective attitudes toward love and relationships.

Eight Types of Love

As with many aspects of life, including architecture and the early foundations of modern medicine, the ancient Greeks identified eight distinct types of love:

1. **Eros** – Named after the god of love, Eros represents sexual passion and the foundation of physical intimacy between people.
2. **Philia** – The love found in deep friendships, including platonic relationships, as explored by Plato.
3. **Ludus** – Playful love, often evident in the excitement and early stages of attraction, where recognition of another takes on a special significance.
4. **Agape** – A universal love that extends to all humanity. This form of love, rooted in empathy, is at the heart of Christian teachings and other spiritual traditions that emphasize a higher, selfless love.
5. **Pragma** – A love of longevity and commitment, characterized by endurance, compromise, and tolerance in long-standing relationships.
6. **Philautia** – Self-love, considered a cornerstone of wellbeing. Healthy self-compassion and self-care enable us to love others. However, in its negative form, it manifests as narcissism—an obsession with oneself that often leads to controlling and toxic relationships.
7. **Storge** – Family love, the foundation of attachment, providing feelings of safety, security, and care.
8. **Mania** – Obsessive love, often found in codependent relationships, as discussed in Chapter 6 on social relationships.

The Impact of Love, Loving, and Not Loving.

Alain de Botton suggests that adult love emerges from a template—a pattern of how we could be loved that is created in childhood and is far more influential than happiness in shaping our motivations within relationships (54). He explains that love is, at its core, a search for familiarity—a longing for comfort that extends beyond simple reassurance and tenderness. It also carries the imprint of past wounds, triggering feelings of abandonment and humiliation. These patterns, whether we recognise them or not, shape the challenges we face in adult relationships.

Natasha Lunn, in *Conversations on Love* (101), observes that we expect so much from love but devote so little time to understanding it. She highlights how individuals often lose confidence in relationships by neglecting their own needs and desires while trying to second-guess a partner's **(WW108)**. She concludes that we often seek answers to the complexities of adulthood and intimacy in each other, reflecting and mirroring one another **(WW103)**. Like de Botton, Lunn suggests that resolving these issues requires courage, self-understanding, perhaps a little loneliness, and a great deal of self-responsibility.

In expanding her definition of love, Lunn finds its presence not just in romance but in friendship, parenting, intergenerational connections, work, cooking, and creativity. Her personal journey to understand love led her inward—to self-reflection and self-acceptance. She emphasises that self-love involves recognising that all human beings have their flaws and imperfections.

Lunn also acknowledges that love inherently involves loss and grief, particularly shaped by our early attachment experiences—our need to feel safe, secure, and loved. These formative experiences influence many of our relationships, especially those that are close and intimate. She concludes that the capacity to love is achieved by overcoming narcissism, as it requires us to truly see other people, their lives, and their feelings as real.

Definitions and perspectives on love would not be complete, in my view, without considering Harville Hendrix, the author of *Getting the Love You Want* (55). This guide for couples remains highly relevant even in the 2020s. Hendrix describes 'romantic love' as an unconscious form of communication between two people, shaped by the emotional patterns and lessons we have inherited from our parents—what can be understood as intergenerational trauma.

He introduces the concept of a 'conscious marriage' or relationship, outlining key characteristics that support its development. His work serves as a practical guide, offering insights that remain valuable in today's world. At its core, a conscious relationship requires the ability to truly listen, to seek understanding, and to build respect and trust through intentional and meaningful communication.

In my own early searches—indeed, my 'awakening' in the 1990s—I produced an anthology of poems titled *Love Is...* I hope it captures some of love's diversity.

LOVE IS...

Love is a passion too strong to hold,
allowing persona to develop, mould.

Love is the feeling deep in the breast,
courageous dealing, an ultimate test.

Love is forgiveness when it hurts most,
celebrating life, upholding a toast.

Love is cherishing all you've got,
sharing with others, accepting your lot.

Love is allowing freedom of speech,
sailing with the wind, reaching the beach.

Love is believing when most are in doubt,
being prepared like a good Boy Scout.

Love is ingenious, a human light,
a pathway to joy, worldly insight.

Love is pleasure, pleasing to do,
an expression of feeling—I love you.

Love is for many a wondrous thing,
healing the hate, soothing the sting.

Love is changing the world and yourself,
respecting Earth, restoring its wealth.

Love is momentus, a spiritual flame,
worshipping God whatever his name.

Love challenges our existence, heaven, and earth—
the story of Christmas, the holy rebirth.

Love is contemplation, thoughts of now,
peaceful thinking, understanding, know-how.

Love is what makes us that different being,
giving us vision, directing our seeing.

Love is mightier than the sword, stronger than the
bow, more defiant than anger, wiser to know.

Love is endless... infinite in time.
Love is yours. Love is mine.

— *Phil Johnson, 1996*

Learning to Love

Alain de Botton, in describing the therapeutic journey of love and relationships, identifies five fundamental 'anchors': non-defensiveness, vulnerability, tenderness, a therapeutic attitude, and enthusiasm (102). While he previously emphasized that love is a skill, he also encourages us to go beyond romanticism and embrace the acceptance of our imperfections.

I believe that self-acceptance is one of life's greatest challenges, and it aligns closely with these ways of being. De Botton also highlights a key insight about trauma: in the present moment, what upsets us most often stems from our own historical disappointments and embarrassments. These past wounds are subconsciously triggered, leading to a response that is disproportionate to the actual situation.

This understanding aligns with the principles of the EMDR and Brainspotting communities. However, recognizing these patterns in ourselves is not always easy.

Love Relationships and Adult Attachment Styles—Intimacy Beyond Self

Adults exhibit patterns of attachment to their romantic and other partners that mirror the attachment styles formed in childhood with their parents. Recognising one's attachment style in adult relationships can provide valuable insight into the challenges that arise and help navigate difficulties more effectively.

There are three primary attachment styles, which parallel those found in children. According to Levine and Heller (103), these are:

1. Secure
2. Anxious
3. Avoidant

Each attachment style influences key aspects of a relationship, including:

- Views on intimacy and togetherness
- Approaches to conflict resolution
- Attitudes toward sex
- Expectations of a partner and the relationship
- Ability to communicate needs and desires.

Research suggests that just over 50% of people have a secure attachment style, while approximately 25% are avoidant, 20% are anxious, and around 5% display a combination of anxious and avoidant traits.

Individuals with a secure attachment style tend to accommodate their partner's needs and foster a balanced, supportive relationship. Those with an anxious attachment style often seek greater intimacy and respond positively to direct and open communication. In contrast, those with an avoidant attachment style may feel uncomfortable with emotional disclosure and increased intimacy, often reacting with defensiveness.

Attachment needs are legitimate and an inherent part of our genetic makeup. When balanced, they contribute to self-confidence and authenticity, ultimately enriching our relationships and personal growth.

We now turn to how 'love' takes place in action. This happens within families—though not in all— and in various kinds of relationships, including marriage, intimate partnerships, friendships, and professional connections. Love can also be present in the relationships we form with work colleagues, with whom we may spend a significant part of our lives, and in the deep sense of care and responsibility that teachers have for their students and coaches for their athletes.

Alain de Botton reflects on the complexities of love, stating that, "To fall in love with someone is such a personal, spontaneous process, yet the history of humanity shows us so many varied approaches to love, different assumptions about how couples are supposed to get together, and so many distinctive ways of interpreting our feelings" (97 p. 129).

Rather than 'falling' in love, perhaps we should consider the idea of 'expanding' the love we already have and directing it in particular ways. This perspective suggests that by not 'falling,' we may feel safer, with hearts that remain open and accessible. In this state, respect, trust, and tenderness can be mirrored mutually and with ease. When love does not flow in this way, it signals that something deeper is at play.

Spiritual Dimensions Emerging

I turn next to Malcolm Stern and Sujata Bristow, two psychotherapists and authors of *The Courage to Love* (104). I completed a synopsis of their book for my clients working through relationship issues. Though written over 20 years ago, their insights remain relevant, embracing modern perspectives and, like de Botton, advocating for a love that transcends 'romantic idealism' and matures into a deeper, more conscious connection. In their view, love has a definitive spiritual dimension.

Their focus is on relationships, which is where I believe the 'action of love' is most evident—how love is expressed in our connections with others, not simply within ourselves. As human beings, we are not designed to exist in isolation; we are meant to be 'attached' to others. This fundamental aspect of the human condition drives us to seek and practice loving connections, fostering intimacy and shared experience.

At its core, love is the 'yearning to be met'—to experience union and togetherness in a way that allows the barriers of self-protection to be lowered. In an intimate relationship, the wounds we have accumulated along the way can be healed and, ultimately, transcended. It is love that serves as the connecting force and, in many ways, an integral part of 'excellence' itself.

In describing the meeting of two people in close friendship or relationship, it becomes a doorway to divinity. Falling in love is often equated to a spiritual experience—one that is 'godlike' in its depth and reverence. It also carries an element of mystery, leading to the soulful question: why this person, and why me? It is believed that at birth, we are all 'divine,' and whether knowingly or unknowingly, we honour and respect that divinity in our connections and unions.

There are frequent references to meeting our 'soulmate.' For a relationship to grow, there must be willingness on both sides, along with the respect and developing trust that Harville Hendrix speaks of—just as Jimi Hendrix expresses through his music.

The capacity to love another person is often considered to be rooted in how we 'love' ourselves. The Beatles capture this sentiment in their lyrics, *"And in the end, the love you make is equal to the love you take"* from their 1969 song *The End*. It is interesting to note how The Beatles, through their connection to the Maharishi Yoga Academy in Rishikesh, India, became leaders in exploring the transformative power of spiritual practice. Salzman describes Transcendental Meditation as something that "naturally takes the mind beyond the present level of experience to eventually reach a pure state of awareness" (105) **(WW109)**. This experience profoundly shaped The Beatles' relationships—

with each other, in their intimate partnerships, and in their evolving worldview—moving them away from materialism and toward the Buddhist principles of detachment and inner peace. They sought to share what they considered to be the 'power' of spiritual practice, distancing themselves from organised religion in favour of a more direct spiritual connection.

The Spiritual Dimensions of Love and Connection

Spirituality is considered to be "a quality that goes beyond religious affiliation, that strives for inspiration, reverence, awe, meaning, and purpose, even in those who do not believe in any 'god.' The spiritual dimension tries to be in harmony with the universe, strives for answers about the infinite, and comes essentially into focus in times of emotional stress, physical (and mental) illness, loss, bereavement, and death." (106)

Definitions of spirituality describe it as encompassing a personal, interpersonal, and transpersonal context within four interrelated domains:

- **Higher power or universal intelligence** – A belief in a higher power or universal intelligence, which may or may not include formal religious practices.
- **Self-discovery** – The spiritual journey begins with inner reflection and a search for meaning and purpose.
- **Relationship**s – An integral connection to others based on deep respect and reverence for life.
- **Eco-awareness** – A profound connection to nature, based on a deep respect and reverence for the environment and a belief that the Earth is sacred.

These four domains are interconnected and interdependent, forming a dynamic relationship.

In their book *Spiritual Dimensions of Ageing*, Malcolm Johnson and Joanna Walker summarise that "the human spirit is capable of responding to the whole range of emotions and experiences that form the lifespan of an individual. It is the agency (experience) that registers emotions across the whole spectrum; from the elation of joy, wondrous experiences, events, achievements, and relationships, to the despair and degradation of profound pain and loss" (108).

So, what's love got to do with it? When all you need is love, and seemingly the courage to do it and be it, love becomes a guiding force, despite the challenges life presents. As I mention earlier in the book, it is noticeable how many professional footballers enter marriage and long-term relationships in their early 20s, often with partners they have known since childhood or from their neighbourhood—someone who understands them and shares a common background. This provides them with a sense of security, trust, and the mutual support of family, in other words, a positive 'attachment.'

Quoted in Johnson and Walker's book on spirituality and ageing, Robert C. Atchley describes spiritual development as a process that "takes the perceptions of our experience in the conscious, forms self-transcendence, goes beyond personal (me), contemplation, the action of looking thoughtfully at something for a long time, and direct experience of the sacred" (106).

In this final exploration of how spirituality deepens our experience of ourselves, we see how it connects us with our personal history and the broader universal self. This midbrain connection with the 'Third Eye' and the pineal gland functions as an internalised radar system, receiving information much like our 'gut feeling.' When activated, the pineal and pituitary glands work

CHAPTER 10: DEVELOPING EXCELLENCE

in harmony, representing the balance of masculine and feminine energies. A belief forwarded by Descartes.

Located in the midbrain, eye positioning and memorised spots in the brain coincide, sending messages to the body. For Brainspotting therapists and their clients, this represents a key point of activation. When Brainspotting and other practitioners refer to using their intuition in sessions, it is part of this neurological system. Additionally, even when working with images and visualisation with the 'eyes closed,' the brain still moves the eyes into position as if they were open. The pineal gland is considered an integral part of this system and is also affected in cases of brain damage, such as concussion. Beyond its physiological role, it is also a mechanism through which we 'connect' with others—energetically, emotionally, and relationally.

My aim here has been to expand our understanding of the many ways in which we 'love'—with whom, in what contexts, and with what depth of meaning and humanity. I have not only presented the philosophy of a 'person-first' approach in supporting individuals toward high performance but also highlighted the deep interconnections between early attachment to primary caregivers and later relationships with others. This extends to interactions with coaches, teachers, instructors, teammates, physiotherapists, sport scientists, fans, media personnel, intimate partners, children, and family—relationships that shape who we become in adulthood.

In nature, we see a fascinating example of connection in honeybee colonies. The queen bee emits a pheromone— a scent that permeates the hive, keeping all 30,000+ bees in harmony. In a sense, this could be considered a form of 'love'—an invisible force that binds individuals together. Scientific study also confirms the 'Mother Tree' in a forest interlinks with all other trees within their 'copse', communicating like an under-World Wide Web (110).

In the same way, love is all-pervasive in human life. It surrounds us, whether we are conscious of it or not. Like the queen bee's role in maintaining connection within the hive, love fosters relationships, supports personal growth, and strengthens bonds. Coaches, for instance, show a form of love toward their athletes, dancers, or violinists—not a romantic love, but a profound sense of care and professional commitment. Their goal is not only personal achievement but the success and wellbeing of those they guide, whether in the classroom, on the football pitch, in the auditorium, the stadium, or the swimming pool.

Parents do the same, believing that their support—however it is expressed—will benefit their children. Yet, just as love connects, its absence creates distance. Some remain disconnected, disinterested, or avoidant in relationships, often mirroring the patterns they experienced in their own upbringing.

SUMMARY:
CONCLUSIONS / REALISATIONS

I trust that in this journey of 'learning,' you can now see how triangular connections—between coach, athlete, and parent—interact and shape each other. These dynamics unfold throughout the lifespan of sport and artistic performance, mirroring the challenges of human life itself. To navigate these complexities, we need both understanding and effective resolution.

The development of Brainspotting as a brain-body trauma therapy is as world-class as the very athletes it helps—desensitising them from broken dreams, fractured bones, concussions, strained parental relationships, and dysfunctional attachments. While the focus may be on performance and the performer, my observations over decades confirm that approximately 75% of performance issues stem from life experiences beyond the sporting or artistic arena (**WW44**). This is why addressing these broader experiences is crucial, not just for peak performance but for a fulfilling life.

Thankfully, a revolutionary way of resolving these psychological challenges now exists—one that works naturally with the body's own healing processes. The journey begins in the body, first as a physiological response, then as an emotional imprint, and only later as a cognitive thought. This reverses the traditional 'top-down' approach of psychology. Rather than trying to solve these issues through conscious thought alone, true resolution comes by engaging the deeper subcortical brain—where memory and history are stored. The amygdala, hippocampus, and hypothalamus hold the roots of disappointment, embarrassment, humiliation, and injury. Through eye positioning, bilateral sounds, and a deep understanding of human behaviour and relationships, lasting resolution and transformation become not just possible, but inevitable.

Spiritual Psychology (which we call "transpersonal psychology" at Meridian University) is a discipline that focuses on the understanding of the human psyche and its relationship with the spiritual dimension. Spiritual psychologists believe in holistic approaches to healing, which includes the integration of mind, body, and spirit into one's daily life. From past experiences, we understand that our thoughts, emotions, and beliefs can impact our physical health by influencing it on a cellular level. (111)

At your fingertips—and through your eyes—are **111 Winning Ways** to enhance your life, artistry, and sport. In numerology, 111 represents opportunity, good fortune, and achievement (109). What a coincidence! These insights, along with additional resources available through social media, offer a pathway to natural, safe, and effective healing.

Above all, recognise that **we ourselves are our greatest resource**. The love we give, receive, and experience—both within ourselves and in connection with others—determines our true success. When we embrace this truth, we are the real winners, no matter the circumstances.

As Al Pacino says, *"That's life... now what are you going to do about it?"*

ACRONYMS

ABCDE: Airway, breathing, circulation, disability and exposure

ADHD: Attention-deficit/hyperactivity disorder

AASP: Association of Applied Sport Psychology

ANIA: Arousal, Numbing, Intrusion, Avoidance

APA: American Psychological Association

BAPAM: British Association for Performing Arts Medicine

BCFC: Bristol City Football Club

BDD: Body dysmorphic disorder

BPS: British Psychological Society

CFS: Chronic fatigue syndrome

CRT5: Concussion Recognition Tool

CSW: Clinical Social Worker

DSM-5: Diagnostic and Statistical Manual of Mental Disorders

DOMS: Delayed-onset muscle soreness

EMDR: Eye Movement Desensitisation and Reprocessing

ENS: Enteric nervous system

FC: Football Club

HPCP: Health Care Professions Council

NICE: National Institute of Clinical Excellence

OCD: Obsessive-compulsive disorder

PDSD: Prolonged duress stress disorder

PNS: Peripheral nervous system

PSNS: Parasympathetic nervous system

REM: Rapid eye movement

SCAT5: Sport Concussion Assessment Tool

SNS: Sympathetic nervous system
SSRI: Serotonin-specific reuptake inhibitors
SFT: Systemic Family Therapy
SUDS: Subjective Units of Distress
STM: Short Term Memory
TA: Transactional Analysis
THC: Tetrahydrocannabinol
UEFA: Union of European Football Associations
VAR: Video assistant referee
WW: Winning Way

GLOSSARY

Abandonment: Emotional abandonment is a subjective emotional state in which people feel undesired, left behind, insecure, or discarded.

Aneurysm: An aneurysm is a bulge in the wall of an artery. Aneurysms form when there's a weak area in the artery wall. Untreated aneurysms can burst open, leading to internal bleeding. They can also cause blood clots that block the flow of blood in your artery. Depending on the location of the aneurysm, a rupture or clot can be life-threatening.

Assertiveness: Ability to represent ourselves positively in the world.

Attunement: The reactiveness we have to another person. It is the process by which we form relationships.

Avoidance: Of people, places, situations, and events.

Bilateral: Sounds which move consistently from left to right, and right to left using headphones, supports the release of trauma, and enables a state of calm.

Bilateral Sounds: Musical and Non-verbal Sounds moving from one hemisphere to the other.

Body Spotting: A Physical touch on the body linked to am activated physiological response in trauma memory.

Boundary: The limits and rules that define what you're comfortable with and how you want others to treat you. They can be physical, emotional, sexual, or workplace related.

Brainspotting Terminology: Eye Positions: Gazing, Proximity, Body Spotting.

Countertransference: In psychoanalytic theory, countertransference occurs when the therapist projects their own unresolved conflicts onto the client.

Dissociative: A pattern of behaviour consistent with dissociative disorders, as evidenced by disruption in the normal integrative functions of consciousness, memory, or perception of the environment.

Dual Brainspotting: Brainspotting working with two people at once.

Dysregulated: Any excessive or otherwise poorly managed mechanism or response. For example, emotional dysregulation is an extreme or inappropriate emotional response to a situation, it may be associated with bipolar disorders, borderline personality disorder, autism spectrum disorder, psychological trauma, or brain injury.

Eastern Philosophy: Philosophical schools of thought that originated in the Middle East or Asia.

Gazespotting: A naturalised position of looking.

Grief: The anguish experienced after significant loss, usually the death of a beloved person. Grief often includes physiological distress, separation anxiety, confusion, yearning, obsessive dwelling on the past, and apprehension about the future. Intense grief can become life-threatening through disruption of the immune system, self-neglect, and suicidal thoughts. Grief may also take the form of regret for something lost, remorse for something done, or sorrow for a mishap to oneself.

Hyper arousal: Brain generated energy through the release of cortisol, and adrenaline released through the SNS Sympathetic Nervous System in Fight and Flight Responses.

Imagework: A system of using imagination to access the subconscious brain to heal past issues.

Inculcate: Implanting, instilling, meaning to introduce into the mind.

Initial Insomnia: Finding it difficult to get off to sleep.

Intrusive Thoughts: An element of trauma including flashback memories, negative self-talk, and dream state.

Loss / Grief: Grief is the emotional response to loss, and it's a natural part of life. It can be a complex and personal experience that affects people in different ways.

Meritocracy: The political philosophy in which political influence and power is concentrated in those with "merit", according to the intellectual talent and achievement of the individual. Michael Young 1958.

MRI Scan: Magnetic resonance imaging (MRI) is a type of scan that uses strong magnetic fields and radio waves to produce detailed images of the inside of the body.

No Assumptions: Remaining in a state of neutrality on and non-judgement.

Numbing: Suppression of unwanted negative emotions, often depressive in nature.

Nurture: The totality of environmental factors that influence the development and behavior of a person, particularly sociocultural and ecological factors such as family attributes, parental child-rearing practices, and economic status.

Panic Attack: An experienced overwhelm of overloaded information from the right to the left hemisphere of the brain.

Paradigm shift: A paradigm shift is defined as an important change that happens when the usual way of thinking about or doing something is replaced by a new and different way.

Paraphrasing: Retelling information given to use in our 'own words'.

Passive aggression: A way of expressing negative feelings, such as anger or annoyance, indirectly instead of directly. Passive-aggressive behaviours are often difficult to identify and can sabotage relationships at home and at work.

Proximity: Moving a pointer or other device closer to the eyes, or away, to induce intensity of release, or calmness in Brainspotting desensitisation and release.

Resource Spotting: An Eye Position linked to a state of calm, pleasure, security.

Self Sabotage: Harming self-opportunities in a form of denial of self. Not self-loving.

Silence WAIT: Why **A**m **I T**alking?

SUDS: The Subjective Units of Disturbance Scale.

Symptomatic plasticity: The brain's ability to reorganize and adapt its structure and function in response to experiences, injuries, or disease, which can manifest as changes in symptoms or behaviours.

Triggered memories: Historical memories found and searched by the subconscious brain activating physical and emotional feelings.

Validated: Representation of words or actions we have given.

Victimisation: The act of treating someone unfairly or being treated unfairly. It can be based on a person's race, sex, beliefs, or other characteristics.

REFERENCES

PREFACE

1. Office for National Statistics. *Divorce Statistics*, 2002–2012. UK Government.
2. Wolfrum, Gerhard. *The Power of Brainspotting*. Asanger Verlag GmbH, 2018.
3. Grand, David. *Brainspotting: The Revolutionary New Therapy for Rapid and Effective Change*. Sounds True, 2013.
4. Swart, Tara. *The Source: Open Your Mind, Change your Life*. Penguin, 2020.
5. American Psychological Association. https://dictionary.apa. org/multidimensionality

CHAPTER 1: INTRODUCTION TO WINNING WAYS

6. Ericsson, K. Anders. "The Role of Deliberate Practice in the Acquisition of Expert Performance." *Psychological Review* 100, no. 3 (1993): 363–406.
7. Green, Chris. *Every Boy's Dream*. A & C Black, 2009.
8. Kane, Harry. "Grassroots Story." *The Times*, March 2023.
9. Specht, Harry, and Anne Vickery. *Integrating Social Work Methods*. George Allen & Unwin, 1977.
10. Mitchell, Joni. *Woodstock*. Track 6 on *Ladies of the Canyon*. Warner Records, 1970.

11. The School of Life. *The Good Enough Parent: How to Raise Contented, Interesting, and Resilient Children.* Edited by Alain de Botton. The School of Life, 2022.

12. Gunston, Jo. https://www.olympics.com/en/news/max-whitlock-mental-health-struggle-paris-2024 17 February 2023.

13. Grand, David. *World Brainspotting Conference 2021 USA.* Dog Ear Publishing, 2021.

14. Henriques, Gregg. "Seven Approaches to Finding the Truth." *Psychology Today,* September 7, 2020.

15. Kalinik, Eve. *Be Good to Your Gut.* Piatkus, 2017.

16. British Psychological Society. "What Is Psychology?" *BPS.org. uk,* 2024.

17. Ruiz, Don Miguel. *The Four Agreements: A Practical Guide to Personal Freedom.* Amber-Allen, 1997.

18. Goldberg, Alan, and David Grand. *Your Brain in Sport.* Dog Ear Publishing, 2011.

19. Young, Michael. *The Rise of the Meritocracy.* Pelican Publications, 1958.

CHAPTER 2: PHIL-OSOPHY

20. de Botton, Alain. *The Consolations of Philosophy.* Penguin Books, 2021.

21. Deci, Edward L., and Richard M. Ryan, eds. *Handbook of Self-Determination Research.* University of Rochester Press, 2002.

22. Gardner, Frank L., and Zella E. Moore. *Clinical Sport Psychology.* Human Kinetics, 2006.

CHAPTER 3: RELATIONSHIPS AND PERFORMANCE

23. Gervis, Misia. "Coach-Athlete Triad." Unpublished manuscript, 2011.

24. Robinson, Ken. "Group Think." *British Journal of Psychotherapy*, Michael Balint Lecture, 2015.

CHAPTER 4: DEVELOPING A POSITIVE IDENTITY OF SELF

25. Delaney, C. H. "The Rites of Passage: Sociology of Adolescence." *British Journal of Sociology*, 1995.

26. O'Rourke, S., et al. The Development of Cognitive and Emotional Maturity in Adolescence and Its Relevance in Judicial Contexts. The Scottish Sentencing Council, 2020.

27. Rogers, Carl R. On Becoming a Person: A Therapist's View of Psychotherapy. Constable, 1961.

28. Deci, Edward L., and Richard M. Ryan, eds. Handbook of Self-Determination Research. University of Rochester Press, 2002.

29. Jones, Graham, and Adrian Moorhouse. Developing Mental Toughness. How To Books, 2007.

30. Hagger, Martin S., and Nikos L. D. Chatzisarantis. Intrinsic Motivation and Self-Determination in Exercise and Sport. Human Kinetics, 2007.

31. Tafarodi, R. W. "Self-Liking and Self-Competence as Dimensions of Global Self-Esteem." Journal of Personality Assessment 65, no. 2 (1995): 332–342.

32. Rogers, Clint G. Ancient Secrets of a Master Healer: A Western Skeptic, an Eastern Master, and Life's Greatest Secrets. Wisdom of the World Press, 2020.

33. van der Kolk, Bessel. The Body Keeps the Score. Penguin, 2017.

34. Wolpe, Joseph. "Psychotherapy by Reciprocal Inhibition." Journal of Psychotherapy, 1958.

35. Nicholson, Paula, and Rowan Bayne. Applied Psychology for Social Workers. Macmillan, 1990.

36. Bruce, Steve, and Steven Yearley. The SAGE Dictionary of Sociology. Sage, 2006.

37. Giges, Bert. My Work in Sport Psychology. CreateSpace Publishing, 2016.

38. Williams, Jean, Linda Bunker, and Nathan Zinsser. Applied Sport Psychology. McGraw Hill, 2006.

39. Higham, Alistair, Chris Harwood, and Andy Cale. Momentum in Soccer: Controlling the Game. Human Kinetics, 2005.

40. Weinberg, Robert S., and Daniel Gould. Foundations of Sport and Exercise Psychology. 5th ed. Human Kinetics, 2011.

41. Berne, Eric. Games People Play: Transactional Analysis in Psychotherapy. Profile Books, 1966.

42. Harris, Thomas A. I'm OK—You're OK. Harper & Row, 1967.

CHAPTER 5: LOST ADOLESCENCE AND PERFORMANCE LIFESTYLE

43. Byrne, D. G., Davenport, S. C., and Mazanov, J. "Profiles of Adolescent Stress: The Development of the Adolescent Stress Questionnaire (ASQ)." Journal of Adolescence 30, no. 3 (2007): 393–416.

44. Tanti, Chris, Arthur A. Stukas, Michael J. Halloran, and Margaret Foddy. "Social Identity Change: Shifts in Social Identity During Adolescence." Journal of Adolescence 34, no. 3 (2011): 555–67.

45. Hackney, Anthony C., Silas N. Pearman III, and Janice M. Nowacki. "Physiological Profiles of Overtrained and Stale

Athletes: A Review." *Journal of Applied Sport Psychology* 2, no. 1 (1990): 21–33.

46. Cacioppo, John T., and William Patrick. *Loneliness: Human Nature and the Need for Social Connection.* W. W. Norton & Co., 2008.

47. Mastrich, Jim. *Really Winning: Using Sports to Develop Character and Integrity in Our Boys.* St. Martin's Press, 2002.

48. Real, Terrence. *I Don't Want to Talk About It: Overcoming the Secret Legacy of Male Depression.* Scribner, 1997.

49. Markway, Barbara, and Celia Ampel. *The Self-Confidence Workbook: A Guide to Overcoming Self-Doubt and Improving Self-Esteem.* Callisto Media, 2018.

50. Agassi, Andre. *Open: An Autobiography.* Knopf Publishing Group, 2009.

51. Efrati, Yaniv, and Yair Amichai-Hamburger. "Adolescents Who Solely Engage in Online Sexual Experiences Are at Higher Risk for Compulsive Sexual Behaviours." *Addictive Behaviours* 118 (2021): 106874.

52. Thompson, Ron A., and Roberta Trattner Sherman. *Eating Disorders in Sport.* Routledge, 2010.

53. Giordano, Simona. *Exercise and Eating Disorders: An Ethical and Legal Analysis.* Routledge, 2010.

CHAPTER 6: PERFORMANCE ISSUES

54. The School of Life. *The School of Life: An Emotional Education.* Introduction by Alain de Botton. The School of Life, 2020.

55. Hendrix, Harville. *Getting the Love You Want.* Pocket Books, 1993.

56. Sleep Apnoea Trust Association. *Sleep Apnoea Trust Association*. 2020. https://sleep-apnoea-trust.org/.

57. Gatens, Katie. 'Wake up to the wonders of a broken night's sleep'. *The Sunday Times*, 20 February 2022. https://www.thetimes.com/article/af635044-91a1-11ec-ba83-35d92f80c266.

58. Australian Institute of Sport. *Concussion in Sport Australia Position Statement*. February 2019. https://www.sportaus.gov.au/__data/assets/pdf_file/0005/683501/February_2019_-_Concussion_Position_Statement_AC.pdf.

59. StopBullying.gov. "What Is Bullying?" U.S. Department of Health and Human Services. Accessed January 10, 2025. https://www.stopbullying.gov/bullying/what-is-bullying.

60. Yahya, Nurul Hayat, and Hajar Abdul Rahim. "Linguistic Markers of Depression: Insights from English-Language Tweets Before and During the COVID-19 Pandemic." *Language and Health* 1, no. 2 (2023): 36–55.

61. BBC Radio 4. "Talking a Good Game." *Word of Mouth*. Aired July 24, 2012. https://www.bbc.co.uk/programmes/b01lodp4.

62. Syed, Matthew. "Narcissistic leader Mourinho out of touch with millennial footballers" *The Times*, March 21, 2018.

63. Jowett, Sophia. "The Coach–Athlete Partnership." *The Psychologist* 18, no. 7 (2005): 412–415.

64. Any Given Sunday. Directed by Oliver Stone. Warner Bros., 1999.

65. Northouse, Peter G. *Leadership: Theory and Practice*. Sage Publications, 2001.

66. Cotterill, Stewart. *Team Psychology in Sports: Theory and Practice*. Routledge, 2012.

67. Walker, Sam. *The Captain Class: The Hidden Force That Creates the World's Greatest Teams*. Random House, 2017.

68. Covey, Stephen R. *The 7 Habits of Highly Effective People.* Fireside, 1989.

69. British Psychological Society. "Definition of Psychology." *British Psychological Society,* 2024. https://www.bps.org.uk.

70. Whyte, Anne. *The Whyte Review: An Independent Review into Gymnastics in the UK.* Commissioned by UK Sport and Sport England, June 2022. https://www.sportengland.org/guidance-and-support/safeguarding/whyte-review.

71. Johnson, Phil, David Grand, and Allan Goldberg. "Sport Trauma." Presented at the *International Conference of Sport Psychology,* Liverpool, 2012.

72. Johnson, Phil, and Stewart Cotterill. "Comfort Zones in Sport Performance." Presented at the *British Psychological Society Conference,* 2010.

73. Hewstone, Miles, Wolfgang Stroebe, and Klaus Jonas, eds. *An Introduction to Social Psychology.* 4th ed. Wiley-Blackwell, 2008.

74. Hawton, Keith, and Kees van Heeringen. "Suicide." *The Lancet* 373, no. 9672 (2009): 1372–1381.

75. Ratcliffe, Susan, ed. *Oxford Essential Quotations.* 4th ed. Oxford University Press, 2016.

76. Bacon, Victoria L., B. Lerner, D. Trembley, and M. Seestedt. "Substance Abuse." In *Applying Sport Psychology: Four Perspectives,* edited by J. Taylor and G. S. Wilson, 229–247. Human Kinetics, 2005.

77. Goodman, Aviel. "Addiction: Definition and Implications." *British Journal of Addiction* 85, no. 11 (1990): 1403–1408.

78. American Psychiatric Association. *Diagnostic and Statistical Manual of Mental Disorders. 5th ed.* American Psychiatric Association, 2013.

79. Grange, Pippa, and John H. Kerr. "Physical Aggression in Australian Football: A Qualitative Study of Elite Athletes." *Psychology of Sport and Exercise* 11, no. 1 (2010): 36–43.

80. Brackenridge, Celia. *Understanding and Preventing Sexual Abuse in Sport*. Psychology Press, 2001.

81. American Psychological Association, OCD updated 15.11.2023 dictionary@apa.org.

82. Emotional Abuse: Journal of Crime and Justice Vol 11, Family Violence 1989 p219–261 University of Chicago Press.

83. Clark, David M., and Aaron T. Beck. *Cognitive Therapy of Anxiety Disorders: Science and Practice*. Guilford Press, 2010.

CHAPTER 7: PSYCHOLOGICAL APPROACHES AND INTERVENTIONS

84. Lavallee, David, and Paul Wylleman. *Career Transitions in Sport: International Perspectives*. FIT Publishing, 2019. In Routledge Encyclopaedia of Sport: Career Transitions, edited by Natalia B. Stambulova.

85. Levelsio. "What happens to your brain when you stop reading the news." X (formerly Twitter), August 18, 2022. https://x.com/levelsio/status/1560486485870141440.

86. Grand, David. EMDR Effectiveness in Treating Trauma. David Grand Trainings, 2017.

87. Kitzinger, Celia, and Jenny Kitzinger. "P.D.S.D.: Prolonged Duress Stress Disorder." The Psychologist, 2010.

88. Klein, Donald. The Theory of Humiliation. Unpublished manuscript, 2003.

89. Grand, David. Brainspotting: The Revolutionary New Therapy for Rapid and Effective Change. Sounds True, 2013.

90. Korngold, Esther. "Brainspotting Therapist, Countertransference." Ask Counselling,

LC, 2020. https://askcounseling.com/therapist-countertransference/#:~:text=Limbic%20 countertransference%20refers%20to%20the,are%20 receiving%20from%20the%20client.

91. Shapiro, Francine. EMDR: Eye Movement Desensitization and Reprocessing. 2nd ed. Guilford Publishing, 2001.

92. Yahya, L., and H. A. Rahim. "Linguistic Markers of Depression: Insights from English-Language Tweets Before and During the COVID-19 Pandemic." Journal of Language and Health, 2023.

93. Drummond, Tom. "Emotional Vocabulary." Tom Drummond, n.d. https://tomdrummond.com/leading-and-caring-for-children/emotion-vocabulary/.

94. "Confidence Definition." Psychology Today, 2022. https://www.psychologytoday.com/gb/basics/ confidence#:~:text=Confidence%20is%20a%20belief%20 in,feeling%20secure%20in%20that%20knowledge.

CHAPTER 8: A PSYCHOLOGICAL REVOLUTION

95. a) Salvador, Mario. *Beyond the Self: Healing Emotional Trauma and Brainspotting.* Independently published, 2017.
b). Schwartzberg, in Mario Salvador. *Beyond the Self: Healing Emotional Trauma and Brainspotting.* Independently published, 2017, p.vii.
c). Antinori, Debora, in Mario Salvador. *Beyond the Self: Healing Emotional Trauma and Brainspotting.* Independently published, 2017, p10.

96. Wolfrum G. Ed. *The Power of Brainspotting, An International Anthology.* Asanger Verlag, Kroning, Germany 2023

CHAPTER 10: DEVELOPING EXCELLENCE / LOVE / RELATIONSHIPS / INTIMACY / SPIRITUALITY / SELF-HEALING

97. De Botton, Alain. *The Course of Love*. Penguin Random House UK, 2016.
98. Dunn, Nicky. "16 Personalities." 16Personalities. https://www.16personalities.com.
99. "Romantic Love Definition." Psychology Today, February 9, 2020. https://www.psychologytoday.com.
100. De Botton, Alain. *Essays in Love*. Macmillan, 1993.
101. Lunn, Natasha. *Conversations on Love*. Viking, 2021.
102. De Botton, Alain. *A Therapeutic Journey: Lessons from the School of Life*. The School of Life, 2023.
103. Levine, Amir, and Rachel Heller. *Attached*. Penguin USA, 2019.
104. Stern, Malcolm, and Sujata Bristow. *The Courage to Love: Rekindling the Magic of Relationships*. London Bridge, 1997.
105. Salzman, Peter. *Transcendental Meditation: The Beatles in Rishikesh*. Penguin Studio Books, 2000.
106. Johnson, Malcolm. *Spirituality and Old Age*. Cambridge University, 2016.
107. Murray RB, Zentner JB. Nursing Concepts for Health Promotion. London: Prentice-Hall; 1989
108. Johnson, Malcolm, and Walker John. *Spiritual Dimensions of Ageing*. Cambridge University Press, 2016.
109. "111 Angel Number." Dictionary.com. https://www.dictionary.com/e/pop-culture/111-angel-number/.
110. Simard, Suzanne. *Finding the Mother Tree: The Uncovering of the Wisdom and Intelligence of the Forest*. Allen Lane, Canada, 2021
111. https://meridianuniversity.edu/content/what-is-spiritual-psychology

BIBLIOGRAPHY

Agassi, A. (2009). Open: An Autobiography. Knopf Publishing Group.

American Psychiatric Association. (2013). Diagnostic and Statistical Manual of Mental Disorders (5th ed.). American Psychiatric Association.

American Psychological Association. (2023, November 15). OCD updated. dictionary@apa.org.

American Psychological Association. https://dictionary.apa.org/ multidimensionality

Any Given Sunday. (1999). Directed by Oliver Stone. Warner Bros.

Australian Institute of Sport. (2019, February). Concussion in Sport Australia Position Statement. https://www.sportaus.gov.au/_data/ assets/pdf_file/0005/683501/February_2019-_Concussion_Position_ Statement_AC.pdf

Bacon, V. L., Lerner, B., Trembley, D., & Seestedt, M. (2005). Substance Abuse. In J. Taylor & G. S. Wilson (Eds.), Applying Sport Psychology: Four Perspectives (pp. 229–247). Human Kinetics.

BBC Radio 4. (2012, July 24). "Talking a Good Game." Word of Mouth. https://www.bbc.co.uk/programmes/b01l0dp4

Berne, E. (1966). Games People Play: Transactional Analysis in Psychotherapy. Profile Books.

Brackenridge, C. (2001). Understanding and Preventing Sexual Abuse in Sport. Psychology Press.

British Psychological Society. (2024). "Definition of Psychology." https://www.bps.org.uk

British Psychological Society. (2024). "What Is Psychology?" BPS. org.uk.

Bruce, S., & Yearley, S. (2006). The SAGE Dictionary of Sociology. Sage.

Byrne, D. G., Davenport, S. C., & Mazanov, J. (2007). Profiles of Adolescent Stress: The Development of the Adolescent Stress Questionnaire (ASQ). Journal of Adolescence, 30(3), 393–416.

Cacioppo, J. T., & Patrick, W. (2008). Loneliness: Human Nature and the Need for Social Connection. W. W. Norton & Co.

Clark, D. M., & Beck, A. T. (2010). Cognitive Therapy of Anxiety Disorders: Science and Practice. Guilford Press.

"Confidence Definition." (2022). Psychology Today. https://www.psychologytoday.com/gb/basics/confidence#:~:text=Confidence%20is%20a%20belief%20in,feeling%20secure%20in%20that%20knowledge

Cotterill, S. (2012). Team Psychology in Sports: Theory and Practice. Routledge.

Covey, S. R. (1989). The 7 Habits of Highly Effective People. Fireside.

de Botton, A. (1993). *Essays in Love*. Macmillan.

de Botton, A. (2016). *The Course of Love. Penguin Random House UK.*

de Botton, A. (2021). *The Consolations of Philosophy. Penguin Books.*

de Botton, A. (2023). *A Therapeutic Journey: Lessons from the School of Life. The School of Life.*

Deci, E. L., & Ryan, R. M. (Eds.). (2002). *Handbook of Self-Determination Research. University of Rochester Press.*

Delaney, C. H. (1995). *The Rites of Passage: Sociology of Adolescence. British Journal of Sociology.*

"Dictionary.com." (n.d.). *111 Angel Number. https://www.dictionary.com/e/pop-culture/111-angel-number/*

Drummond, T. (n.d.). "Emotional Vocabulary." *Tom Drummond. https://tomdrummond.com/leading-and-caring-for-children/emotion-vocabulary/*

Dunn, N. (n.d.). "16 Personalities." *16Personalities. https://www.16personalities.com*

Efrati, Y., & Amichai-Hamburger, Y. (2021). *Adolescents Who Solely Engage in Online Sexual Experiences Are at Higher Risk for Compulsive Sexual Behaviours. Addictive Behaviours, 118, 106874.*

"Emotional Abuse." (1989). *Journal of Crime and Justice, 11, Family Violence, 219–261. University of Chicago Press.*

Ericsson, K. A. (1993). *The Role of Deliberate Practice in the Acquisition of Expert Performance. Psychological Review, 100(3), 363–406.*

Gardner, F. L., & Moore, Z. E. (2006). *Clinical Sport Psychology. Human Kinetics.*

Gatens, K. 'Wake up to the wonders of a broken night's sleep'. *The Sunday Times, 20 February 2022. https://www.thetimes.com/article/af635044-91a1-11ec-ba83-35d92f80c266*

Gervis, M. (2011). *"Coach-Athlete Triad." Unpublished manuscript.*

Giges, B. (2016). *My Work in Sport Psychology. CreateSpace Publishing.*

Giordano, S. (2010). *Exercise and Eating Disorders: An Ethical and Legal Analysis. Routledge.*

Goldberg, A., & Grand, D. (2011). *Your Brain in Sport. Dog Ear Publishing.*

Goodman, A. (1990). *Addiction: Definition and Implications. British Journal of Addiction, 85(11), 1403–1408.*

Grand, D. (2013). *Brainspotting: The Revolutionary New Therapy for Rapid and Effective Change. Sounds True.*

Grand, D. (2017). *EMDR Effectiveness in Treating Trauma. David Grand Trainings.*

Grand, D. (2021). *World Brainspotting Conference 2021 USA. Dog Ear Publishing.*

Grange, P., & Kerr, J. H. (2010). Physical Aggression in Australian Football: A Qualitative Study of Elite Athletes. Psychology of Sport and Exercise, 11(1), 36–43.

Green, C. (2009). Every Boy's Dream. A & C Black.

Gunston, Jo. https://www.olympics.com/en/news/max-whitlock-mental-health-struggle-paris-2024 17 February 2023.

Hackney, A. C., Pearman, S. N., III, & Nowacki, J. M. (1990). Physiological Profiles of Overtrained and Stale Athletes: A Review. Journal of Applied Sport Psychology, 2(1), 21–33.

Hagger, M. S., & Chatzisarantis, N. L. D. (2007). Intrinsic Motivation and Self-Determination in Exercise and Sport. Human Kinetics.

Harris, T. A. (1967). I'm OK—You're OK. Harper & Row.

Hawton, K., & van Heeringen, K. (2009). Suicide. The Lancet, 373(9672), 1372–1381.

Hendrix, H. (1993). Getting the Love You Want. Pocket Books.

Henriques, G. (2020, September 7). "Seven Approaches to Finding the Truth." Psychology Today.

Hewstone, M., Stroebe, W., & Jonas, K. (Eds.). (2008). An Introduction to Social Psychology (4th ed.). Wiley-Blackwell.

Higham, A., Harwood, C., & Cale, A. (2005). Momentum in Soccer: Controlling the Game. Human Kinetics.

Johnson, M. (2016). Spirituality and Old Age. Cambridge University.

Johnson, M., & Walker, J. (2016). Spiritual Dimensions of Ageing. Cambridge University Press.

Johnson, P., & Cotterill, S. (2010). "Comfort Zones in Sport Performance." Presented at the British Psychological Society Conference.

Johnson, P., Grand, D., & Goldberg, A. (2012). "Sport Trauma." Presented at the International Conference of Sport Psychology, Liverpool.

Jones, G., & Moorhouse, A. (2007). Developing Mental Toughness. How To Books.

Jowett, S. (2005). The Coach–Athlete Partnership. The Psychologist, 18(7), 412–415.

Kalinik, E. (2017). Be Good to Your Gut. Piatkus.

Kane, H. (2023, March). "Grassroots Story." The Times.

Klein, D. (2003). The Theory of Humiliation. Unpublished manuscript.

Kitzinger, C., & Kitzinger, J. (2010). P.D.S.D.: Prolonged Duress Stress Disorder. The Psychologist.

Korngold, E. (2020). "Brainspotting Therapist, Countertransference." Ask Counselling, LC. https://askcounseling.com/therapist-countertransference/#:~:text=Limbic%20countertransference%20refers%20to%20the,are%20receiving%20from%20the%20client

Lavallee, D., & Wylleman, P. (2019). Career Transitions in Sport: International Perspectives. FIT Publishing. In N. B. Stambulova (Ed.), Routledge Encyclopaedia of Sport: Career Transitions.

Levelsio. (2022, August 18). "What happens to your brain when you stop reading the news." X (formerly Twitter). https://x.com/levelsio/status/1560486485870141440

Levine, A., & Heller, R. (2019). Attached. Penguin USA.

Lunn, N. (2021). Conversations on Love. Viking.

Markway, B., & Ampel, C. (2018). The Self-Confidence Workbook: A Guide to Overcoming Self-Doubt and Improving Self-Esteem. Callisto Media.

Mastrich, J. (2002). Really Winning: Using Sports to Develop Character and Integrity in Our Boys. St. Martin's Press.

Meridian University: https://meridianuniversity.edu/content/what-is-spiritual-psychology

Mitchell, J. (1970). Woodstock. Track 6 on Ladies of the Canyon [Album]. Warner Records.

Murray, R. B., & Zentner, J. B. (1989). Nursing Concepts for Health Promotion. Prentice-Hall.

Nicholson, P., & Bayne, R. (1990). Applied Psychology for Social Workers. Macmillan.

Northouse, P. G. (2001). Leadership: Theory and Practice. Sage Publications.

Office for National Statistics. (2002–2012). Divorce Statistics. UK Government.

O'Rourke, S., et al. (2020). The Development of Cognitive and Emotional Maturity in Adolescence and Its Relevance in Judicial Contexts. The Scottish Sentencing Council.

Ratcliffe, S. (Ed.). (2016). *Oxford Essential Quotations* (4th ed.). Oxford University Press.

Real, T. (1997). *I Don't Want to Talk About It: Overcoming the Secret Legacy of Male Depression.* Scribner.

Robinson, K. (2015). "Group Think." *British Journal of Psychotherapy, Michael Balint Lecture.*

Rogers, C. G. (2020). *Ancient Secrets of a Master Healer: A Western Skeptic, an Eastern Master, and Life's Greatest Secrets.* Wisdom of the World Press.

Rogers, C. R. (1961). *On Becoming a Person: A Therapist's View of Psychotherapy.* Constable.

"Romantic Love Definition." (2020, February 9). *Psychology Today.* https://www.psychologytoday.com

Ruiz, D. M. (1997). *The Four Agreements: A Practical Guide to Personal Freedom.* Amber-Allen.

Salvador, M. (2017). *Beyond the Self: Healing Emotional Trauma and Brainspotting.* Independently published.

Salzman, P. (2000). *Transcendental Meditation: The Beatles in Rishikesh.* Penguin Studio Books.

Shapiro, F. (2001). *EMDR: Eye Movement Desensitization and Reprocessing* (2nd ed.). Guilford Publishing.

Simard, Suzanne. *Finding the Mother Tree: The Uncovering of the Wisdom and Intelligence of the Forest.* Allen Lane, Canada, 2021

Sleep Apnoea Trust Association. (2020). *Sleep Apnoea Trust Association.* https://sleep-apnoea-trust.org/

Specht, H., & Vickery, A. (1977). *Integrating Social Work Methods.* George Allen & Unwin.

Stern, M., & Bristow, S. (1997). *The Courage to Love: Rekindling the Magic of Relationships.* London Bridge.

StopBullying.gov. (n.d.). *"What Is Bullying?" U.S. Department of Health and Human Services. Accessed January 10, 2025. https:// www.stopbullying.gov/bullying/what-is-bullying*

Swart, Tara. *The Source: Open Your Mind, Change Your Life.* Penguin, 2020.

Syed, M. (2018, March 21). *"Narcissistic leader Mourinho out of touch with millennial footballers." The Times.*

Tafarodi, R. W. (1995). *Self-Liking and Self-Competence as Dimensions of Global Self-Esteem. Journal of Personality Assessment, 65(2), 332–342.*

Tanti, C., Stukas, A. A., Halloran, M. J., & Foddy, M. (2011). *Social Identity Change: Shifts in Social Identity During Adolescence. Journal of Adolescence, 34(3), 555–67.*

The School of Life. (2020). *The School of Life: An Emotional Education. Introduction by Alain de Botton. The School of Life.*

The School of Life. (2022). *The Good Enough Parent: How to Raise Contented, Interesting, and Resilient Children. Edited by Alain de Botton. The School of Life.*

Thompson, R. A., & Sherman, R. T. (2010). *Eating Disorders in Sport.* Routledge.

van der Kolk, B. (2017). *The Body Keeps the Score.* Penguin.

Walker, S. (2017). *The Captain Class: The Hidden Force That Creates the World's Greatest Teams. Random House.*

Weinberg, R. S., & Gould, D. (2011). *Foundations of Sport and Exercise Psychology* (5th ed.). *Human Kinetics.*

Whyte, A. (2022, June). *The Whyte Review: An Independent Review into Gymnastics in the UK. Commissioned by UK Sport and Sport England. https://www.sportengland.org/guidance-and-support/safeguarding/whyte-review*

Williams, J., Bunker, L., & Zinsser, N. (2006). *Applied Sport Psychology. McGraw Hill.*

Wolfrum, G. (2018). *The Power of Brainspotting. Asanger Verlag GmbH.*

Wolfrum, G. (Ed.). (2023). *The Power of Brainspotting, An International Anthology. Asanger Verlag, Kroning, Germany.*

Wolpe, J. (1958). *Psychotherapy by Reciprocal Inhibition. Journal of Psychotherapy.*

Yahya, L., & Rahim, H. A. (2023). *Linguistic Markers of Depression: Insights from English-Language Tweets Before and During the COVID-19 Pandemic. Journal of Language and Health.*

Yahya, N. H., & Rahim, H. A. (2023). *Linguistic Markers of Depression: Insights from English-Language Tweets Before and During the COVID-19 Pandemic. Language and Health, 1(2), 36–55.*

Young, M. (1958). *The Rise of the Meritocracy. Pelican Publications.*

ABOUT THE AUTHOR

Phil Johnson – Unlocking Potential, Transforming Performance

Phil Johnson is a world-renowned psychologist, trauma therapist, and performance expert with over 25 years of experience spanning 25 sports and 16 countries. As a trusted advisor to Olympic champions, professional footballers, and performing artists, he specialises in removing mental barriers and unlocking peak potential.

His ground-breaking new book, *Winning Ways: A Psychological Revolution for Excellence in Life, Art & Sport Performance*, offers parents, coaches, and educators powerful strategies to nurture talent while safeguarding mental well-being. Rooted in his expertise in Clinical Mental Health, Sport Psychology, and cutting-edge trauma therapies like EMDR and Brainspotting, this guide empowers readers with the tools to cultivate resilience, confidence, and sustained success.

Based in Bristol, UK, Phil delivers his expertise globally through virtual coaching. Join the movement to rethink performance, ambition, and success.

Find out more at **www.winningways.uk**

\

BV - #0109 - 091225 - C0 - 210/148/20 - PB - 9781917056663 - Matt Lamination